AMONGST THE MARINES

Amongst The Marines

The Untold Story

STEVEN PREECE

MAINSTREAM
PUBLISHING

EDINBURGH AND LONDON

First published in Great Britain in 2004 by
MAINSTREAM PUBLISHING COMPANY (EDINBURGH) LTD
7 Albany Street
Edinburgh EH1 3UG

ISBN 1 84018 852 9

Reprinted 2004, 2005

A catalogue record for this book
is available from the British Library

Typeset in Apollo and Stone Sans

Printed and bound in Great Britain by
Cox & Wyman Ltd

CONTENTS

FOREWORD

As a child, I read comics about war stories and enjoyed watching war films. My favourite war film actors were John Wayne and Audie Murphy, whom I idolised. When I was awarded the coveted Green Beret at the age of 18, I had achieved my childhood ambition. My training had been long, challenging and arduous. I'd seen a lot of people fall by the wayside, but I'd worked extremely hard and made it through. I was a Royal Marine Commando.

At the time, I didn't fully realise how much being a Marine would change me as a person. However, I have no regrets about this. If I could go back and choose a career all over again, I would still choose to be a Marine. I wouldn't change that for the world.

Some people tell me I was brainwashed. If I was, then I can honestly say I enjoyed being brainwashed. Personally, I'd like to call it conditioning. The world that Marines live in is often violent. Danger is an accepted hazard and, in order to stay alive, a Marine must think on his feet, react on impulse, and kill without hesitation.

One of the watchwords of the Marines is 'controlled aggression'. I should state from the outset, though, that the story I am about to tell you is far more about aggression than it is about control.

INTRODUCTION

The Royal Marines are widely known as one of Britain's finest fighting forces. Marine Commandos are trained to the very highest of standards, and face roles and situations which only the most dedicated and exceptional of troops can handle. Because of this, Marines are a breed apart from regular soldiers, and have their own ways of getting things done. This is no less true of their social lives than it is of their hours of service.

This story portrays the social side of an elite soldier's life. It does not focus on the special demands and dangers of battle situations, or the heroics of military glory. Instead, it portrays the private life I experienced as a Royal Marine Commando, after the day's work was complete and the battles were won.

My story begins with a snapshot of Marine life, in describing the reception that lay in store for me – and for all newly trained Marines – at my first commando unit in Arbroath. I then go back to describe my childhood and the events leading up to this moment, including my rigorous Marine training at the commando training centre near Exeter.

What follows from this point is a blow-by-blow insider's account of the social life of the Marines, spanning the seven years of my career. I have it on authority that things are very different in the Marines today, and that violence among their ranks and other kinds of bad behaviour are no longer tolerated. I can only narrate what happened to me, however, and what life was like there as I found it.

To those outside Marine culture, these pages will be more than an eye-opener. Some may find certain parts of this book both disgusting and disturbing. These episodes, though, give vivid insights into what makes a Marine tick. What others would call dangerous and repellent, we Marines called entertainment.

I joined the Royal Marines on 7 February 1983 and served with several different units until 8 May 1990. During this time, I changed from being a quiet, sensible young man into an aggressive fighting machine.

CHAPTER ONE

45 COMMANDO – THE BEGINNING

On 27 October 1983 I passed out of Marine basic training at the Royal Marine Commando Training Centre in Lympstone, near Exeter. Leaving the training centre as a trained Marine for the first time gave me a great feeling of satisfaction. My face shone with pride and I felt ten feet tall. I was one of seven people from an original intake of fifty-six men who had managed to pass this rigorous course and be awarded the esteemed Green Beret. I had finally completed what must have been the hardest thirty weeks of my life and was now ready to take my place in a commando unit (a Marine regiment of front-line troops). I had been assigned to 45 Commando Unit in Arbroath, Scotland, whose Marines had recently played a major part in winning the battles of the Falklands War in the South Atlantic. I was ready for anything, or so I thought. Unknown to me at that time, I was heading to the home of hundreds of Marines whose nature and culture were completely different from anything I had experienced. I wasn't aware of it then, but being accepted as one of them was going to be a long and painful process.

I was 18 years old, a young and amiable man, straight out of the factory and still in the box. The factory is a term for the Commando Training Centre, which produces Marines like factories produce shiny new cars for the showrooms.

It was a dark November evening when I boarded a train in my home town, destined for Arbroath on the east coast of Scotland. The train was full of young men with short military haircuts, the majority of whom were asleep. The shelves above our heads were packed solid with green bergen backpacks, so I was fairly sure that these men were fellow Marines or soldiers from different army regiments. I found a space for my bergen on the shelf above my seat and placed my kit bag beside it. Rain thrashed against the windows and the train wheels rattled loudly beneath the carriage. After several hours and a lot of stops, we finally arrived at Arbroath train station and everybody still on the train grabbed their bergens from the shelves above and got ready to get off.

I was expecting a big rush for the taxis when I passed through the exit of the train station, but everybody seemed to be entering the surrounding pubs. I caught the attention of a taxi driver, who pulled over and opened his rear cab door. I put my bergen and kit bag on the back seat and climbed in beside them.

It was dark and I could hardly see the taxi driver sat in the front seat of the cab. He spoke in a quiet but broad Scottish accent.

'Condor.'

I looked at him and felt slightly confused.

'45 Commando Royal Marines, please,' I replied.

He nodded and repeated his last word, 'Condor,' before putting the car into gear and driving off.

After about twenty minutes we arrived outside a prominent military barracks. It had a single-storey guardroom, heavily lit by powerful floodlights. It had black-painted iron bars on the windows and a pair of large white wrought-iron gates in front of it. A small sentry box was attached to the building with a Marine on guard who stood alert inside. I could see a wooden sign attached to the wall at the end of the gate with the words '45 Commando Royal Marines, Condor Barracks' inscribed in gold letters. I then realised that the word the taxi driver had said was the name of the barracks.

'Condor. Condor Barracks. That'll be three pounds, please,' said the taxi driver.

'Oh yes, Condor,' I replied.

I paid the fare, climbed out of the car and swung my bergen over my shoulder. I watched the taxi pull away and disappear into the darkness.

'Have you got an ID card, mate?' asked the Marine guarding the main gate as he left the sentry box and walked towards me.

'Er yes, I have, mate,' I replied anxiously and produced my new white Royal Marine ID card from my wallet.

The sentry looked a lot older than me and had a thick, bristly dark moustache. He looked at my ID card and scrutinised the small photograph on it, checking that it matched my face.

'Guardroom's over there.' He grinned and pointed to the guardroom door.

'Thank you,' I replied, and dragged my kit bag behind me.

I felt nervous and knocked lightly on the door before entering the room. Inside, I saw a Marine sat behind a wooden desk. He was dressed in the usual military clothes – green woollen jumper with Royal Marine Commando flashings on his shoulders, green trousers and highly polished black boots. I noticed he had two stripes on his right shoulder, which identified him as a corporal. He was the duty guard commander.

'Come in, young man. Don't be shy,' he said.

I smiled and moved towards him.

During our basic training we were trained by corporals and always had to put our heels together when we spoke to them. I had heard previously that these rules didn't apply once you got posted to a commando unit, but still felt unsure. If he'd said, 'Get your heels together,' at that point, I would have quickly stood to attention.

Two other Marines then entered the room. They too were a lot older than me. They both grinned at each other. Then one spoke to me.

'Hhhhmmm, a bit of skin, eh?' (a term for a young and inexperienced Marine).

I nodded to acknowledge his comment.

'Leave it out, you,' interrupted the corporal. 'Go and put the kettle on.'

The Marine laughed loudly and disappeared through a door at the far end of the room.

I explained to the corporal that I had just passed out of basic training and been assigned to this commando unit. It was late, too late for him to arrange for me to collect some bedding from the bedding store and be allocated a bed. He explained that he had no choice but to put me up in one of the empty prison cells for the night. I agreed, but that didn't matter anyway.

The prison cell was painted white and had a small window, which had bars on the outside. The room had nothing inside it but a single bed with two sheets and a couple of blankets folded neatly on top.

I lay awake for most of the night and stared at the ceiling and the window with bars on it. I felt lonely. Everybody I had seen so far was a lot older than I was. I tried to imagine what it was going to be like the following day, but I had nothing to base things on. All my friends, my fellow recruits from the training centre, had gone. They had been assigned to other commando units in other parts of the United Kingdom. I was all alone and stared into the dark shadows of the cell, feeling unsure and uneasy.

The following morning I awoke around 6.30 a.m. and went through the unlocked cell door and used an adjacent shower. Once I'd finished washing I got dressed into my uniform and asked the guard commander for directions to the dining hall so I could get some breakfast. When I entered the dining hall, heads turned and stared at me. I felt strange and a bit like an impostor. Did I look different from them or something?

On completion of breakfast I had to report to the regimental sergeant-major, who would decide which troop and rifle company I would be assigned to. A troop consisted of thirty Marines and a rifle company consisted of three troops. The rifle companies of 45 Commando Unit were called X-Ray, Yankee and Zulu companies. I was slotted into Six Troop in Yankee Company. I knew I had to make new friends and there was no time like the present to get acquainted.

The accommodation blocks were shabby, unlike the new luxurious accommodation at the commando training centre I had just left. They were old worn-out huts that looked like they were left over from the Second World War. Everything was on one floor and there was no upstairs. The walls were paper-thin and water dripped through the asbestos sheeting which covered the roof. It looked in a bad state of repair. Inside there were long empty corridors, which made even the slightest sound echo. Six long rooms ran off each corridor, with a big washroom/shower block housed in the centre.

Inside each of the barrack rooms there were fifteen beds, each with a bedside cabinet and a large wardrobe secured by a padlock. The wardrobe was your locker, and the area around your bed was your bed space.

I went to the bedding store and collected a set of bedding, which consisted of one single white mattress, one mattress cover sheet, one pillow with a pillowcase and two thick blankets. When I entered the Yankee Company accommodation block for the first time I pushed a red wooden door open and stepped inside a long corridor. I had to find the middle room on the right-hand side of the block to reach the bed and locker I had been allocated. It only took me about a minute or so to find the room as the layout of the building was very simple.

The door to each room was bright yellow and had a black latch-type handle on it. The words 'SIX TROOP' were painted black on all of them. I pushed down the latch to my room and stepped inside. It was occupied by several Marines, all of whom stopped what they were doing and turned their attention towards me.

'Knock when you enter this room, you ill-mannered little bastard,' a deep voice called out.

I was startled, but quickly replied, 'Sorry.'

I informed them that I was a new joiner and didn't know the routine yet. I proceeded into the room and looked for my bed space. There was only one space empty so it was obviously mine. I sorted out my pile of bedding and made up my bed. I then collected my bergen and kit bag, which were still at the guardroom, and unpacked them into my locker.

I paused for a few moments and looked around the room. There were lots of Union Jack flags and pictures of Page 3 girls above other Marines' beds. This time, nobody appeared to be paying any attention to me.

'Excuse me, lads, could you tell me where the toilets are,

please?' I asked, while looking in their general direction.

Once again, everybody stopped what they were doing and stared at me. I could feel the hairs on the back of my neck stand up on end. One of the Marines raised his hand and pointed towards the open door leading on to the corridor. Nobody spoke; there was complete silence.

I felt nervous and uneasy and quickly made my way through the doorway and into the toilet, wondering if I had done something wrong.

When I returned to the room, I found my bedding, and all my personal belongings that had been in my locker, scattered around on the floor. I didn't understand why, but decided to say nothing and picked everything back up.

By nightfall, the barrack room was quiet. Everybody had either gone ashore (into town) or into the barracks' NAAFI bar (Navy, Army & Air Force Institution). Things were quiet and peaceful. Nothing stirred except the odd bird chirping outside a small window near my bed space. I switched off my bedside light and drifted off to sleep.

A loud banging noise echoed in the corridor. I opened my eyes. What's going on, I thought. It was very late and a thick darkness filled the room. Somebody was in the adjacent corridor and was shouting something, but it wasn't very clear. At that moment I was still only half awake and switched on my bedside light. It gave off a limited beam of light and only lit up the area around my bed space. A clock on the wall above me ticked away quietly. It was two o'clock in the morning.

Then the door at the end of the room crashed open and a large figure of a man stood in the doorway. His shape was silhouetted against the light coming from the toilets in the corridor behind him.

He was breathing heavily. 'Where are you? Where are you, you little bastard?' he yelled in a loud and angry voice.

I cowered below my bed sheets and curled up into a ball. It couldn't possibly be me he's looking for, I've only just arrived, I thought.

I could hear him coming closer and then my bedside light was switched off. My bed crashed over onto its side and my naked body spilled out from under the sheets and onto the cold slippery floor. The large stocky man stood above me. I couldn't see his face in the dark, but could sense his anger.

'Get up now and stand to attention,' he shouted. 'Get up and stand by your bed.'

By this time I was absolutely terrified and still confused. Did he have the right person? Was it really me he was looking for?

He continued to shout orders at me.

'Get up or I'll fucking cripple you.'

I stood up, trembling.

'Stand to attention and don't move.'

I stood to attention and watched him move away into the darkness where he seemed to be searching for something.

My naked body made me feel defenceless. I felt like a knight without his armour. The cold air circulated around me and chills ran up and down my spine. My underwear was on a chair close to me. Maybe he wouldn't notice if I put them on, I thought, and quickly climbed into them. Thwack!! A blunt object hit me hard on the right side of my jaw, almost knocking me down to the floor. My assailant had obviously found what he had been looking for.

'I told you not to move,' he shouted angrily, and struck me again.

This time my legs gave way and I screamed with pain. He repeatedly kicked me around on the floor. Blood oozed from a gash on the side of my head and down my face onto the floor. A heavy numbness ran through my body. I thought he would stop if I didn't try to react, but he didn't.

Then the door to the room swung open.

'Leave him alone, he's had enough,' a male voice called out.

The two men stood above me. Their voices sounded distant.

'He has to learn. He has to learn,' replied my attacker.

'He's had enough, leave him.'

Blood and tears streamed down my face and I whimpered like a child who had just been punished for doing something wrong. I looked up and could only see one person. One of them had left.

'Come on, young man, let's get you cleaned up,' the man said in a friendly and reassuring voice.

He led me into the toilets and helped me bathe my wounds and clean the blood from my face and head. I saw my reflection in a mirror above one of the many sinks. My face was black and blue and badly swollen. I felt and looked dreadful. He told me to put the incident down to experience and to keep my mouth shut, and also to go back to bed and that everything would be OK in the morning.

I did as he said and went back to bed. I lay on my back and stared at the ceiling. I couldn't stop the tears, which flowed freely down my face. I was shocked and found it hard to understand what had just happened. Why, I thought. Why me? What have I done wrong? I'm a Marine the same as they are. Aren't I?

The sound of a radio playing music awoke me the following morning. I could hear other people moving around, getting ready to fall in for roll-call. I squinted just in case it had all been a bad dream. My face and head ached badly. I looked at my white pillowcase and saw that it was soaked with blood. The clock on the wall behind my headboard ticked quietly against the background of the radio's music. It was seven o'clock. I got out of bed and took my wash kit from my locker and went into the toilets to wash. Other Marines stared at me as I walked towards a vacant sink. Some smirked. I could see them pointing at me.

I looked at my reflection in the mirror and saw that my face was a mess of bruising and swelling. I had a huge lump on my right cheekbone. This made shaving very difficult and painful. When I had finished I returned to my bed space and got dressed. Nobody spoke to me; they just acted as if I wasn't there.

Just after eight o'clock everybody started to leave the building. I knew it was for roll-call so I followed. I walked with my head down and stared at the ground. I didn't feel proud. I felt sick.

The place where we fell in for roll-call was called the company lines. This was Yankee Company lines. It was a small office block with an equipment store attached to it. Outside the block, all the Marines stood at ease in three neat lines and chatted casually. I stood somewhere in the middle. There were about ninety Marines present. Thoughts shot through my mind. Why me? Why was I beaten up? What was I doing here? Did I want to be here? Would it always be like this? A tall ginger-haired sergeant emerged from the company office carrying a clipboard under his left arm.

'Right, gentlemen, listen in for your names,' he shouted in an authoritative voice.

Everybody stopped talking and turned their attention towards him. The sergeant started to call out Marines' surnames. As each Marine heard his name, he quickly stood to attention and shouted, 'Yes Sergeant'. I listened for my name, but it wasn't called. At the end of the roster the sergeant asked if he had missed out anybody's name. I was stood almost opposite him so I stood to attention and raised my hand into the air. He saw me and walked closer. I hoped he would see my wounds and say something like, what happened to you? He looked at the wounds on my face and grinned as if he was admiring them.

'Good here, isn't it?' he smirked.

I just stared at him. I couldn't believe my ears.

'Name,' he continued.

'Preece, Sergeant,' I replied.

'Have you just joined Yankee Company?'

I nodded slowly and he laughed loudly. Bloody hell, what sort of men are these, I thought.

Several weeks later, I was beginning to get used to the way things were. Nobody had spoken to me yet, but that was the way new Marines were treated. These extra few weeks had taught me a lot. I learned that you had to gain the respect of the older, more experienced Marines and the best way to do this was to do as you were told and to keep your mouth shut. In other words, you had to learn to fly with the turkeys before you were allowed to soar with the eagles.

It wasn't long before several other young Marines joined 45 Commando Unit and were assigned to Yankee Company. Two of these men were assigned to Six Troop and were both allocated bed spaces next to mine. The older Marines looked at them, but didn't speak as they watched them unpack their kit bags and make up their beds, just as I had done several weeks earlier.

One of them was called Neil. I heard the other newcomer call him that as they talked and unpacked. He was around eighteen years old, 5 ft 4 in. tall and of stocky build, with short brown hair. He looked at me and smiled. I knew he wanted to say hello, but I turned away. I dared not speak for fear of what the older Marines might say or do. Neil's face dropped and there was a silence between him and his friend. They could feel the tension as I had done when I first arrived.

23

I wondered if they would get the same treatment. Time will tell, I thought, time will tell.

A few days later, it was Tuesday, 20 December 1983 and the evening was set to be Yankee Company's Christmas celebration party. The ginger-haired sergeant had told everybody that they had to attend. The function was held at a local social club, which was situated several miles from the barracks.

On arrival, the troop sergeant approached the two new Marines and myself. He suggested that we should sit at a table in the far corner of the room as he thought it would be best to keep us away from the older Marines.

The place was a tip. It was a large room filled with tables and chairs that were in a bad state of repair. It was badly lit and had a highly polished red floor, similar to the one in our barrack room. The only area that was well lit was the bar, which had three barmaids stood behind it. These were the only women, but others would turn up later on, civilians from the surrounding areas who liked to hang around with servicemen.

Before long, the place was littered with Marines and none of them wasted any time getting into the swing of things. All the beer was free, as it had been paid for out of the Company funds. We sat quietly together in the corner and sipped our beers. We talked about basic training and what it was like when we were awarded our Green Berets. I didn't mention the beating I had received, as I still didn't know whether I had been singled out. We got on quite well. The other young Marine was called Simon. He had short brown hair and was tall and skinny. He told me he was from London and that Neil was from Manchester.

We watched in amazement as the older Marines swilled their beer as if there was no tomorrow. The more they drank the louder they got. They spat beer at each other and hurled abuse at any nearby women.

I saw one Marine pick up a handbag belonging to a girl who had gone to the bar. He proceeded to urinate and then crap in it. He wiped his behind with some tissues he had taken from the handbag, then he stuffed them back inside it and snapped the top shut before placing it back onto the table. I later found out that this was common practice and was called a grand slam. A short time later, after the girl had returned, she opened her handbag and placed her hand inside to pull something out – probably her purse or handkerchiefs. She was talking to her friend who was sitting next to her when she pulled her hand from the bag and looked at her palm. She was holding a turd. She screamed and went absolutely berserk, shrieking at everybody who was sitting around the table.

A little later in the night a fight broke out between two Marines on the far side of the room. Both men threw punches, kicks and head-butts in an attempt to defeat each other. Blood was splattering all over the place. Finally, they scuffled together against the far wall and the winner stood up victorious. He looked pleased with himself and wiped the blood from his face with his T-shirt, before calmly walking to the bar for another beer. The thing that fascinated me the most was that, even though this vicious fight was taking place, nobody except Neil, Simon and myself took any notice or even seemed the slightest bit interested.

The victor was called Jacko. I had heard the other Marines talk about him on previous occasions. He was quite short but very well built, with a bald head and a long bulbous nose that was broken and twisted. He was renowned for fighting and also for his antics with a machete, with which he terrorised young Marines.

All of a sudden a glass came hurtling across the room and smashed onto our table. It was thrown by Jacko. For him, the fight was only the start of his fun, and now he had turned his attentions to us. He stood a few feet away and stared wildly at us. His dark eyes were filled with anger and an evil grin covered his face. He clenched his fist and shook it angrily at us. Then he turned to his friends and laughed.

I fearfully walked into the nearby toilet to gather my thoughts. Whilst I was sat quietly in a cubicle, I heard Jacko and a couple of other Marines enter. They stood urinating into the urinals and were laughing. 'Are you going to beat them up?' asked one of them. 'Yeah, are you going to golok them?' laughed another ('golok' was another word for machete). 'I'm going to cut them to pieces,' Jacko replied, and laughed wildly as they all walked out the door. The room was silent. Without hesitation I got up and left quickly by a side entrance. I wanted to get out of there before anything else happened, so I caught a taxi to take me back to Condor Barracks.

As I walked towards Yankee Company's accommodation, I thought about my previous experience and the horrible bastard who had dragged me out of bed. This was called a midnight shake. With this in mind, I decided not to spend the night there and headed down to a toilet block, which was situated a few hundred yards away on an old airfield near the perimeter fence of the barracks. The toilets were dimly lit. I walked in and pushed open one of the wooden doors to the cubicles. Another young Marine, from one of the other companies, was already in there. I couldn't see his face as a blanket covered him. When I opened the door he peered out.

'Find your own place, this one's taken,' he said quietly.

I tried the next cubicle door and found that it was empty. It was cold, however, so I quickly nipped back to the barrack room and collected a thick blanket.

During the night, I was cold and very uncomfortable, but this I felt was better than being the victim of a violent attack once again. I felt as if I had outfoxed them and was quite pleased with my new hiding place.

Birds sang out the dawn chorus from the roof of the remote toilet block. I opened my eyes and looked at my watch. It was 6.30 a.m. I stood up and stamped my feet on the floor. My legs felt numb and tingled with a pins and needles sensation. The thick blanket I had wrapped around me fell to the floor. It was bloody freezing. I opened the door and stepped out of the cubicle. Next door was empty, as the other young Marine had already left. He had been courteous enough to close the outside door on departure, which helped retain a little heat from the lukewarm radiator attached to one of the walls.

I got the circulation back into my legs and opened the outside door. The air outside was absolutely freezing, which made me realise that the night may have been cold, but not as cold as being outside in the open. The frozen grass made a crisp crunching noise as I walked back across the airfield towards Yankee Company's accommodation. I wasn't sure what to expect on arrival, but felt a dread in my stomach.

The corridor was very quiet as I walked through it. Normally there would be plenty of activity at this time. Everyone must still be in bed after drinking so much beer last night, I thought. The door to Six Troop's room was ajar. I walked in and looked around. I saw fragments of smashed glass and broken furniture scattered all over the floor. Both Neil and Simon were in bed and their bedclothes were covered in blood. Simon's headboard had been hacked to pieces. My bed had been tipped over and I felt glad that I had slept in the toilet. It was Jacko's work. I knew it because of the handiwork on the headboard. I wasn't sure if I felt sorry for the other two young Marines. I was more pleased that it wasn't me and that I had found a good hiding place to get away from it all.

Roll-call had a familiar ring too. The two Marines' names weren't on the register, and the troop sergeant was grinning broadly at them. I received no acknowledgement from the older Marines, and this was a relief. I was focusing on the fact that it was Wednesday, 21 December and the Marines in 45 Commando Unit were going home on leave for Christmas. I was excited and couldn't wait to return to the safety of my parents' home. I had some much-deserved sleep to catch up on.

CHAPTER TWO

CHILDHOOD

I grew up on a headland in a town in the north-east of England. It was only a small place with a few thousand residents. Most of the workforce there were either fishermen or dockworkers. During the early years of my life, we lived in a council flat. It was on the ground floor with another flat above it. It had one big living-room, two bedrooms and a bathroom. The rooms were so damp that the wallpaper was always wet and had black mouldy patches all over it. All our furniture was bought second-hand or given to us. The flat was heated solely by an open fire, which we fuelled with scrap pieces of wood collected from a local wood mill on the docks, topped up with sea coal. This was oil-covered coal that was washed up onto the beach from the nearby coal mines that were close to the coast. We used to enjoy sitting around the fire together holding bread over it on the end of a fork to make toast.

There were five people in my family: my mother, who had long ginger hair and a heart of gold; my father, who had jet-black curly hair and tattoos on his hands – he was a short stocky man who worked at the docks; and two older brothers, Martin, who was five years older than me, and Peter, who was two and a half years older. We were a very poor family. Our father usually spent what money we did have on beer or betting on horse racing. To prevent us from starving, he used to catch crabs on the nearby rocky beach and was also given fish from the local fish quay by his drinking partners. We also got cheap dented tins of soup from a food factory that our mother used to work in. My father was a womaniser and didn't hide it from our mother, whom he often beat up for no reason at all. Our clothes were always cheap and got passed down from one brother to the next. By the time I got the clothes, they were usually badly damaged or well stitched together. When other kids got leather jackets, we got PVC. When they got leather boots we got plastic, or cheap plimsolls. The flat only had two bedrooms. My two brothers and I used to share the same bed. This had its good and bad points. It was good because our combined body heat used to help to keep us warm and it was bad because Peter was forever wetting the bed in his sleep.

My worst memories of that flat are from when I was between four and six years old, on the many occasions when my father took out his moods and violence on my mother after he had been out drinking. One night he came home in his usual angry mood and started an argument with my mother. Then he head-butted her and repeatedly punched and kicked her around on the bathroom floor. There was blood everywhere and she screamed incessantly. I stood next to them, pleading that he would stop beating my mother, but this, as always, fell on deaf ears. One memory from those times which had puzzled me for many years was that, on Christmas day, Martin never got up early like Peter and me, and he always opened his presents in private a few days later. It wasn't until I asked my mother at the time of writing this book, some thirty-plus years later, that I found out why.

Mother told me that, one year, when my father had been out drinking late, he came home and beat her up so badly that she couldn't get up to put Martin's presents out. This was how Martin found out that Santa Claus didn't exist, and from that year on he had lost all interest in getting his presents.

On 5 November 1970, when I was six years old, we finally moved into a three-bedroomed terraced house. It was opposite a busy main road and had a new type of coke (smokeless fuel) fire, which was lit by a gas poker (a gas tube that attached to a gas pipe and was placed under a grate beneath the coke to ignite it). The extra bedroom meant that Martin got his own room and Peter and I got bunk beds. This was good news as this house wasn't as damp or as cold as the flat. I made sure that Peter occupied the bottom bunk just in case his bed-wetting habit continued.

At school I was fairly tough and willing to fight with literally anybody my own age. I seldom lost a scrap, but if I did I always went back a few days later for another try. I hardly ever saw Martin during my childhood. The reason for this was that if Peter or myself ever did anything wrong then Martin would be punished for it by our father. He had obviously decided that if he didn't play with us at all then he couldn't be held responsible for anything we did wrong.

At the age of ten, I was on the nearby docks with my friends and our Peter, playing around the huge fires that were always burning there. The fires were set by workmen to get rid of thousands of wooden beams that were remaining after they had knocked down all the old disused coal stays. The coal stays had been wooden structures approximately forty feet high, and were once used by trains to drop off coal into the holds of merchant ships. There were about ten of us in total and we messed around with the fires and threw things like rubber tyres onto them. The workmen who were supposed to watch and control the fires were never anywhere to be seen and were probably frequenting some of the many pubs in the area instead of looking after the fires.

On this particular day, I was stood next to a kid called Freddy. We saw a rusty old oil barrel near one of the fires. It was lying on its side and had small flames coming from inside it that slowly flickered around the hole where its sealing cap should have been. Freddy said that it could explode and suggested that we should move it away from the fire. I pushed it with my foot and it rocked away from me and shuddered. I could hear the liquid splashing around inside. I moved in behind it to push it again, but unfortunately for me it rolled back towards me and splashed some of its liquid onto my left trouser leg. My trouser leg instantly caught fire and flames roared around my leg.

My first reaction was to take the trousers off, but my belt was so tight that I couldn't undo it. I then thought about running a hundred yards or so and diving into the dock's water. However, for a few moments I was in a state of panic and ran around in circles and screamed for help. One of the other kids, who was a couple of years older than me, ran at me and pushed me to the ground. He then scattered a combination of mud and sand onto my leg and extinguished the flames.

I saw my brother Peter looking at me. Like me, he was in a state of shock. He was on his knees, crying uncontrollably with his head in his hands. A man and a woman seemed to appear from nowhere and asked if I was OK. I told them yes and said that I just wanted to go home. The man asked to look at my leg and helped me undo my tightly fastened belt. The skin on my leg had melted and was all wrinkly, like melted plastic.

A short while later, I was taken to the hospital, where the skin was removed. I had lots and lots of very long blisters that caused excruciating pain, hurting like nothing I had ever experienced before.

I spent the next three months in hospital and had skin grafts with skin that was taken from both of my thighs. The pain I endured was indescribable and constant. I had a daily dressing of gauze bandages that were covered in a yellow jelly-like substance. It cooled the burnt part of my leg, but always stuck hard and fast to my legs where they had removed the skin. Each morning, this was literally torn off like strong masking tape to make way for each new dressing. I used to dread being wheeled into the first aid room and cried and screamed throughout the ordeal. Two nurses would hold me down, whilst a third tugged the dressings away from my legs.

It had been suggested to my parents that they take the matter to court to seek damages for my injuries. However, they had little or no money for any such action and were nervous of any mention of law courts. Later it transpired that the missing workmen should have been watching the fires, and their employer organised a meeting. At this meeting, they offered us £500 compensation, which we gratefully accepted. The money was put into a trust fund and was to remain there until I reached the age of eighteen. Fortunately for my father, there was a clause which stated that I could withdraw small amounts before this time if I needed to. He would encourage me to take out some money and lend it to him to pay for his beer. The loaned money was never returned and two years later the whole amount had been spent.

Our father's violent behaviour continued and he constantly beat our mum. He was a pure bastard and Martin didn't hide the fact that he hated him. When he punished us, he used to smack us hard with a thick leather belt, which had metal studs on it. He didn't care where the belt hit us and just lashed out with it. He generally aimed for our backsides but quite often whacked us in the face or over the back with it. The worst I ever saw him do was to lift Peter off the floor by grabbing hold of his hair with one hand and then repeatedly punch him in the face with the other. Another of his bad habits was to come home drunk after a lunch-time drinking session and throw his full steaming-hot dinner plate against one of the walls in the living-room.

Both my brothers and I had to work for our pocket money, so we took on newspaper delivery jobs. Later, we went on to a job delivering milk each day before going to school. Firstly, Martin got a newspaper delivery job, then left for the milk delivery job and handed the newspaper round over to Peter. Then Peter also left for a milk delivery job and handed over the newspaper delivery job to me.

My first go at delivering milk was with a different supplier to my two brothers. However, I got fed up after the first day as the owner only paid me four pence for working on a Saturday from 4.30 a.m. till 1 p.m. I was disgusted at being ripped off in such a way and occasionally stole his takings from a tin that he kept hidden in his milk cart whilst he was doing street deliveries. I saw this as a type of personal justice.

Later, we all worked for the same milkman. We used to start at 5.30 a.m. and finish at 8.00 a.m. We earned around £5 per week each and all had to endure the regular attempts of our father to borrow it to buy some beer.

On a Sunday, we raced whippets and occasionally won a few trophies and some prize money. The prize money went the same way that all of our money went, on our father's fags and booze, and then to the bookies if there was any left over.

A few years later, our mother wised up and divorced him. However, they continued to live under the same roof. On returning from court that day they broke the news to me and I wept inconsolably. I was still only nine years old and too young to understand what was going on. My father saw the opportunity and used my sadness and emotion to bribe my mother into letting him stay with us.

I turned my interests to pigeons and kept a small loft in the garden. Peter and I joined our local church choir, where we stayed for a couple of years. A humorous moment I recall is the time when Peter put his hand in the collection bag that was being passed amongst the members of the choir and took money out instead of putting it in. The choirmaster swiftly clipped him around the ear, and then Peter put the money back and a few of his own pennies to go with it.

My eldest brother Martin became some sort of tough guy. He was on a quest during his last year at school, beating up everybody who had bullied him in the past. One of the fights he had was against one of the reputed toughest men in the town. It lasted a full forty-five minutes in an underground car park. Martin was finally defeated and his opponent said openly that it had been the toughest fight of his life and that he felt he was lucky to have won.

Martin carried on his violent ways. One day he had had yet another argument with our father, who always picked on him. He took an axe from the garden shed and went upstairs. A moment later, I heard him shouting like a madman and smashing something with the axe. I was frightened and made a quick exit out of the front door. I stayed out of the way for a few hours until things calmed down and returned when the house was quiet. I walked upstairs to see what had happened and saw that his bedroom door had a hole in it. I pushed the door open and looked inside. The inside of the room looked like a bomb had just exploded. His bed, wardrobe and chest of drawers were smashed to pieces and scattered all over the place. He had vented his frustration and anger on his furniture. Later that night, we were all in bed. Around 11.30 p.m., there was some sort of commotion outside. Peter and I walked into our parents' bedroom at the front of the house to find out what was going on.

'Get down,' said our father hastily. 'He's stoning the fucking house.'

We could hear Martin shouting outside. He was angry.

Outside the front of the house there was a main road. On the other side of the main road was a six-foot wall, which led to the docks. Martin and a friend of his were on the other side of the wall in view from the upstairs window and throwing big stones at the house and windows. A lot of the bricks they threw missed the windows and made loud banging noises as they bounced off the walls.

The result was almost amusing. The police were called and Martin and his friend had disappeared. My father told the police that he didn't want to press charges against the culprits if they were caught, and said he wasn't sure who it had been. The only windows they had managed to smash were two of the small sheets of glass that made up Martin's bedroom windows. In a single day's work, then, he had smashed both the interior and the exterior of his bedroom.

The lack of our father's love and guidance during our childhood affected us all in the years that followed. Martin had no pride and very little confidence. He took on job after job and left each one after a few weeks. He used to just lie in bed and tell our mother that he wasn't happy with his job and didn't want to go to work. Then, a short time later, he would be out of work until he could find another job. Once he was working on a building site, which I walked past on my way to school. I saw him and shouted, 'Hiya Martin!' and smiled. He just looked at me as if he wanted to beat me up. Then he shouted angrily, 'Fuck off. Fuck off, you little bastard.' I was startled, I only wanted to say hello to my big brother. Then he threw his sandwiches at me, followed by a couple of building bricks. 'Fuuccckk oooorrfffffff!' he screamed at me. I ran off.

Well, fuck you too, I thought. I hope your job is shite.

He was courting strong and had an argument with his girlfriend. She upset him, which wasn't difficult, and he beat her up. She pressed charges and he acquired a criminal record for actual bodily harm (ABH).

A while later, he opted to join the Royal Marines and applied at the local Royal Navy & Royal Marines careers information office. He was turned down because of his recent conviction and told to try again a couple of years later. He told me that his closing words were, 'If there was a war on you would fucking drag me through that door,' and the answer he received was, 'Yes, we would'.

Peter took a different path during his teenage years. He often played truant and hung around with the wrong kind of people. He strayed on the wrong side of the law, illegally entering into youth clubs and schools, usually to sample the contents of the tuck shop and occasionally causing some criminal damage. This used to sicken me as I attended a couple of the youth clubs he had 'visited' and saw the damage that he and his so-called friends had caused. I knew it was him because he used to boast about it when we were alone. I obviously didn't repeat what he told me but I felt ashamed of his actions.

The police became regular visitors to our house and usually took Peter away for further questioning. My father used to kick the living daylights out of him, but this didn't seem to have any effect. His choice of friends was not to my liking. They would talk about breaking into places and stealing things as if it was great and the in thing to do.

Peter and I were always very close and my father soon realised that if I was with Peter then he was less likely to break the law, as he didn't want me to get into trouble. However, he quickly got fed up with this and used to throw stones at me to persuade me to go home. I would cry when this happened, as I enjoyed being around him and didn't want him to get into trouble or get beaten up by our father again.

Eventually, he went to borstal and served a sentence of around three months. This didn't seem to have any impact on his behaviour, as he carried on the way he'd left off on his return home.

When he turned eighteen he discovered women and got a job at the local steelworks. This was finally the recipe that was needed to keep him on the straight and narrow.

In my early teens, I joined the Boys' Brigade, where I participated in all kinds of sports. I didn't have time to hang around on street corners looking for something to do, as the youths I attended with were good-natured and were focused on the brigade and its related activities. I still went to church every Sunday, carrying on from my choirboy days, as this was a requirement of our membership.

Also, I started playing football on a regular basis: initially behind some shops against old council garages, and then for a local team on a proper football field. I excelled at this and was eventually chosen to represent my home town.

I then discovered rugby. One of my schoolteachers asked me to turn up for a trial at a local club that he played for. I did as he requested and was chosen to play in the colts' team (under 18s). The sport was a lot tougher than football and had a stronger team spirit. I preferred it and gave up the football.

At the age of sixteen, I left school with five O levels and attended a number of interviews for jobs. Things were difficult, as apprenticeships were in the process of being scrapped by the government and places on them were limited.

The best I could do to find work was to take a Youth Opportunities Programme (YOP). This was the name of the system introduced by the government in 1978 and expanded in 1980. A company could employ you to work for them and pay you £25 a week. They were given this money by the government at no cost to themselves. The company who employed you were to give you a job for six months, with the possibility of taking you on permanently at the end of it. It was really a way of fiddling the unemployment figures as you were classed as employed whilst on the scheme. The public saw it as slave labour as the companies who employed you on the scheme very rarely took you on permanently at the end of the term. My job was as an assistant to a car mechanic in a local garage. The garage consisted of a big workshop, which was used to fix both cars and big trucks. At the back of the workshop there was a red steel door. It had 'Fire Exit' marked on it, but was actually used to access a large tank that held diesel.

The diesel tank was just outside the door and had a tap attached to it to extract the fuel. The tap was high up, which meant that whoever had to fill up a big diesel can had to hold it up high and struggle with the weight as it filled up. It was always myself or another young man who was also on the YOP scheme who had to do this task. The pitfall was that the older employees used to boot the door open and it would hit you in the back as you struggled with the weight of the diesel can.

In my spare time, I took up sea fishing and purchased a fishing rod from a catalogue. The only problem was I tended to lose a lot of lead sinkers when my line became snagged on the rocky beaches. A friend of mine called David Strange had a lead sinker mould, so we decided that we would make our own. There was an old housing estate nearby, which was being demolished, and David said the lead pipes and guttering would be a good source of the lead needed to solve our sinker problem. I agreed and we both headed down to the estate.

Only a few streets were still upright, as most had been knocked down. It was a weekend and the site was quiet. A cool breeze whistled through the empty rooms and blew dust into the air. We entered a couple of the derelict buildings and found lead pipes hanging out of the kitchen walls. We wrenched them off and put them into a hessian sack. After a while we had enough lead to make an ample amount of sinkers and left the building by an open door.

Outside, we heard a van accelerating behind us. The noise got louder as the vehicle got closer. We turned around and saw a police van, which pulled over beside us. Two police officers were inside. One of them leaned out of the window.

'Now then, lads, what have you got there?' he asked and pointed to our hessian sack.

We both stared at him, speechless, and then stared at each other.

'Come here and show me what's in the sack,' the policeman continued.

I walked towards him and handed over the sack. When he took hold of it the weight nearly pulled him through the open window. I saw this as an opportunity to escape and bolted, sprinting up the street. David had the same idea and ran the other way.

'Stop now!' shouted one of the policemen as they exited their van.

I heard the doors slam shut behind me as I continued to

run. The two coppers split up in pursuit of both of us. I could hear the footsteps of the one who was chasing me. He was getting closer and closer. The streets were long and consisted of rows of terraced houses. I saw an open door and ran through it, dodging the gaps between some missing floorboards. I quickly reached the back door and wrenched it open. He was right behind me; I could sense it. The back door led to a small back yard with a wooden gate and a six-foot brick wall. I pulled at the gate and saw that it was nailed shut. Then the door behind me slowly opened and the copper appeared in the doorway. He was sweating and breathing heavily.

'Got you,' he panted.

No you haven't, I thought, and ran at the wall before leaping into the air and pulling myself up and over it. The policeman grabbed my jumper just as I started my descent, but his grip gave way to the pull of my body weight and I landed smoothly on the uneven ground below. I sprinted off and headed across some unused railway lines in the direction of home. I stood on top of a railway embankment and looked down onto the estate below. I could see the police van driving up the few remaining streets and David was sat in the back. I knew I was clean away and that David would not tell on me.

I thought for a while and felt nervous. What if David did tell on me, though? I could picture the police van pulling up outside our house, just like it had done on numerous occasions when Peter had been in trouble. My father would go mad. He would half kill me. I decided to give myself up and walked back down the embankment towards the empty streets and the area of the police van. They saw me and one of them ran towards me.

'Its OK,' I said. 'I want to give myself up.'

He grabbed me and twisted my hand behind my back,

before pushing me into the back of the van and slamming the door shut.

We were then driven to the police station. Once inside, we were taken into separate rooms and asked to make a statement. The policeman who interviewed me was in plain clothes. He was around forty years old with short dark hair. He had a deep voice and was very firm with his questioning. I didn't hide anything and answered all his questions truthfully before completing a statement of the events that took place. On completion, he asked what I was doing hanging around with David and said I seemed too intelligent to be on the wrong side of the law. He asked about my employment situation and I told him that I didn't like being on the YOP scheme and wanted to join the armed forces. He supported this and suggested that I keep my nose clean for a while. I was then taken to another room, where I was photographed and fingerprinted like a criminal.

I was then taken to an empty room where I was left to sit on my own, whilst the policeman went to telephone my father to come from his work and collect me. I sat patiently and stared at the wall. I could feel the emptiness of the room, which had only a table, two chairs and a clock on the wall. I was worried about what my father would say when he arrived and felt sure he would give me a good hiding.

The door opened and my father peered in. I immediately saw the look of disappointment on his face.

'Not you,' he snarled. 'The other two I can accept, but not you. Have you been charged?'

'Yes, with theft,' I replied, with a feeling of shame.

'All these years and you haven't been in trouble. Why now, son, why now?'

'I'm sorry, Dad, I only wanted some lead for sinkers.'

'Come on, let's go home and tell your mother.'

I got up and we left.

I went back to work the following day and felt totally hacked off that I had let my parents down and got into trouble. I grabbed hold of a diesel can and went through the steel fire exit door to fill it up. I turned the tap on and could hear the footsteps of someone approaching the door. Every time this had happened previously the door would hit me in the back and the mechanic who kicked it would stand there and laugh at me. Balls to this, I thought. When he kicks that door open I'm going to move. We'll see who laughs then.

The door was kicked and I moved out of the way. Diesel gushed out from the tap and somebody stood there cursing. I looked in the doorway and saw the garage owner, who was dressed in a three-piece suit. He stared at me and shook his head. He was lost for words.

'Don't tell me, I'm leaving,' I said. 'Shove your stupid job scheme up your arse.'

Several weeks later I was still jobless, and was walking down the main high street in the town centre. I passed the Royal Navy & Royal Marines careers office, which was on a street corner. There was a wooden bench on the opposite side of the road. I walked across the road and sat down on it and stared at the careers office, trying to paint a mental picture of what I would look like in a uniform, as I had wanted to be a Marine ever since I was a kid. This is it, I thought. I'm going for it. I stood up and walked across the road, pushed the door open and walked in. Inside, there was a small room with a brown carpet, a few wooden seats and a table full of military magazines. There were pictures of warships and Royal Marines all over the walls and models of grey Navy ships in glass cases. I took a seat and picked up a magazine. A fat gentleman in a naval uniform entered the room via an internal swing door. I looked up and he smiled at me.

'Hello, young man,' he said in a warm and welcoming voice. 'Do you want to join the Navy?'

'Er, no,' I replied. 'I want to join the Marines.'

I half expected him to come out with an old John Wayne quote: 'So you want to be a Marine, uh?' Instead, he frowned and questioned me. 'How old are you?' 'You don't look big enough.' 'How fit are you?' I felt nervous and looked at his fat belly. He wasn't a Marine. He was a big fat sailor.

I stood up and stared him right in the eyes.

'I'm nearly eighteen. I'm still growing and I'm a lot fitter than you are.'

He grinned. 'OK, let's see you do fifty press-ups.'

'No problem.' I got down on the floor and did what he requested.

'OK, OK. You can sit the entrance test.'

He gave me an A4-sized question booklet and a pencil and rubber. I found the paper quite easy and completed it in around half an hour. I handed it back to the fat sailor and he told me that I would hear something in a couple of months. As I was leaving, he handed me a small pamphlet. It was a greenish colour and had a picture of a Royal Marine holding a rifle on the front. The title read, 'What it takes to be a Royal Marine Commando'. I took it home and read it from start to finish. I felt excited. This is what I want to do with my life, I thought. I want to be a Royal Marine Commando.

I proudly walked into the front room to tell my mother and father. I knew they would be proud of me. My father had a look of horror on his face. He took the booklet from me and read through it. He then scratched his head and looked at me.

'I don't want you to do this, son,' he frowned.

I was speechless and could hardly believe my ears.

'I'm old enough to make my own mind up and anyway, I can't find a decent job around here.'

I didn't hear anything from them for about a year. During this time, the Falklands War was fought and won and I longed to be a Marine more than ever. Finally, I got a letter, which requested my attendance for a medical. I passed the medical and waited a few more months before I got my acceptance letter to join up. My instructions were clear. I was to report to the Commando Training Centre Royal Marines (CTCRM) in a place called Lympstone, near Exeter, on 7 February 1983.

That morning, I picked up my suitcase and left home very early, around 5.30 a.m. It was about four miles to the train station and, unfortunately, the local buses didn't start running until 6.00 a.m. Consequently, I walked the distance. It was dark, but warm and quiet. I felt quite chuffed with myself and whistled the tune to the song 'Pack up your troubles in your old kit bag'. My ambition had finally come true. I was going to train to be a Marine.

CHAPTER THREE

BASIC TRAINING

The train journey to the Commando Training Centre in Lympstone took most of the day and I had to change trains at several different stations. By the time the last train had pulled up outside of the training centre it was dark and raining. As everyone disembarked, you could tell which of us were the new recruits as we all had long hair and stood out like sore thumbs. A big sergeant stood on the platform to greet us. He was dressed in a khaki uniform, with the coveted Green Beret on his head. He had highly polished boots and was stood with a clipboard in one hand and a big wooden stick tucked under his other arm. One of the young men who got off the train with me took one look at the sergeant and then got back onto the train and left.

An hour later, we swore allegiance to the Queen and commenced the long, arduous nine-month training course of the Royal Marine Commandos. We were shown to an accommodation block and allocated a bed, bedding, a bedside table and a kit locker.

The accommodation blocks were fairly new. All the walls

were painted cream and the floors were red and highly polished. Lots of little rooms filled the block and six people were allocated to each room. We were then told that each of us was responsible for the cleanliness of our own bed space.

I felt very nervous the first night. Another recruit in the next bed was groaning all the time and talking in his sleep. He awoke several times shouting out loud and complaining of headaches. Then a couple of Marines came in and took him away. I never saw or heard of him again.

The following morning we were woken by a corporal from the recruit training team at exactly 5.30 a.m. I was sure of the time as I'd spent most of the night watching the clock on the wall. On this first day we were issued with our military kit, including a black beret with a red patch in front bearing the Marine Corps cap badge. In addition, we had to complete loads of paperwork, which was then followed by the traditional Marine haircut. The camp barber shaved off all our hair. I watched each shear and felt as if all my previous life was being erased. Then came the funny part. We had to pay the barber £1 for the pleasure.

There were fifty-six recruits when we started and all were highly motivated and keen to be Marines. We all came from different walks of life and from lots of different parts of the United Kingdom. Whatever our backgrounds, however, the fifteen weeks that followed were torture.

In the months between receiving my acceptance letter and arriving at the training centre, I had asked a Marine from my home town (whom I'd known up until then just to say hello to) for advice about preparing for my imminent training. As a result, we'd soon became training partners and good friends. He had helped me to build up my stamina with lots of running, weight training and various physical exercises. However, he'd said to me that no matter how hard I trained, once I started commando training I would feel like I had not trained hard enough. He was right; that's exactly how I felt.

The physical demands of the course were unbelievable. The physical and psychological pain experienced on long-distance runs and in the gymnasium was immense. Everything was hard work and we were always pushed to the limit. After physical training sessions we had to sit in the classroom and study weapons, field craft, camouflage and the principles of concealment. Being able to hide in the undergrowth of woods and grassed areas and being expert with numerous weapons was an essential part of the training. Our personal weapons were called self-loading rifles and were issued without slings. Everywhere we went, our weapon had to go with us. Anyone found away from their weapon would be punished. We spent hours on the drill square and in the drill sheds during wet weather, constantly rehearsing drill routines until we could do them perfectly. The Marine recruits were nicknamed nods, because they were pushed so hard that they would often nod off to sleep. If you were caught asleep at any point, you would be told to run down to the assault course and dive into a big tank full of water and then return. This was nothing difficult, but it meant you were soaking wet for the rest of the day and had even more kit to clean during the evening.

Above all, you had to keep going when anybody else would have given up. You needed vigour and determination that was second to none. After each day's training had finished, a new phase of responsibility would commence. We had to keep our accommodation block spotless and inspections were carried out daily. Our weapons had to be thoroughly cleaned, as well as our bed spaces, our clothing, our accommodation block including the toilets, and also ourselves. Unfortunately, we were not allowed to use washing machines at this stage of training and had to wash everything by hand. We were given a photograph of a kit locker showing all the clothes and kit folded neatly away and every shirt and jumper folded exactly the same size as a monthly Marines magazine called the *Globe and Laurel*. This was measured using the actual magazine, and if the measurements weren't correct the whole contents of the locker were emptied out of the window into the elements and mud outside. This meant that the whole process of cleaning had to start again before you could go to sleep.

All points of hygiene were covered. We were taught how to shave, wash, shower, iron and keep everything clean. The reasoning for this was that more people were killed in the Second World War from hygiene problems, food poisoning, etc., than were actually killed on the battlefield. Sometimes, this meant that we would not get to go to sleep until around 2 a.m. and yet we had to rise at 5.30 a.m. to start the next day. This got even worse when we occasionally had to carry out security guard duties of the establishment and got no sleep at all through the night.

Each day, we had to make our beds in different kinds of ways or make bed packs with our bedding. Later, we would have to stand to attention by our beds and undergo our daily inspection by the training corporals. During the inspections, they quite often rubbed their fingers around the areas of our bed spaces looking for even the slightest speck of dust and sifted through our lockers and bed packs looking for faults. If they found anything at all, they emptied the whole contents either onto the floor or out of the window. They constantly screamed in our faces and sometimes pushed us around. Initially, I found this hard to take but, after a while, I got used to it and it didn't bother me any more. You just accepted that you had not attained the required standard and put it right as soon as possible.

We were introduced to the field (the wilderness) and taken through the steps to put what we had learnt in the classroom into action. We also started to spend a lot of time on the firing ranges and had to pass lots of tests with numerous weapons. The training team always treated us worse in the field. There was no one around to see what they did, so they often ran us ragged until most of us dropped and kept us awake all through the night. Our inspections were just as strict in the field as they were at the training centre, but it was harder to keep yourself, your weapon and your kit clean in the outdoors. If we were caught out, we were punished with more physical training; this was called a beasting and was common practice during basic training.

Our numbers became fewer as the weeks went by. A lot of people dropped out of training and decided this wasn't the life for them. This was called opting out. However, we also lost a lot of recruits through various injuries. These men were taken out of our troop and placed in a special troop, called Hunter Troop, until their injuries were healed and they were fit again. At this point they would be pushed back into mainstream training with another troop who were at the stage of training they were at when they had been injured.

Personally, I found the first half of training very difficult. Every day seemed like a great effort. The training was hard and the training team treated us like pieces of shit. We were constantly evaluated and tested on what knowledge and military skills we had gained, and also had to keep passing physical training tests and producing the high training standards required to be a Marine. I often felt like opting out and often thought to myself, WHAT THE HELL AM I DOING HERE?

No matter how pissed off I became, I just got on with it. I wanted to achieve my ambition and pass out at the end of basic training with a Green Beret. I honestly felt that I would not be able to face the people back at home with the news that I couldn't hack the Royal Marine Commando training course.

After fifteen weeks, we were assembled for a halfway passing out parade. We had been taught the basics. Our parents were invited, but I didn't ask mine, as I was only halfway to winning the coveted Green Beret. A revealing measure of the difficulty of our training was that, of the original fifty-six men that had started the course fifteen weeks earlier, only twelve were left.

During our halfway passing out parade, our drill sergeant described us as being in a similar state to a blunt sword and said that the next fifteen weeks would be spent pushing us harder, to sharpen the sword.

The second phase of training was different, as it encompassed commando-training skills. For a start, the physical fitness side became a lot tougher. We went from working in the gymnasium wearing shorts, a sweatshirt and white plimsolls, to working on the obstacle courses carrying a fighting order (pouches which weighed around thirty-six pounds, containing ammunition, water bottle and food rations), and a self-loading rifle that weighed nine pounds and nine ounces.

Carrying the extra weight made me feel as if we had started all over again. Initially, I struggled with climbing the thirty-foot ropes. We were taught a technique to do this, but climbing with all this extra weight was a new and arduous experience. We were introduced to the assault course, which consisted of a series of walls, nets, climbing frames, rope bridges, a hill and a tunnel. We also had to run a distance of 200 metres with another recruit held up on our shoulders like a fireman's carry. This meant you were then carrying this man's kit and rifle, along with your own kit and rifle and the man himself! We also trained on the Tarzan course, made up of a set of rope obstacles, and the endurance course, which consisted of a couple of miles of deep pools, water tunnels and obstacles followed by a four-mile run back to camp and a test of marksmanship at the end of it. More emphasis was put on speed marches (running as a body of men in full kit over distances of between four and nine miles). All of these physical tasks were timed and if you didn't pass each one in a given time you were given extra physical training at the end of the working day.

I found the second phase of training more enjoyable. My level of fitness had risen sharply and I measured my performance in terms of time, distance and effort (the amount of time it took me to cover the distance and the amount of effort required to do it). No matter how fit I became, the effort required was always 100 per cent, as the course was devised to constantly push us, and nothing else was deemed to be acceptable.

Our classroom work moved on to more advanced techniques of stealth and weapons training, and great emphasis was put on teamwork and commando assault skills. We moved on to using lighter weapons and also started to spend more time in the field. The field exercises were never easy. The elements were always against us: it always seemed to be very hot, very cold or very wet. On one occasion the training team told us to fix bayonets and charge into a six-foot-high clump of gorse bushes. We did as we were told and charged in, screaming blue murder. The razor sharp thorns on the bushes made huge gashes in our skin but we all pressed on until we came out the other end. On another occasion, we were made to run about twelve miles, wearing nuclear, biological and chemical warfare suits and gas masks. The terrain on these runs was never flat, consisting of series after series of granite tors. On this occasion, one of the recruits collapsed and was later diagnosed as having a collapsed lung. Quite often, we were told that we had to run five or six miles to rendezvous with some four-ton trucks that would transport us back to base after a week in the field. When we got close to the trucks they would drive away and we would be given a new location where we could find them, only to receive the same treatment again and again.

One day, we were carrying out a live firing exercise at a place called Torpoint in Cornwall. We fired at targets from distances of up to 600 metres using a variety of weapons. The firing range was on a steep hill and the targets were at the bottom of it. Our training team, as usual, ran us ragged and made us run up and down the hill and then crawl up and down it.

Then we started firing light machine guns down the range before being told to cease fire and leave the weapons pointing down the range. At this point, all the training team went down onto the firing line to discuss something about the targets. We all hated them and watched them as they moved into the line of fire. For a moment, I stared at the weapon I had left pointing towards them and thought of manning the gun and firing a hail of bullets into them. I looked around and several of us grinned at each other. We were all thinking the same thing.

Blisters became a common sight, as our webbing equipment, which held our ammunition and survival kit, generally rubbed the skin off our backs. The blisters and sores were very painful, but I had literally got to the stage where I had learnt to just ignore them.

The weeks rolled on and we were given extended shore leave passes. This meant that we could go into town more often and also return back to base a lot later than previously allowed. The training team gave us a list of pubs that the trained Marines socialised in and told us to stay clear. They said that until we had passed out of training we would not be given the same privileges. The only night we actually drank was a Saturday night. This was because we had to do the endurance course every Saturday morning and spent every Saturday afternoon cleaning our kit.

Sunday was seen as a rest day and was a good opportunity to just lie on your bed and suffer the hangover from the night before. We didn't have to go into town to socialise as there was always a disco held on the base on a Saturday night. This was called the Gronk's Ball: a gronk being a nickname for an ugly woman. The women were ferried in by a free bus and took the opportunity to get all these recruits to buy them lots of cigarettes and beer and frequently have sex with them. Although I attended the disco when I didn't feel like going into town, I stayed clear of the loose women as I didn't want to catch any of the sexual diseases that were passed around by them.

In the last few weeks of training, shore leave was cancelled and more emphasis was put on preparing us for the final set of commando tests. We needed to pass these tests to move into the King's Squad. This was the most senior of the troops in training and consisted only of the recruits who had passed all the commando tests and were now preparing for their passing out parade and the official presentation of the coveted Green Beret.

The commando tests were carried out over five days, but a week prior to this we had to complete a final five-day field exercise. During this exercise we were assessed on all of our infantry and commando skills. If we failed to reach the required standard we would not be allowed to attempt the commando tests.

The final exercise was as tough as expected, but our skills and fitness were at the required level to meet any military tasks given to us. We had bonded strongly as a team during our training and worked together to achieve all of our objectives. Even though the demands of the exercise were tough, they weren't as tough as having to wait until the day after the exercise was complete to be given our results. We were each to be told individually whether we had passed through to the commando tests, or whether we would be back-trooped (put back in training) and made to undergo the rigours of the exercise again.

Thankfully, we all got through, and started the tests as planned. The first test was the assault course and all of us managed to pass well within the required time. This was followed straight away by the Tarzan course, which we all passed without a problem. We also had to complete the series of high-up rope obstacles at night, but this wasn't timed.

Next day, we had to complete both the Tarzan course and the assault course together, which was very difficult. This was made even more difficult by heavy rain, which made all the obstacles slippy. All of us, except one, passed this test. Unfortunately, one of our colleagues could not get over the six-foot wall on the assault course. This was something he had never struggled with before, but on this occasion he just couldn't get over it. Ten minutes later he was given a second attempt, but this meant that he would have to do it all again. When he hit the wall he struggled to climb over it, but we saw him grit his teeth and drag himself over it, showing guts and determination, and he continued through the remainder of the obstacles within the time allowed. Straight after this, we had to run 200 metres carrying another recruit and, as with all the tests, we were carrying full kit. I had become good at this and was quite quick to the finish. Then we had to climb the thirty-foot ropes. The extra weight didn't bother us now and we used our well-rehearsed climbing technique to achieve the objective easily. Lastly on that day we had to cross the big water tank that we were made to dive into on the occasions when we had fallen asleep in the classrooms. There were two ropes suspended over the tank and we had to cross them on our bellies and then drop below the ropes in a hanging position, before climbing back on top and pulling ourselves to the end of the rope. This was known as a regain.

The nine-mile speed march was as tough as ever and it took a lot of high spirits and determination to keep going to the end. Running nine miles would be hard work for anyone but we had to run in combat boots, wearing and carrying weapons and our full combat kit. The total weight including our SLR rifles was around forty-two pounds. The task was made harder as the long country lanes acted like heat traps causing us to suck hard when inhaling air. The course wasn't flat either and had a good number of very steep hills. One of the hills was called killer hill. During our run up this hill we unexpectedly encountered a civilian coming down the hill around a corner towards us. He accidentally ran straight into two members of our troop. Our troop sergeant acted quickly and kept the rest of us moving whilst one of the corporals checked that the civilian was OK and that the two men he had collided with were fit enough to carry on. Unfortunately, one of them wasn't and had to drop out, along with another two who failed to complete the test. At the end of the route we had to get organised and carry out a mock troop attack on a given position. This was to prove that our fitness level was high enough for us to cover the nine miles and still be fit enough to fight at the end of it. On completion we were ferried back to the commando training centre in a four-ton lorry and dropped off outside the main gate, where we were assembled once again into a body of men. Two Royal Marines bandsmen who beat their drums and led our march back to our accommodation block met us here. This was a great feeling. We marched along with our heads held high and a great feeling of pride lifted our tired spirits.

Next it was the endurance course, which is an infamous part of the Royal Marines' training. The start was four miles from the training centre, which we always had to walk to. We were generally given a time to be there and had to set off early, bearing in mind what time we had to muster and start the test. The weather was damp and wet and cloudy. I felt butterflies in my stomach as I prepared myself for the start. We commenced in groups of three and ran side by side where possible. We were told that we had to go at the pace of the slowest man, so encouraging each other to keep up was imperative. Most of the water obstacles were covered in ice and I had to grit my teeth as I waded through, holding my weapon above my head. We cleared the obstacle part of the course in good time and headed off downhill to start the four-mile run back. Our kit and clothing felt like it weighed a ton as it was totally wringing wet. Steam came off the top of our heads from the heat produced by all the running. Then, tragedy: I slipped on a raised root from a nearby tree. It was wet and slippy with ice. The momentum from the pace I was running at caused me to fall flat on my face and hit the ground with a great thud. I gasped heavily and felt a numbness through the front of my whole body. My two colleagues sat me up and checked I was OK.

I was numb and winded and blood trickled from cuts on my hands and face.

I stood up and sucked in the air with a few deep breaths. My colleagues looked at me, with frowns covering their faces. Although they were concerned that I was hurt I also knew how much they wanted me to carry on and complete the course with them. I nodded my head and started to run again. The numbness started to go away and my sights were set on Heartbreak Lane, which was the last lane on the home straight.

I looked up and saw the customary picture of a Royal Marine cartoon character with a pot-belly and the words 'IT'S ONLY PAIN' written on it. I smiled to myself as I passed it and then it was the last stretch to the firing range where we had to prove our marksmanship with the weapons we had carried around the course. We got to the range well inside the time allowed and prepared to fire. This part wasn't timed but it was difficult because the sights of your weapon moved up and down as you struggled to steady your breathing. As I fired each shot I held my breath in order to steady my aim. I breathed out, then in, and then paused before firing. We all fired well and congratulated each other when we were given the scores by one of the training team.

I felt excited. There was only one test left between me and the coveted Green Beret I had always dreamed about wearing. I was so close now I could almost taste it.

The thirty-miler was the longest and hardest commando test. This was thirty miles across the dense terrain of Dartmoor, using maps, instinct, common sense and a lot of guts and determination. The start was at a place called Okehampton, which was in the middle of the moors. We arrived the night before and were issued radios, maps, compasses and survival gear. On top of this we had to carry a pack full of safety equipment, which we would pass around en route and as usual we had our fighting orders and our weapons. The terrain across Dartmoor was difficult and there were a lot of really steep looming hills, which would be just as painful coming down as jogging up. Some of the ground was boggy and some was hard. There was some flat ground but most of the course was up- or downhill. The whole task was usually made harder by the inclement weather conditions of thick fog, rain and snow.

We set off in groups of six and got a good pace going. The weather was damp and wet and it seemed to rain constantly. We took turns with the navigating using a map and compass. We covered the first twenty miles in good time and kept everybody together. After this, the going seemed to get a lot harder. The hills seemed steeper and the fatigue from the week of tests began to set in. Both my heels and some of my toes were bleeding and covered in blisters. They were agonising, but I found that as long as I kept moving they stayed hot and caused me less pain. Realistically, it would take a lot more than blisters and bleeding feet to stop us now. We all pushed on hard and I thought deeply about our Green Berets being presented at the end of this final test.

The last five miles were the hardest for some of our group. Two of them were suffering badly from fatigue so we took their fighting orders and weapons off them to reduce their load and distributed them around the rest of us. This helped for a couple of miles but they were both really starting to fade on the last three miles. We stopped for a few minutes and checked our watches. Our time was still good so we decided to stop for a few more minutes to let them catch their breath. This was just as hard for the rest of us because it meant that our swollen, blister-covered feet would cool down and the pains would set in. We gave them back their kit and pressed on for the home straight. My feet were absolutely killing me and I started to limp. Then my feet warmed up again and the pain from the blisters sort of numbed itself, allowing me to press on. One of the two recruits who had been struggling started to fade again as we jogged along a dirt track. We shouted encouragement, as we wanted everybody to pass the course. He shook his head and said that he had had enough, so I kept pushing him along. I found this very hard as the energy I was using was starting to sap my strength. To get around this problem, one of my colleagues took hold of one of the man's fighting-order straps and I grabbed the other side. Then we all ran along together. After a while, we could see the finishing line, but this made little difference to our colleague as he was practically on autopilot and words just weren't registering any more.

We crossed the line and stopped to check we were all in one piece. We first saw that our fading colleague was OK and gave him a cold drink. We waited for the rest of the groups to finish and were told to fall in for the formal presentation of our Green Berets.

For this task, the commanding officer from the training centre was present and he made a speech that I had kept in mind to inspire me throughout my trials. He said the following:

'This is the coveted Green Beret of the Royal Marine Commandos. It is a symbol of the commando around the world. Your achievements today are not to do with winning the right to wear this Green Beret. They are not just to do with getting through one of the longest and hardest training courses in the western world. But they are to do with that thing inside your head that says, "I DON'T GIVE UP". Well done gentlemen, and welcome to the world of the elite Royal Marine Commandos.'

At this moment in time I felt on top of the world. I just wanted my family to see me now. I'd done it. I was now a Marine and had achieved my childhood ambition. So many times along the way I'd felt like giving up, but I couldn't. My pride wouldn't let me. I didn't know whether I wanted to laugh or cry. The feeling was overwhelming for all of us.

That night we were told that we could keep our berets and hand them back the following morning so that they could be presented to us during our passing out parade a couple of weeks later. We were shattered and our feet were in shreds. I ached all over as I lay in bed. I was excited but well and truly exhausted.

We were in the King's Squad now, the most senior recruit troop at the training centre. This was the troop that we had all watched and dreamed about being part of. The next two weeks were going to be easy. No guard duties, very little physical training and very little class work. The emphasis now was on the drill square, in preparation for our final passing out parade, and lots of unarmed combat.

However, even though we had passed the commando tests, we were constantly reminded that we would not be classed as Marines until we marched off the drill square two weeks later. The preparation for the big day was classed as being just as important as all the other stages of basic training. Our uniforms, boots and kit had to be in immaculate condition and we also had to work hard on the drill square to repeatedly practise our sequences of arms drill for the final big day. There was no room for mistakes; it had to be perfect.

We worked hard for the next two weeks and filled out the paperwork to request which commando units we would prefer to be posted to. The units were spread out around the United Kingdom and I requested 45 Commando Unit in Arbroath, Scotland, which had gained a reputation for its toughness in the Falklands War. The Marine from my home town who had prepared me for the training course was from this unit, and I strongly wanted to be a part of it.

The morning before our last day at the training centre we paraded on the drill square in front of the regimental sergeant-major. He was a big tall Scotsman with a thick walrus moustache and a deep thunderous voice. He had a wooden pace stick tucked neatly under his arm. He screamed at us to stand firmly to attention with our necks pushed hard into the backs of our shirt collars. Then I heard a clattering noise as the recruit next to me dropped his rifle onto the ground. The regimental sergeant-major was furious. He briskly marched up to the recruit and prodded him with his stick.

'There's a piece of shit on the end of this stick,' he growled.

'It's not on this end, sir,' answered the recruit, who then started to yelp, as the regimental sergeant-major proceeded to beat him hard with his big pace stick.

The sun shone brightly on the day of our passing out parade. There was a cool freshness in the air and the mood of the King's Squad was electric. Firstly we dressed in our number two uniform, which was called Lovats and was a dark khaki colour. We wore our dark blue recruit berets as the new green ones were to be presented during the morning of our passing out ceremony. The beret presentation was held in the drill sheds in front of our families. All of my family except Martin were present. I felt a little disappointed, but he obviously didn't want to be here for me. Not to worry, I thought, it's the Green Beret I want.

We were marched into the drill shed together and brought to a halt in front of a makeshift stand where our parents sat watching. As we halted we slammed our studded boots into the concrete floor and caused a huge thunderous noise to echo around the building. A corporal from our training team made a speech, saying that the blunt sword that we had resembled halfway through training was now sharp and ready to be used in combat in any corner of the world.

Then our names were called out one at a time and we each

had to march out to be officially presented with our Green Beret by the commanding officer. After a handshake and a few words of congratulation we each marched off to the side and threw our blue berets into a bin, before placing our new Green Berets onto our heads. I felt great and smiled in the direction of my parents.

Next we promptly marched out of the drill sheds and back to our accommodation block to get changed into our number one Blues uniform in readiness for the arms drill parade. We were led by a small contingent of the Royal Marines band and marched smartly onto the drill square to begin the well-rehearsed sequences. The whole thing went really well and we all felt great as we fired our volley of shots into the air. The adjutant (senior disciplinary officer) came onto the square riding his horse and holding his sword in his right hand. He gave instructions for us to march past a group of senior-ranking officers who had come to inspect the parade. This was followed by the words we were all waiting to hear:

'Royal Marines, to your duties, right wheel [turn right], quick march.'

We marched off the parade ground in disbelief that our training was finally over. The song 'Auld Lang Syne' was played and we all stared towards our training team. Let all the past things be forgot, I thought, I fucking hate them bastards.

We had finished. Everything had gone according to plan. We were Marines now and had a long weekend's leave before reporting to our assigned commando units. I was chuffed that I'd got what I'd asked for: 45 Commando in Arbroath, Scotland.

CHAPTER FOUR

NORWAY 1984 – SETTLING IN

The Christmas break after my first spell in Arbroath had been all too short. It was back to reality for me. Personally, I felt as if I didn't want to go back to 45 Commando Unit. I wondered how long it would take before I was accepted as one of the lads. Would things be different then?

The barracks were deserted when I returned. Only a small skeleton crew of Marines had stayed behind to guard it. The rest of the Marines returned from leave at different times of the night and early hours of the morning. The first two weeks back were all work and no play. There was an emphasis on preparation for the forthcoming deployment to Norway. We were going there to train in arctic warfare to protect NATO's northern flank during the Cold War. Physical training in these weeks was intense; muscles were toned up and the extra pounds of body fat gained over Christmas burned off. It was called clearing the cobwebs away. Some of the Marines suffered with exhaustion and were seen vomiting during long runs, probably because they spent more time enjoying themselves over Christmas than keeping fit. Suffer they did, but nobody fell behind on the long runs or dropped out of a hard training circuit. There was an unwritten rule: a Marine could enjoy a full social life as much as he wanted to, but only as long as he could still hack the physical training the following day and give 100 per cent at his job. If he failed to maintain the appropriate standard, not only would his pride be hurt but also a beating off the other Marines would be inevitable. The reason for this was that your life could depend on the professionalism and ability of your colleagues.

Several new faces now littered Yankee Company. I wondered how long it would be before they got their initiation beating. It would only be a matter of time but it was more or less a formality. We were about to spend the next three months in Norway. The older Marines would work hard, train hard, drink hard and play hard. The new Marines would be their source of entertainment. It would be like watching kestrels swooping down on unsuspecting field mice.

I didn't have much time to dwell upon this, because before I knew it I was in the mountains of Norway, and arctic warfare training had begun in earnest. It was work, work and more work. The only break we had was from a Saturday afternoon until early on a Monday morning. This was back at a hostel, which had nice warm rooms and clean bedding. By the time the weekend came along, the Marines were ready for a good session on the beer. There was a cellar in the hostel, which was turned into a makeshift bar. When it was opened, nobody wasted any effort just purchasing one bottle of beer at a time. Instead, they all bought themselves a 24-pack of Pilsner lager. The conversations between the Marines ranged from war stories from their experiences in the Falklands War or Northern Ireland to other past encounters generally to do with women or fighting. They drank heavily and were soon well under the influence of alcohol. This brought out the animal in them; they were full of mischief and hell.

After a while, they became bored with conversing and turned their attentions to other forms of entertainment. Tonza, a large bulky man from London, stood up, dropped his trousers and underpants and crapped on the table in front of everybody. He then placed his dirt between two slices of bread and added some tomato sauce and black pepper. To my astonishment, he proceeded to eat it. He laughed loudly and swiftly swilled down a bottle of beer, whilst everybody cheered and clapped to show that they were impressed with his performance. A plastic container which had been placed on top of one of the wooden tables was the target for all the vomit that followed. It was the younger Marines that used it, including myself. Our stomachs were weaker and still unused to this kind of behaviour.

Tonza suggested that each man should contribute a bottle of lager to pour into the container. Two of them also urinated into it.

'Now we're going to have some fun,' shouted Jacko, the Marine with a fondness for machetes.

The objective was to get all the young Marines to fill a pint glass full of the obscene mixture, as part of their initiation into Yankee Company. It had to be gulped down without pausing and without throwing it back up again. If any of us refused to drink it or failed to keep it down, a kangaroo court (a mock committee-like court made up of older Marines) would form and decide on a penance.

We were told to form a line next to the container, so I stood next to the table first to get it over with as soon as possible. I couldn't believe my ears when, to my surprise and good fortune, I was told that I didn't have to take part and should take a seat with the older Marines and watch the others do the deed. I felt good inside. It was the beginning of my acceptance into the company. Four young Marines remained in the line. The first was handed a glass of the filthy mixture. He lifted the glass to his lips without looking at it and began to drink it. Instantly, his insides erupted. Everybody jeered because he had failed his task. The kangaroo court assembled and quickly came to a decision. His hair, eyebrows and pubic hairs were shaved off. He had, by all accounts, gotten off lightly, but the penalties got worse as the court got more drunk and the queue got smaller.

The second man failed too, and was stripped naked and covered from head to toe in very strong insulation tape. For a few moments he resembled an Egyptian mummy. Then several of the older Marines began to viciously rip the tape from his body. He screamed out loudly with the pain it caused and even more when it was torn from his private parts. Cheers filled the room as the young Marine rolled around the floor in agony. He looked deeply shocked and tears streamed down his cheeks.

The third man, who also failed the test, was told to eat a large piece of glass from the debris that littered the floor. At first, he refused to carry out the task and said it was impossible to do. Jacko stood up and snatched the piece of glass from his hand. He bit into the glass and crunched it and then swallowed it down. There was no blood and he drank another bottle of beer and gurgled it to a rapturous round of applause.

There was obviously a knack to the way in which it was done, because the young Marine's attempt was in vain. Blood poured from his mouth and everybody laughed.

The next and final young Marine bluntly refused to even attempt to drink the concoction. He said he would gladly carry out any other task. A worrying silence filled the room.

The kangaroo court was not impressed with his suggestion. To them it was a sign of weakness and inferiority. They argued over numerous suggestions as to what they were going to do. We all knew the result would be more of a punishment than an arduous task.

The court's decision was that he would be punched in the face twice. The punches would be thrown by the weakest member of the court and the strongest member of the court in turn. To give him a chance, it was also decided that both punches would have to be delivered with their left hands. The first punch was thrown and successfully connected with his jawbone. He shook his head and absorbed the blow with very little fuss. The second punch came from Jacko. He was left-handed and threw his punch with immense force and aggression. There was a big cracking noise and the Marine hit the floor like a ton of bricks. His nose was broken and blood poured from it and from his mouth. Everybody cheered like a crowd of Romans watching gladiators engaged in mortal combat. Two of them grabbed hold of him and lifted him to his feet. One of his front teeth fell out of his mouth and down into a pool of blood on the floor. Everybody cheered – at least, everybody who was still conscious.

The weekends that followed had similar outcomes, up until early March. Then, 45 Commando Unit had a long weekend break – Thursday night until Tuesday morning.

By this time, I was well acquainted with everybody in Six Troop and with the other troops in Yankee Company. I always worked hard at my job and achieved good results. This earned me the admiration and respect of the other Marines. Amongst ourselves, we decided to spend the long weekend in Narvik.

On arrival, we headed for the biggest and noisiest nightspot, The Beer Keller. The price of beer was outrageous. It was three times the price that we paid in the UK and the measure was only two-thirds the size of a pint glass.

To the more experienced Marines, the answer was easy. They would steal the local Norwegians' beer whilst they were busy dancing with girls or visiting the toilet. This tactic was used for most of the night. It was called mine-sweeping. However, it confused and upset the Norwegians and made them angry towards us.

After going through the expense of purchasing a couple of beers, I decided to get in on the act and try mine-sweeping myself. I saw an unattended pint and took it from an empty table. I headed back to where I was previously sitting, unaware that the beer's rightful owner had seen me and was coming to get it back.

'That's my beer, you thieving English pig,' he shouted.

'Fuck off, shitface, it's mine now,' I sharply replied.

The Norwegian raised his hand and slapped me across the back of my head.

'It's my beer, Englishman.'

By this time he had become extremely angry and agitated. Several of his friends came rushing over and stood on both sides of their fellow countryman.

Jacko stood close by. He was in the company of several Norwegian women and was entertaining them with his party trick — eating glass!

He casually glanced across in our direction and noticed the build-up of Norwegians around the area of our table. The smile on his face dropped and, without hesitation, he walked in our direction. He pushed his way through the Norwegians and stopped next to the one who was opposite me. The atmosphere was filled with tension and trouble was imminent.

'What's the problem?' asked Jacko in a loud aggressive voice.

His back was to the wall. This was a tactical move to prevent being attacked from behind.

After a short silence, one of the Norwegians replied, 'I hate you English pigs.'

Jacko's reply was not one of words but of actions. He head-butted one of them and then swiftly threw a volley of punches at the others. Three of them went down onto the floor and held their heads. The whole place seemed to erupt into sheer chaos. Marines all over The Beer Keller were lashing out at anybody they didn't recognise. The room practically resembled a cowboy saloon; chairs and tables were flying everywhere. Windows, mirrors and pint glasses were smashed all around the place, and everybody was going wild. I felt more excited than frightened and joined in the fun. I could feel the adrenalin pumping through my veins. I was exchanging blows with the big guy whom I had previously been arguing with. I took one step back and then threw my next punch with as much force as I could muster. Blood splattered across his face and he fell down onto the floor. A sharp pain shot through my right arm and blood was dripping all over it. I realised that when I had drawn back my arm to throw the punch my elbow had gone through a plate glass window. The blood on the Norwegian's face had come from my arm.

'MPs!' somebody shouted.

I looked through one of the broken windows and saw a military police van pull up outside. The bar lights were turned off and then everybody scattered.

We all dispersed via an exit door at the rear of the bar and made our getaway into the night. All that the military police could do was pick up the pieces and make a note of the damage.

Much later, back at Yankee Company's location, all the

Marines were summoned for a roll-call. News of the fracas had reached our commanding officer and he wanted to know who was responsible. Fortunately, there was no evidence to prove that it had been Royal Marines who had caused the disturbance. Everybody denied any knowledge of it; our lips were sealed and we all felt chuffed with ourselves. The night had been eventful and, as far as we were concerned, a morale booster and a damn good way of letting off some steam.

There were no more social activities for the remainder of the deployment as preparations and involvement in the final NATO war exercise were more important.

A couple of weeks later, we arrived back in Arbroath. All the Marines were excited. They had worked extremely hard for the past three months and now had a lot of socialising to catch up on.

Condor Barracks was a sight for sore eyes. I never thought that one day I would welcome the sight of the place, but it was our home from home. At least, that is, it was more homely than living in the snow. The main objective on everybody's mind now was to unpack our kit, get a shower, get dressed, go into town, get a woman and get drunk.

Tonza ran through the accommodation's corridor and pushed open Six Troop's room door, followed closely by myself.

'I suggest you knock when you come in here,' somebody shouted.

The voice came from one of a group of men who were sat around a table on the right-hand side of the room. They were all young Marines who must have joined the commando unit whilst we had been away in the arctic.

The look on Tonza's face said it all. He exploded with a foul temper.

'Shut your fucking mouth. We live here.'

The young Marines were silent. Tonza then proceeded towards his locker and unpacked his kit. I did the same. I knew that they would be dealt with later and that they would regret the reception they had given us.

After a quick shower and change of clothes, we called a taxi and headed into town. We spent the evening in a pub called Breakers. It had a long bar and a couple of pool tables. It was quite plush inside and was a popular place with most of the Marines.

Throughout the night, Tonza repeatedly told me that he was not very impressed with the homecoming reception that we had received earlier. He had been in Six Troop for a number of years and was generally not the quietest of men. He was renowned for speaking his mind and being able to back it up with his fists. His tough stance earned him the respect of a lot of his comrades and most people tended not to get on the wrong side of his quick temper.

Tonza spent most of this night standing alone at the bar and drinking heavily. He was deep in thought and could not blot out of his mind the insult he had received earlier.

'Last orders, please,' the barmaid called out.

He declined another drink and walked back towards me.

'I'm leaving now. I'm going to teach those bastards a lesson they'll never forget.'

I could see he was annoyed. He looked like a bomb that was about to explode. He then left and caught a taxi back to Condor Barracks.

There was only one thing on my mind. I felt like I would be willing to screw anything that moved or at least had a pulse. I wasted very little time in getting fixed up with a loose woman. She wasn't particularly good looking, but that didn't matter. She knew what I wanted and had no objections about giving it to me.

Later, I was told what Tonza had got up to when he left Breakers in a taxi. He had paid the cab driver and declined to wait for his change. He ignored the greeting given to him by the Marine on the main gate whom he knew very well and walked past quickly like a man with a purpose.

The door to Yankee Company accommodation block slammed open under the force of his boot. It echoed loudly throughout the building. He stormed towards Six Troop's room with a brush shank firmly housed in the grasp of his right hand. He stopped outside the door and knocked several times in a quiet and polite fashion. The only people in the room were the three new guys; all the other Marines had gone out to paint the town red.

'Come in,' a quiet voice called out.

Tonza stood back and then charged forward in an aggressive fashion and smashed the door open as he reached it. The force smashed it from its hinges and onto the floor.

'That's how I knock on the door, you fucking cheeky bastards!' Tonza screamed.

There was no escape for the three young men. Tonza was lethal with the brush shank he had acquired and lashed out with it like a madman. He didn't care how much damage he did to them or to the room. His pride was hurt and they had to learn some respect.

The following morning, I returned to the barracks. The damage to the troop's door was the first thing that caught my eye. I stepped over the debris and entered the room. Tonza was lying awake with his arms tucked neatly behind his head watching the television. The three young Marines were also in the room and were sat watching the television with their backs towards me.

Tonza smiled. 'Do you want a cup of tea, Steve?'

'Yes, please,' I replied.

He clicked his fingers and shouted to one of the men watching television. 'Make me two cups of tea, now.'

A tall thin man with blond hair stood up from his chair and switched on an electric kettle. He held his head down, not daring to look in our direction. A minute or so later, he passed us both a cup of steaming hot tea. His face was black and blue with bruising and swelling. I instantly knew that Tonza had patched up the hole in his pride and given the new kids on the block the customary reception that was dished out to new arrivals.

CHAPTER FIVE

EASTER LEAVE

I enjoyed a good social life when I went home on leave and went out every night with my family and friends. I chose to remain in the background during most conversations with the local townsfolk, as they were usually about local current events which I had no knowledge of. I felt that I was on a different wavelength to everybody. Most of my friends at home did the same things week-in and week-out, while I was living a very different lifestyle in very different places.

Through experience, I learned it was best not to tell them about the antics that the Marines got up to. They found it hard to believe that people could live so wildly. I didn't try to change their view, as I knew they wouldn't understand. They lived their lives their way, with their own beliefs and ideas.

Whilst on leave, I ran into an old acquaintance called Barry Dodson. He was twenty-eight years old, short and plump. The locals thought he was very immature for his age. He was renowned for being a compulsive liar and tended to exaggerate a lot when he spoke to people.

Barry told me that he had joined the Army and was enlisted

in the Royal Army Ordnance Corps. He also told me he was getting married in a couple of days' time and invited me to come. He requested that I wear my best uniform on the day, as it would look good in the photographs. I tactfully declined his request and lied to him, telling him that it was in the tailor's shop being adjusted. My thoughts were, why should I show some respect for a man who didn't deserve it? He was literally the local village idiot, so I didn't want people to think I was a close friend and potentially tar me with the same brush. Rather than totally fob him off, I agreed to turn up for the wedding reception, which was held in one of the local working men's clubs.

On the day of the wedding, I went to the working man's club along with my father, who was also invited. I didn't dress in smart clothes for the event but chose to wear the customary serviceman's casual clothes of jeans, T-shirt and desert boots. My desert boots were well worn-in and covered in piss, blood and beer stains. This was called giving them character.

The club was crowded when we arrived and there had been a good turn-out from the married couple's family and friends. I recognised a lot of people with whom I had grown up and also a few I normally drank with when I came home on leave. Barry was busy on the far side of the room conversing with a couple of his military colleagues, who, like him, were dressed in their regimental uniforms. I made my way to the bar and ordered a couple of beers for my father and myself. A guy called Johnny, whom I'd known since I was a young kid, waved his hand for me to go over and talk to him. I could read his lips. He wanted to tell me something. I passed a beer to my father and told him I would be back in a couple of minutes. When I walked over there, Johnny shook my hand and suggested that I take a seat next to him.

'I've been talking to Barry,' said John.

'I bet that was eventful,' I replied with a smirk on my face.

'You're going to love this.'

'Love what?'

'About half an hour ago, I heard Barry talking to his squaddie mates. He told them there was a Marine coming to the reception and that it would be a good laugh if they embarrassed him in front of everybody.'

'OK, Johnny, I've got the message. Thanks for telling me,' I said, frowning.

I stood up and rejoined my father. He'd overheard the conversation and didn't look too happy either. He'd done two years' national service himself, serving in the Royal Artillery. He was down to earth and really popular with the regulars. A few other local lads joined us and we had a laugh about Barry. They found it hard to believe that the local village idiot had joined the Army and was now married. They joked that his new wife either needed a white stick or that Barry must have a huge penis. Everybody laughed loudly.

When Barry noticed that I had arrived at the function, he headed towards me. I saw him signal to his two friends by nodding his head in my direction. They both returned a smile to him and also walked over to speak to me. I gave a warm smile and cautiously gestured to shake his hand to congratulate him on his special occasion. However, he didn't accept my handshake and stopped about a foot or so in front of me along with his two friends.

'The commando tests are a piece of piss,' he sneered, in a harsh and serious voice.

I looked at him and felt my anger starting to rise. I felt insulted and that he was trying to wound my pride. His two friends burst into laughter. They were highly amused at their colleague's comments. My father saw the look on my face and knew that I wasn't very pleased.

'Steven, don't do it, son,' he said, shaking his head from side to side. 'He's not worth it.'

He could see that I was going to snap, but his words weren't enough to contain my rage. 'I'm going to fucking pulverise him,' I shouted in an aggressive manner at the top of my voice. Within seconds, I had grabbed hold of Barry's throat with my right hand and squeezed his windpipe. His face turned deep red as he struggled to breathe. He started to choke and splutter.

A woman screamed and everybody moved back. The music stopped, but nobody spoke. Barry's newly-wed was on the other side of the room. I don't know how much she saw, but it would have been hard to miss the commotion going on. Everybody just stared, unsure of what they should say or do. The other two squaddies moved in to help their friend and approached me from both sides. I maintained my grip on his throat and used my other arm to elbow the first one that got close in the face. His nose burst open and blood splattered across his face. He fell backwards and onto the floor. Chairs and glasses crashed and smashed as he fell and a few women started screaming. A few seconds later, the second squaddie closed in on me. I grabbed the skin under his chin and pulled it downwards. This caused his face to smash into a table below us and he screamed with pain. I then kicked him in the face and he too fell on the floor.

After a few more seconds there was a silence. Most of the guests had cleared out of the room and down the stairs into another function room below. I was boiling with temper and watched for any other forms of attack.

'Come on, son,' said my father. 'They're not worth the effort.'

I turned my attention to Barry. I still had a hold on his throat but with a lighter grip. He looked sorry. I believed he had realised he had bitten off more than he could chew. My father was right. They weren't worth the effort. I released my grip on his throat and took hold of his hair. He pleaded for me to stop and started to cry like a child.

'You're an arsehole, Barry. Everybody knows that,' I said calmly.

His two friends remained motionless on the ground. They looked at each other and then put their heads down, not daring to look at me. I let go of his hair and slapped him across the face with the back of my hand.

'Keep out of my way in future,' I said in a threatening voice.

'Yes, I will, I will,' he murmured.

My father and I then left and walked home, as I wanted a couple of hours' sleep before going out for the night.

If that wasn't enough to keep the locals gossiping, then the following evening's events certainly were. It was my last night of leave and I had decided to spend it socialising with some former school friends in our home part of town, where there was a good choice of public bars. This made the area a great pub-crawl. We usually started at one end of a long street and finished at the other, visiting around ten bars and drinking a pint of beer in each. The last bar we went into was called The Ship Inn. We arrived there around 10.15 p.m. and it was quite busy because most people used to end up there for last orders and the occasional drink after closing time.

We stood at the bar and were all soon served with an ice-cold pint of beer, which was a strong brand that the pub was renowned for keeping. Whilst listening to a conversation between my friends, I could not help overhearing another conversation that was being held by a small group of men in the opposite corner of the room. A couple of them were local to the area and were familiar to me. One of the strangers in the group seemed to be the centre of attention. He was a tall well-made man with short hair and looked like a serviceman. He raised his voice when he spoke to his friends and attracted the attention of a lot of other people who were stood next to him. One of my friends told me that the stranger was a Paratrooper and was a member of the Second Parachute Battalion from Aldershot. This became clear when I noticed a badge bearing the Parachute Regiment's emblem on his jumper.

The Paras and Marines had always been the greatest of rivals and were both elite soldiers with similar reputations for their levels of professionalism and toughness. They hated each other but only because each thought they were better than the other.

After a while, one of his friends told him that I was a Royal Marine Commando and pointed in my direction. I could overhear their conversation and watched out of the corner of my eye as the Para stared in my direction. I was alert and ready in case something was going to happen and pretended to be unaware of his presence as I chatted to the people who were sat around my table. The Para decided it was time to impress his friends.

'Is that a bootneck over there?' he shouted in my direction. (Bootneck is a nickname for a Royal Marine, in a similar fashion that Para is a nickname for a Paratrooper.)

I pretended not to hear his question and continued talking to my friends. One of them also heard his question and asked me if I had heard it too. I nodded my head and told him to ignore him. At first, he seemed a little surprised with my answer, but smiled when I gave him a reassuring wink and a smile. I swallowed what was left of my drink and made my way past the Para and his friends to the bar to purchase another.

'Hey, Marine,' he called out.

This time I looked in the direction of the Para. He signalled with his hand for me to wait for a moment and got up and approached me. When he reached where I was standing, he poked me in the chest with one of his fingers.

'Are you in the Marines, mate?' he questioned in a sarcastic manner.

'Yes, I am, but I'm not your mate,' I replied.

'I'm in the Parachute Regiment,' he continued.

'Yeah, OK. So what do you want me to do about it?'

He asked if I'd been watching a recent television series that was being screened about the training of the Paras. I immediately got the impression he was trying to prove something and decided to end our conversation quickly.

'Piss off, I don't watch comedies,' I snapped at him.

He stared hard into my eyes and looked offended by my comments. I didn't care and was more interested in purchasing another beer before the bar closed. When I got another beer I moved away and ignored him. This seemed to offend him, as he moved to confront me whilst his friends looked on and stood between me and my path to my friends' table.

'The Paras hit harder than the Marines,' he snarled.

I could see him causing friction between us and knew it wasn't going to stop here. I wasn't happy about the situation, as I wanted to stop back in the bar after closing time and have a few more drinks. I thought about what he said and acted quickly.

'Watch this,' I said in a calm voice.

I drank my pint of beer in one go and then threw my empty glass up into the air. He took the bait and followed the glass upwards with his eyes. I threw a hard right-hand punch and hit him square on his chin, which caused him to stumble backwards and into a seat as if he had just sat down. The glass bounced down on the floor beside him without breaking. He was dazed and the blow had almost knocked him unconscious. His friends moved quickly to his aid and checked to see if he was OK. They gave him a drink of water and lifted him up out of the chair and put his arms around their necks before leaving the bar.

I looked at my friend whom I had been talking to earlier and winked and smiled in the same way I had done before. I then casually made my way back to the bar for another drink. My friends seemed astonished with my actions, but impressed with my cool and controlled temperament.

CHAPTER SIX

THE ROYAL GUARD

Back in Arbroath at 45 Commando Unit, things were all go once again. Yankee Company had been asked to provide a Royal Guard to put on a display of commando skills for Her Majesty the Queen. The display consisted of a number of activities, such as abseiling from helicopters, beach landings on assault landing craft, parachuting and a ceremonial parade of the whole of Yankee Company for inspection by the Queen and Prince Philip. It took place at Poole in Dorset, but the rehearsals and training took place at a land naval base in Portsmouth called HMS Excellent. The base was situated on a small island called Whale Island and was also the home of one of the Royal Navy field gun crews. This was a group of men who got together each year and trained rigorously for the field gun display competition, which was held annually at the Royal Tournament in London. They came from all parts of the Royal Navy and had a good reputation for their fitness and strength.

When we arrived, we were accommodated in a huge two-floor building. The inside was very similar to our barrack rooms with the highly polished floors and a locker and bed space for each man. The rooms were very long and broken up by the personal lockers pushed side by side to act as dividers. There were three of these rooms, one for each troop of men.

Two four-ton military lorries arrived at the base and stopped outside of our accommodation block. They were carrying all our kit, including our best Blues uniforms, which were to be used for the ceremonial parade, after the commando skills display. They were all hung up neatly on coat hangers as they had just been pressed at the tailors. Everybody took their turn to climb onto the lorries and collect their uniforms.

Jacko and myself were the last two to do this, as we'd waited for the rush to die down. One uniform still remained on one of the lorries and no one had come to collect it. We both had a closer look and saw that it had a sword attached to it, which meant that it belonged to an officer. The sword was housed in a smart leather scabbard and had a shiny metallic handle, which gleamed as it reflected the bright rays of the sun. Brown cardboard nametags were tied to both the sword scabbard and the uniform. We read them and saw that the officer they belonged to was in Four Troop. Jacko made it crystal clear that he didn't like this officer and referred to him as a fucking wanker. He smiled and then removed the sword from its scabbard. He looked excited and started to wave it about in a simulated sword fight. I decided it was time to leave and took my uniform back to my room.

Jacko was later seen chasing some of the resident sailors around the establishment with the sword, apparently amusing himself with his new-found toy. Also, the officer's Blues uniform was later found in a gutter outside our accommodation block. It was smeared in excrement and was soaking wet with urine.

The following day, an investigation was started by the naval police. However, it was never proven who was responsible for the removal and damage caused to the sword or the ruining of the officer's Blues. My lips were sealed . . .

We had a whole week of rehearsals to prepare for the display and ceremonial parade. This gave us ample time to enjoy the nightlife of Portsmouth and let off some steam.

The main social event of the week took place in a nightclub called Bistros. It was a small seedy joint with a bad reputation for trouble and whores. This made it a perfect venue for men of our nature.

I arrived there late in the evening and was accompanied by Tonza. Inside, the atmosphere was wild. People were dancing everywhere, cigarette smoke filled the air and the music was deafening. There was no shortage of women; in fact I think the men were outnumbered two to one. Before long, I started chatting with one of them. She was tall and skinny, about forty-one years old with long streaky hair and a bulbous nose. She was no oil painting, but that didn't matter. The saying was, 'you don't look at the fireplace when you're poking the fire', meaning that good looks came second in importance to getting laid. I talked to her for a while and found it quite bizarre that she lived in Portsmouth but actually grew up in the same town as me. This gave me a good grounding to get my patter going and gain her confidence. Tonza, meanwhile, had other ideas and ventured upstairs into one of the other bars in the nightclub.

I found it easy to converse with the woman and soon managed to talk my way into her knickers. She was very excited about the blunt proposition I made, asking if I could sleep with her, and she invited me to accompany her back to her flat for a 'coffee'. Another saying the Marines had at the time was, 'Women are like pieces of dog shit: the older they get, the easier they are to pick up'. I accepted her offer and got ready to leave.

'Steve . . . Steve . . .' a familiar voice called.

I looked towards the direction of the voice and saw that it was Tonza. Blood trickled from his nose.

'Come on, Steve, give me a hand, there's trouble upstairs,' he continued, and he beckoned me to follow him.

Oh shit, just my fucking luck, I thought. I sighed deeply and walked away from the willing woman, without even bothering to tell her why. I continued to curse and swear as I followed Tonza up the stairs.

At the top, there was another small room. It was mainly made up of a wooden dance floor with mirrors on all the walls and had a well-lit discothèque at the far end. There was a mass of people fighting with each other all around the room. I recognised some of them as Marines and quickly joined in. The strange thing was that a few of the opposition were women. They were prostitutes and were built like brick shithouses. They fought like men and gave as good as they got. Fists and glasses were flying everywhere and yet the music kept playing. Several doormen appeared on the scene dressed in tuxedos and charged into the crowd. Unusually, they declined to join in the fight and started to push everybody down the stairs and out of the exit door. Their chosen tactics paid off and everybody was outside within minutes, where the fight continued. The big women made themselves scarce and there appeared to be evenly matched numbers who fought on.

I easily overpowered my first opponent and left him on the ground in a pool of blood. Then I began to fight with another and took hold of his clothing around his neck and forced him to the ground. Suddenly, I felt a hand grab hold of the back of my clothing and was pulled backwards away from the man on the ground.

I turned around and saw a policeman restraining me by twisting my right arm behind my back. Then, more policemen arrived and swarmed amongst us in vast numbers, quickly bringing the fight to a standstill.

'What's this all about?' asked one of the policemen.

Everybody who was involved in the fight looked at each other. Blood covered a lot of their clothing and bruised faces. For a few moments, there was total confusion and nobody seemed to know why we were fighting. There was a total silence.

'I know why it started,' a voice called out.

A young man was sat several feet away on the edge of the pavement. He had dyed red hair and was wearing a pair of jeans and a T-shirt. We all looked at him, waiting for his explanation. He rolled up his left trouser leg and revealed he had an artificial limb. He explained that the cause of the fight was because Tonza had tried to remove the artificial leg from him.

'I wanted it for our barrack room wall,' interrupted Tonza.

Everybody, including the policemen, burst into laughter and found the reason behind the brawl very amusing. Fortunately, the policemen allowed us to make our way back to the naval base without being arrested and told the other group of men to leave in the opposite direction.

The entrance to Whale Island was via a small bridge which spanned an inlet from the sea and led up to the main entrance gate of HMS Excellent. We made our way across the bridge to the entrance of the base, where a Navy sentry who was on guard duty challenged us.

'Can I see your identity cards, please?'

'Yes, come closer,' I replied and saw an opportunity for some fun.

The sentry walked the few paces needed to reach me and I

held out my hand as if to show my identity card. He stared at my empty palm and looked puzzled. I took hold of him by his uniform and threw him over my shoulder in a similar fashion to a fireman's carry.

'Put me down,' he shouted. 'I'm the duty watch main gate sentry. Put me down.'

'Down?' I replied.

'Yes, down.'

I stepped forward a couple of paces and threw him off my shoulder and over the side of the bridge.

'Aaaaaaaaaaarrrrrrrrrgggggghhh!' he yelled, and splashed into the deep dark water below. We all burst into laughter and were highly amused.

The door to the well-lit guardroom sprung open and two more uniformed Navy guards ran towards us, but they soon met the same fate as the main gate sentry and splashed into the water.

'It looks like the fun is over,' said one of the other Marines, as the door to the guardroom remained shut. We then made our way back to the accommodation block.

Before turning in for the night, I went to the vending machine room, which was housed in an opposite building. The room was brightly lit and had several vending machines which contained food and soft drinks, and there were also a couple of small-change machines.

I got myself a cup of coffee and a meat pie and sat down on one of the small plastic chairs. I was alone and thought about the events back at the nightclub. I felt disappointed that I had got involved in the fight when I could have been between the sheets with the willing woman. The door to the room slowly creaked open and a man with short black hair and a moustache staggered in. I recognised him as a Marine from one of the other troops. He had a bed space opposite mine in the accommodation block. He looked heavily intoxicated – so much so that his face muscles were relaxed and he slurred when he made an effort to say hello. He inserted a coin into the slot of one of the small-change machines. The machine made a noise as if to eject small change, but no money came out. This annoyed him and he reacted by repeatedly slamming his hand against the side of it. This had no effect.

'Fucking stupid machine,' he growled in disappointment. He turned and slowly staggered towards the door.

'I won't be long,' he said. 'I fucking hate being ripped off.' The door creaked shut after he made his exit.

I continued to enjoy my meat pie and coffee and thought nothing more about it. However, several minutes later the door creaked open again and the same guy staggered back in. I couldn't believe my eyes when I saw what he was carrying. He had a heavy-looking sledgehammer in the grasp of his hand and smiled at me as he prepared to swing it. Instead of waiting to see the inevitable, I made a quick exit and headed into the accommodation block.

Sounds of banging and glass breaking filled the air. Nothing to do with me, I thought, as I undressed and got into bed. I fell sound asleep as soon as my head touched the pillow, until the door to our room banged open. I opened my eyes and rubbed them with my fingers and saw four uniformed Navy policemen walk into the room. Their boots thudded against the bare floor and gave off a sense of urgency.

'Bloody hell. Just look at that,' one of them said, and he pointed to the bed space opposite mine, which was now occupied by the Marine I had seen earlier with the sledgehammer. His bed space was literally saturated with hundreds of coins. They woke the sleeping Marine and told him to get dressed. He looked around and rubbed his eyes in disbelief.

'It's a plant. I didn't do this. I've been set up,' he insisted and shook his head from side to side.

He was then escorted out of the room and one of the Navy policemen remained behind. He pulled a pair of white gloves out of his pocket and put them on before he picked up the coins.

The Marine later admitted the offence because his fingerprints were all over the inside of the change machines and also on some of the coins that were scattered around his bed space. He was convicted of criminal damage and theft and was subsequently sentenced to sixty days' confinement at Portsmouth naval detention quarters.

A few days later, we completed our rehearsals and the display successfully took place in the presence of Her Majesty the Queen and Prince Philip. She later commented on the high level of professionalism and sheer determination shown by the Marines who took part and commended our efforts to our superior officers.

CHAPTER SEVEN

THE QUOTA SYSTEM

After my first active tour of duty to Northern Ireland, I was really beginning to enjoy being a Marine. It had been all work and no play for three solid months, but it had given me the excitement I had joined up for as well as a strong bond with my Marine colleagues. One mistake or mishap could have resulted in the death or serious injury of myself or one of my colleagues, so we were constantly watching each other's backs and trusted each other with our lives. I knew I was with some of the best soldiers in the world and honestly wouldn't have changed places with anyone.

At roll-call back in Arbroath one morning, I learned that my location was about to change again. We were briefed by our sergeant-major, who said there was a shortage of manpower in a number of technical branches throughout the Marine Corps. We were told that the manpower shortage problem had to be resolved and the introduction of the 'quota system' was explained to us. This system was a means of detailing the required amount of men to fill the vacancies in shortage-category branches, whether they were volunteers or not. You would still be required to fulfil the primary role required as a Royal Marine Commando but you had to fulfil a secondary technical role for which you would be trained and specialised.

On completion of his briefing, the sergeant-major told two other Marines and me to stay behind after Yankee Company had been dismissed. For a moment, I wondered why it was us three who had been singled out. Then a tall sergeant from the Royal Marines military police came out of the sergeant-major's office and stood in front of us. The sergeant-major told us to stand at ease and to listen to what the police sergeant had to say.

'Whilst you men have been away in Northern Ireland, we have been carrying out investigations about the events that took place at HMS Excellent during the preparations for the Royal Guard,' said the sergeant. 'Although we cannot prove who threw the three members of the duty guard over the side of the bridge, we know you three were involved.'

The sergeant-major cleared his throat and cut in: 'We could continue the investigation and we feel fairly confident that we can prove it was you three who committed the offence. However, I've decided to volunteer you all for the quota system. Call it your punishment; it'll be a lot better than a military prison. Do any of you disagree?'

There was complete silence. The military police sergeant smiled, whilst the sergeant-major just stared at us with a very serious look on his face.

'Good,' continued the sergeant-major. 'Preece, Black, you two are assigned to the clerks branch. Picknett, you are assigned to the signallers branch.'

Although they had no proof it was us, they were clearly onto us and could quite possibly have pinned it on us with a little more effort, so we weren't tempted to argue with them.

We were all told to report to the signallers' and clerks' training wing back at the Commando Training Centre (CTCRM) at Lympstone in Devon.

One of the other Marines was Paddy Black, who was from County Down in Northern Ireland. He was around twenty-two years old, around 6 ft 3 in. tall and heavily built. He had virtually no eyebrows and always laughed very loudly. At that time, he'd been in the Marines for four years and had fought in the Falklands conflict. His family still lived in Northern Ireland and he went home several times a year to visit them. Because of the Troubles there, servicemen like him were allowed to grow their hair long prior to going home. This was so that they didn't look like servicemen, as this would be a recipe for disaster if any of the terrorists or their supporters ever found out their true identities. Like the majority of Irishmen who ventured out of Ireland, he was nicknamed Paddy.

Paddy and I travelled on the train together from Arbroath to CTCRM. It was a long and boring journey and the train was old, noisy and uncomfortable. It took around fourteen hours to reach our destination from start to finish.

A chill ran down my spine when I walked back through the gates of the Commando Training Centre for the first time since basic training. Memories clamoured in my head as I peered down onto the assault course and saw the thirty-foot climbing ropes blowing in the wind. I frowned and thought of the intense physical pain I had endured there. It was strange being back. I felt like an ex-convict returning to prison after being convicted of another crime. The difference now was that I was a trained Marine and was treated like a person as opposed to being a recruit and treated like a piece of shit. We collected some bedding and were allocated bed spaces in one of the accommodation blocks.

The following morning, we assembled in a classroom situated in the signallers' and clerks' training wing and were greeted by our instructor. His name was Sergeant Smith and he looked around forty years old. He was fit-looking and had short dark hair and a thinly groomed black moustache. He introduced himself and gave us a presentation on the length and content of the course. The course would last for three months and I would be trained in IT within the clerical branch, which would involve a great deal of work with computers. He questioned us in turn as to whether we had volunteered for the course or been detailed to attend it. The delegates were made up of ten Marines, four of whom, including myself, were victims of the quota system.

Clerical duties were generally not what people had joined the Marines for (and nor for that matter were the other two branches of the quota system – chefs and signallers), and we were told that some previous course delegates had done some damaging things in an attempt to get themselves thrown off the course. Sergeant Smith added, however, that he would not tolerate any further behaviour of this kind and warned that any offenders would be severely punished. He even sympathised with us and agreed that the quota system was unfair, but informed us that it was now Marine Corps policy. As he spoke, he knew that we were not the least bit interested in what he had to say and that problems from the four of us were imminent.

In general, life as a trained Marine was a lot more relaxed at the training centre than it was as a recruit, and I often smiled to myself as I watched the day-to-day movements of the recruits under training. Socially, especially, there was no holding us back and we went into town literally every night, frequenting the pubs we used to use as recruits.

One night, I met with a couple of Marines who had been in

the same troop as me during training. Their names were Justin and Tom. They too were victims of the quota system and had to specialise as signallers. We were pleased to be reunited again and exchanged stories of our experiences at our respective first commando units. We drank a few beers together and arranged to meet up the following evening to drink a few more.

Around 6.30 p.m. the following day, I left my room and headed for their accommodation block. These blocks were much better than the ones back at Condor Barracks. They were four floors high and square-shaped, with winding staircases that ran up the middle of their interiors. They had several four-man rooms on each floor.

When I entered the building, I was faced with the task of finding my friends' room. This meant that I had to stop at each room and read the nameplates that were attached to each door. Just my luck, I thought, as I reached the last door on the top floor and found the nameplates with their names on them. The door opened and a short stocky man with a spotty face stood looking straight at me.

'Could you tell me if Tom and Justin are in this room?' I asked him.

'Och yes,' he muttered. 'They'll be back in a few minutes.'

He spoke with a broad Scottish accent and had a sense of urgency in his voice. His face was flushed and, for some reason, he seemed nervous. He then walked past me and headed down the stairs.

I entered the room and found that it was unoccupied. Inside there were four beds and four lockers. Two of the lockers had been left open, so I assumed that Tom and Justin must be somewhere close by or else they would have secured their lockers with the available padlocks. I leaned against the window ledge and peered out of the window. I could see lots of recruits in the opposite blocks. They were ironing clothes and cleaning their field kit, weapons and boots.

A few minutes later, the door opened and Tom entered the room.

'Hello, Steve. Have you been waiting long?'

'No, only a few minutes,' I replied.

'I've just got to collect my wallet and then I'll be ready,' continued Tom.

The door to the room opened again and Justin entered.

'Hello, Steve,' he grinned. 'Let's go and get drunk.'

'Oh fuck, I don't believe it,' frowned Tom.

'Believe what?' Justin asked curiously.

'There's ten pounds missing from my wallet.'

My stomach turned when I heard his comments. A horrible sinking feeling ran through my body, as I'd been alone in the room before they had returned. I hope he doesn't think I've taken it, I thought.

'Tom . . . Tom, I haven't taken it. You know me better than that, mate,' I sighed with a sorry look on my face.

He calmly assured me that the thought hadn't crossed his mind and that he had a fairly good idea who had taken it. I told him about my initial entrance to the room and about the spotty Scotsman whom I had met.

'That's the guy I suspected,' remarked Justin. 'Everybody here knows he's a thieving git.'

We discussed the matter no further and left the building. We had more important things to do, like getting drunk.

Throughout the evening, we discussed at great length the experiences and hardships we had endured since leaving basic training. It felt good to be reunited with my two friends and I knew the feeling was mutual. We drank heavily and laughed together, enjoying the banter. Within myself, I couldn't help feeling guilty about the missing ten-pound note. After all, I was the only person in the room when Tom had returned to find the money missing. I let both my friends know how I felt about the incident and we all agreed that, on our return to base, I alone would be allowed to question the Scotsman about the disappearance of the money.

A few hours and a lot more beer later, we returned to the training centre. Tom and Justin said they would give me a few minutes' head start to carry out my task and told me where the thief's room was located.

The accommodation block was quiet when I entered and dimly lit by a single light bulb on the wall of the stairwell. My footsteps echoed as I walked up the stairs. I stopped outside the Scotsman's room and saw his name inscribed on the nameplate. I braced myself and kicked the door hard with the sole of my shoe and it crashed open, making a loud banging noise that seemed to thunder around the building. I saw him standing at the end of the room. He was dressed in white shorts and a turquoise rugby shirt and had a startled look on his face. He had a metal steam iron in his right hand and was stood behind an ironing board, ironing a pair of trousers.

Anger raged through my body, like a flame landing on a petrol can. I surged forward and kicked the ironing board out of my path. It smashed against the wall, as did the steam iron, which was knocked out of his hand.

'Where is it, you thieving bastard?' I screamed at the top of my voice.

Then, to my total surprise, he didn't deny any knowledge of the money but produced it from a small cardboard box, which he took from his locker. He held out a ten-pound note. His hand was shaking.

'Here it is,' he said trembling. 'I'm really sorry . . . I didn't mean to take it.'

For a few moments, I glared at him and was undecided

what to do. My anger ebbed away and I felt calm. I almost felt sorry for him.

'Why did you take it?' I asked him.

'I don't know, I just did,' he replied desperately.

He could see I had calmed down and moved towards me. I saw the expression on his face change and sensed his intention to attack me. I moved quickly. His nose cracked loudly under the force of a head-butt, which I launched on him with a considerable amount of force.

'Aaarrrgggggghhh!' he screamed and blood splashed into the air.

'I'm going to fucking hammer you, you thieving bastard,' I yelled aggressively, before pushing him back towards the wall.

Then there was a loud clatter as he stumbled backwards over the ironing board and fell down onto the floor where he grabbed hold of the metal iron. When I saw this I reacted quickly and picked up one of the metal bed frames, which had no mattress on it, and raised it above my head. It was quite heavy but I didn't care. I prepared to launch it at him. He couldn't escape . . .

The door to the room suddenly opened and Tom and Justin entered the room.

'Steve . . . leave him, he's had enough,' said Justin in quite a friendly voice.

'Put the bed down, don't throw it at him. He's not worth it, mate,' added Tom, shaking his head.

I looked at the Scotsman. He was a mess and was sat on the floor against the wall with his blood-covered hands covering his face. They're right, I thought. Time to stop.

I slowly put down the bed frame and looked around the room. It was a mess and pieces of smashed furniture were scattered everywhere. The Scotsman slowly lowered his hands and exposed his battered face. Blood oozed from his nostrils and dripped onto the floor.

'OK, here's your money,' I said to Tom and handed over the ten pounds. 'I'm going to bed. Sort this bag of shit out,' was all I could say to them, as I pointed at the thief.

As I left the room, my two friends smiled at each other. They were clearly satisfied with the carnage I had left behind.

The following morning, all the students on our clerical course, including me, assembled with our kit and boarded a four-ton lorry bound for Plymouth. The next phase of our course was at HMS Raleigh. It was the Royal Navy's basic training centre.

CHAPTER EIGHT

HMS RALEIGH (TORPOINT)

HMS Raleigh was located at a place called Torpoint. It was a short ferry ride across the River Tamar from Plymouth's Devonport dockyard.

During our first week, Paddy and myself spent all our spare time making use of the base's excellent sporting facilities, which were much better than those provided in a commando unit. We were like two kids playing with new toys at Christmas time.

Our accommodation was practically brand new and, for the first time since I had enlisted in the Marines, we had carpets on the floor. The food in the dining hall was of an excellent standard and offered plenty of choice at meal times. Again, this was a lot better than that offered back at the commando units as we usually had only two choices: take it or leave it.

Nevertheless, Paddy and I were not happy with having to undergo a training course for which we did not volunteer. We missed being back at 45 Commando and actually doing the kind of work we had originally joined up to do. When payday came around we headed into town to drown our sorrows in as much beer as we could possibly consume.

The venue was the main high street in Torpoint. It wasn't very big and only had a handful of pubs and a small dingy nightclub called the Harbour Lights. Most people generally caught the nearby ferry into Plymouth, except for most of the new Navy recruits and a few trained ranks. During the night, we had two or three pints of beer in each of the pubs before entering the pub next door to the nightclub.

'Steve, I'm just going to the toilet. Get the beers in,' said Paddy as we entered the dimly lit pub.

The lounge was half-full of people and the atmosphere was warm and friendly. I watched Paddy as he turned and walked towards the toilets and saw him take an ice bucket off the side of the bar and disappear through the toilet door with it tucked neatly under his arm.

I laughed to myself. He's going to urinate into it and place it back on the bar, I thought, and ordered the beers ready for his return. After several minutes, he returned with the ice bucket and casually placed it back on the bar. He was grinning like a Cheshire cat and looked quite pleased with himself.

'You've pissed into it, haven't you?' I asked him.

He grinned even more. 'You'll see.'

We moved away from the bar and sat on a couple of stools around a small wooden table. We were facing the bar and watching the ice bucket. Paddy still looked very excited and continued to smile.

Half an hour or so later, a group of middle-aged people entered the pub and stood at the bar to order some drinks. A tall man, dressed in a smart suit, with curly brown hair and a thick bushy moustache ordered several glasses of whisky. When he received his order, he placed one of his hands into

101

the ice bucket and removed a handful of ice cubes and placed them into the whisky glasses. He then passed a glass to each of his friends and proposed a toast in celebration of something.

By this time, Paddy was holding his sides and rolling around in laughter. Whatever he had done had now started to take effect. The group acknowledged their friend's proposed toast and drank from their glasses. Then they curiously raised their glasses against the light and stared at them.

I continued to observe the group and looked at the tall curly-haired man. I could see something that looked like a gooey substance clinging to his moustache.

I burst into laughter. 'You dirty bastard, Paddy. You've shit in the ice bucket, haven't you?'

He laughed loudly. 'Yes, and I've got diarrhoea.'

We both howled with laughter and then quickly left the pub to go to the nightclub next door, before anybody realised what we were finding so amusing.

The Harbour Lights nightclub was very busy when we entered and was bustling with servicepeople. Inside was just a huge hall with a wooden floor and a disco that was more like the type of disco you saw when you were at school. Most of the people inside were naval personnel from HMS Raleigh. This was their local nightspot and hardly anybody from Plymouth on the other side of the river ever came across.

For some reason or other I decided to telephone home and say hello to my family, so I looked for and quickly located a phone whilst Paddy went to the bar to buy a round of beer. I dialled the number and waited for an answer. After about four or five rings, someone answered the phone.

'Hello?' It was my brother Peter; I recognised his voice.

'Hello, Peter, it's Steve. How are things at home?'

'All right at the moment. But have I got news for you!' he answered in a cocky tone of voice.

'What news?' I was curious.

'Can you remember Marilyn, who you slept with when you were last home on leave?'

Marilyn was a middle-aged woman whom I had slept with after a heavy night on the beer. She had a terrific figure, but wasn't the best-looking creature in the world. She'd been the only one available at the time, though. I suppose the saying was 'any port in a storm'.

'Yes, I remember her. What about her?'

'She's pregnant.' He howled with laughter.

I paused for a moment and tried to gather my thoughts. I could hear Peter sniggering on the other end of the telephone. Fucking bollocks, I thought, and slammed down the telephone to go to drink some more beer with Paddy. I was quite shocked at the news. Oh shit, I thought, I don't even like her.

Paddy just laughed when I told him the news. 'Is she ugly?' he asked.

I nodded my head. 'Yes, very ugly. Where's my beer?'

He passed me a pint of beer. 'Fuck it, Steve. Let's get drunk.'

We drank several more pints of beer and joked about the ice bucket from the previous pub. Paddy later acquired himself a woman and danced the night away on the dance floor. I left about half an hour before closing time and stood outside looking for a taxi. It was raining heavily so I stood in a nearby shop doorway. I was alone at first but was joined by another Marine who was on the same course as me at HMS Raleigh. He kindly offered to let me share his waiting cab rather than leave me to queue for another. I accepted and was very grateful.

We got out of the taxi and entered the naval base via the main gate. The sentry checked our identity cards and allowed us to proceed into the establishment. We were both very hungry and headed straight for the vending machine cafeteria. Unfortunately, there were no lights on inside and the outside doors were locked.

'It's locked, Steve. We can't get in,' said the other Marine with a big frown on his face.

'Oh yes we can,' I replied.

CCRRRAAAASSSSHHHHH . . . .

The double doors to the cafeteria crashed open under the force of my right boot. Their window frames shattered inwards and smashed onto the floor inside. I looked around. The other Marine had disappeared. Only the splashing of the rain could be heard and this was quite heavy.

The beer I had consumed through the night had taken its effect and I felt quite drunk. I didn't care if anybody had heard the noise or came to investigate it. I was very pissed off with the news I had received earlier in the night and was past caring.

Inside the darkened cafeteria I made short work of a couple of glass-cased vending machines. I smashed them open and took a couple of pies and pasties and then calmly placed them into a microwave oven, which was housed on a shelf fixed to the wall. There was no noise apart from the rain pouring down outside. I still didn't care if somebody came and caught me, but nobody did. I took my time and ate the food I had stolen before calmly leaving the building.

A short time later, I arrived back at our accommodation block. I was soaking wet and in a really bad mood. As I walked up the stairs I felt angry. I saw a glass window and kicked it without thought. It smashed and I just laughed and carried on walking up the stairs. Each time I came to a window, I did the same thing over again – either smashing it with my foot or with my fist. Blood slowly trickled between my fingers from a resulting small laceration on my right hand. I licked the wound and laughed hysterically.

At the top of the stairs, I stood outside the door to my room. Then I heard voices coming from the television room, which was at the other end of a long corridor. I saw a fire hosepipe fixed to the wall opposite the television room. Hhhmmmmm, time to have some fun, I thought.

I uncoiled the hosepipe and turned on the water stop tap. Water gushed out rapidly as I held the hose and ran towards the door.

THWACK . . . .

The door burst open under the force of my boot and several startled sailors, who were watching the television, all looked towards me.

'Have some of this,' I shouted and waved the gushing hose from side to side. They dived for cover and hid behind some chairs. I wasn't stopping yet, the fun was just beginning. Anyone who dared to peer over the top of the chairs fell foul of a further burst from the hosepipe.

I quickly got bored with this and left the room, dragging the hosepipe with me. I then carefully rehoused the hosepipe and wound it back onto the hose reel attached to the wall.

I turned to walk back to my room and suddenly noticed that there was a fire extinguisher right next to my leg. Yeah, why not, I thought. I picked up the fire extinguisher and pulled out the safety pin.

'Yeeeeaaarrrrrgghhh!' I yelled wildly and pounded back towards the television room. A sailor peered around the door, which was slightly open.

'Oh, fucking hell. I don't believe it, he's back,' he shouted to the other occupants of the room.

The sailor fell to the ground as I shoulder-charged him on re-entry to the room. I then discharged the extinguisher all over everybody until it was empty. Foam was everywhere. Then I felt angry again and lifted the extinguisher above my head in preparation for smashing it into the television screen.

'Steve, no,' somebody shouted.

I recognised the voice and turned around. It was another Marine who was on my course.

'No, Steve. Don't smash the fucking television, we won't have anything to watch.'

'Er, OK,' I replied and threw the fire extinguisher onto the floor.

I left the room and walked down the corridor. Every few feet I came to a door, which accommodated four naval personnel. I kicked each door open, switched on the light and tipped the sleeping residents' beds over and onto the floor. Then I switched off the light and left the room.

After four rooms I stopped, because the next room was mine. Time for bed, I thought, and entered my room. Paddy wasn't back yet, so I got undressed and got into bed. I lay awake for a while and stared at the stars through an open window. The door creaked open slowly and several uniformed naval ranks stood in the doorway and looked around the room.

'Yes, gents, can I help you?' I asked in a polite and calm manner.

One of them stepped in front of his colleagues and introduced himself as the duty petty officer before taking a few more paces into the room. I wasn't familiar with naval ranks at the time, but later learned that a petty officer is an equivalent rank to a Marine sergeant.

'Who are you?' he asked.

'Marine Preece. Why?' I replied.

'Have you been outside your room tonight?'

'No. I've been in bed all night. I've got a bad back.'

The petty officer looked confused with my answer.

'I'm very sorry. There must be a mistake,' he said and left the room and closed the door behind him.

Stupid fucking sailors, I thought.

Several minutes later, the door opened again. It was the same group of naval ranks led by the petty officer.

'Get dressed, Marine Preece, and come with us,' he shouted in a serious manner.

'Fuck off,' I replied.

'Do you know who I am?' he continued.

'No, I don't. Fuck off, I'm trying to sleep.'

'You had better get dressed. You're in serious trouble.'

I knew I was in deep trouble, but I didn't care.

'OK, I'll get dressed,' I said.

I then got out of bed and put my clothes on. As I dressed, I pointed towards the petty officer.

'I don't know who or what you are. I'm not familiar with naval ranks.'

'OK, OK, let's go,' he ordered.

Two naval policemen along with the duty petty officer then escorted me to the guardroom. Inside, it was well lit and the dark blue floors were heavily polished. Lots of pictures of warships covered the light grey walls.

I was stood in a corridor outside the petty officer's office. I had my back to the wall with the two naval policemen standing guard over me.

'Can I use the toilet, please?' I asked politely.

There was no reply. The petty officer walked into the corridor, so I repeated my question.

'Can I use the toilet, please?'

'No, you cannot use the toilet,' he replied harshly.

Fuck you, I thought, and relieved my bladder of its now

heavy load. Two wet patches immediately appeared on my jeans. Urine dribbled its way down my leg and formed a small pool on the floor.

'You dirty bastard,' the petty officer exclaimed.

I grinned at him. 'Sorry . . . I needed a piss. Couldn't wait.'

He then told me that he was going to have me put in a cell for the night and had one of the naval policemen search me before I was marched into a small room for a brief interview.

'Did you break the glass windows in the accommodation block?'

'What windows?' I replied.

He stared at me in silence. 'Did you set off the fire hosepipe?'

'Yes, I did.'

'Did you extinguish the fire extinguisher?'

'Yes, I did.'

I knew I couldn't really deny these offences. But I also knew that nobody had seen me breaking the windows. If they had, he would have told me that he had a witness or witnesses. He never mentioned the doors to the cafeteria, the vending machines or the fact that I had wrecked a lot of the rooms and tipped people out of their beds. The petty officer tried another tactic.

'OK, you've admitted two of the offences, so you might as well come clean and admit you smashed the windows and be done with it.'

'I've told you, I don't know anything about breaking windows,' I replied cautiously.

He sat back in his chair. For a few moments, he was motionless and looked to be in deep thought. Then he rubbed his chin.

'It's the cells for you,' he snarled. 'We'll sort this out in the morning.'

He shouted for the two guards outside the room to enter. They came in and then escorted me to a cell.

My cell was small and lit by a bright light, which was housed high up against the ceiling, out of reach. There was a small window, which was also high up and was covered by three iron bars. My bed was a long narrow wooden bench, which was situated only a few inches off the cold concrete floor. It had a mattress, a sheet and a thick blanket.

The guards removed my belt and both of my laces. This was standard procedure for prisoners, just in case they tried to hang themselves. They then slammed the door shut and locked it. A loud bang echoed around the cell and the keys rattled as they removed them from the lock. Then there was a silence.

I removed my clothes and climbed into bed. Oh well, bollocks, I thought. Another night in the life of Steven Preece. I was tired and fell asleep as soon as my head hit the pillow.

The following morning, I awoke early and felt confused. At first, I didn't know where I was or how I had got there. I sat up and rubbed my hands over my face. My head ached and I felt like shit. I sat up and put my feet on the floor. The events from the previous night came flooding back.

Keys rattled in the lock of the cell door. The door opened and a young uniformed sailor entered. He was carrying a tin breakfast plate, which consisted of egg, bacon, beans, tomatoes and two slices of fried bread.

'Here's your breakfast, Royal,' he said smarmily and held out the plate at arm's length. Royal was a shortened term for a Royal Marine used by the Navy.

I stared at him. He was grinning at me.

'Fuck off,' I shouted and kicked the plate out of his hand. It landed against the wall and fell onto the floor. The plate rattled and rolled away from the food.

He bolted for the exit and quickly locked the door behind him. There was an eyehole on the door covered by a small steel plate. This was pulled to one side and his eye was pushed firmly against the hole so that he could peer into the cell. He screamed as I poked it hard with my index finger, and the steel plate was drawn shut across the hole again.

I stared at the food on the floor and my stomach rumbled because I was hungry. Oh well, I thought. The cell floor is clean and it all comes out the same way. I began to eat the food off the floor. The egg was a bit dirty but I still consumed it, and the rest of it posed no problems. Unfortunately, there was no coffee to wash it down with, but you can't have everything.

When I was released from the cells, the naval police escorted me to an interview room for further questioning. I was left alone in the room for about half an hour, which gave me time to think. The room was bare apart from a table, two chairs and a clock on the wall.

A short fair-haired naval policeman entered the room and sat in the chair on the opposite side of the table. He looked directly into my eyes. 'OK, young man, tell me all about it?' he asked.

'I have nothing to say until a Royal Marine officer is present,' I promptly replied. I knew that I was entitled to have one present and that he would advise me as to my answers during the course of the interview. He nodded his head and acknowledged my request.

'Very well, there are a couple here at present.'

Approximately one hour later, the naval policeman returned, accompanied by a Royal Marine officer. He was a young lieutenant who was staying at the establishment with a Marine recruits' training team. They came here to use the firing ranges at a place called Tregantle Fort.

He introduced himself and asked me to explain in detail the events from the previous night. I told him exactly the same story I had told the naval police.

'What about the windows?' he asked.

'No, sorry,' I replied. 'I don't know anything about any windows.'

He wasn't sure whether or not to believe me and tried again.

'Look, we both wear the Green Beret. We're not like these stupid sailors. If you admit to me that you smashed the windows, I promise you that it will go no further.'

He sounded very sincere. I briefly looked at his Green Beret. I wanted to tell him the whole story. Maybe he'd understand, I thought. I paused for a moment, before telling him about the phone call and the news I had heard from my brother, but I declined to admit responsibility for the windows. The risk was too great to tell him the whole story. Why would he ask me to trust him with this information if his intentions were not to reveal it?

'I am sorry, sir, but I really am not responsible for any damage done to some windows. I've admitted what I am responsible for and will accept the consequences,' I finished.

'OK,' he replied. 'Wise move.'

The following day, I was brought before the Navy commanding officer and charged with the following offences:

1. Extinguishing a fire extinguisher without just cause.

2. Misuse of a fire hosepipe.

3. Causing a disturbance.

4. Insubordination to a superior non-commissioned officer.

The process of passing judgment in the Navy was quite different from that in a Marine commando unit. The Navy commanding officer held what was called a 'captain's table'. The officer stood behind a large wooden table and was presented with the case to be tried. It was a fair process, where the accused were given a fair chance to state their defence. (Back in the commando units, by contrast, we were hauled in front of the commanding officer and screamed at by the RSM (regimental sergeant-major). Your fate was usually decided before you even marched through the door.)

I pleaded guilty to all the charges except the last one: insubordination to a superior non-commissioned officer. The petty officer stated that I had stuck one finger up in his direction, when he originally challenged me in my room. This was when he identified himself and I pointed at him and told him I didn't know who he was.

I emphatically denied this, as my action was not intended as he had indicated, and to my delight I was supported by the commanding officer. He fined me £160 for the offences and also imposed fourteen days' restricted privileges – called number nines – on me. Luckily, the damage caused to the cafeteria was never linked to me and the smashing of the windows could not be proved. I occasionally wondered how different the outcome would have been if I had admitted responsibility to the Royal Marine officer.

A few days later, I telephoned home and spoke to my brother again. He told me that the pregnancy comments were all a big joke and asked if I thought it was funny. I laughed loudly: 'You didn't really think I would fall for that, did you?'

CHAPTER NINE

AN EYE FOR AN EYE

Thank the stars that's over, I thought. I had finally finished my restricted privileges. For the past fourteen days and nights I had been kept busy cleaning, mopping and polishing floors, scrubbing huge gas cookers and washing vast amounts of pots and pans, along with polishing brass handrails and cannons. The only thing on my mind now was to go out on the town and get drunk again with Paddy. He had missed my company and told me that his social life had been quiet and uneventful.

It was a Thursday night; Paddy and I had a lot to celebrate and headed into the high street at Torpoint. It was the usual busy night on a Thursday, as a lot of naval personnel went out for a few beers prior to going home on a weekend's leave.

We met a few of the other Marines who were on our course in one of the pubs and joined their company. They continually joked about the antics for which I had been charged and seemed highly amused. Some of them bought me a drink and congratulated me on the occasion of finishing my punishment routine. Beer flowed throughout the evening and once again we ended up in the Harbour Lights nightclub. Our group had grown in numbers to about seven Marines, most of whom were now in a drunken and abusive state. This was to the dismay of some of the other people socialising, as they were on the receiving end of a lot of the abuse.

Back inside the nightclub, we split into two separate groups. This was because there were so many people inside the club that it was practically impossible to stay together. The volume of the music was extreme. We could hardly hear ourselves talk and had to shout in each other's ears to make some form of conversation.

Paddy was with the other group, who were stood about ten feet away from us. I looked in their direction and caught his attention. He smiled and pointed at the numerous groups of women that littered the dance floor. I nodded my head and smiled back at him, before continuing to converse with other members of my group.

A more easy-listening record was being played, which reduced the heavy volume of the music. Then I heard Paddy's voice.

'Hey, watch where you're going,' he shouted.

A tall well-built man dressed in jeans and a dark blue sweatshirt pushed Paddy aside and continued to barge his way into and through our group.

'Get out of my way, I hate Marines,' he snarled.

I took an instant dislike to his sullen and aggressive attitude and stood in his path, staring at him face to face. He was much older than I was and a lot taller and broader in the shoulders.

'Get outside, I'll fight you,' I shouted and beckoned him to follow me as I turned towards an exit door.

His face dropped and he reacted quickly by grabbing hold of my jumper around the shoulder area and pulling me backwards towards him. Attack was my only form of defence, so I turned around and adopted a boxing stance before quickly launching a powerful head-butt directly into his face. His nose crunched under the blow and blood splattered into the air. The force of the head-butt sent him reeling backwards and onto his back. Two doormen dressed in tuxedos and dickey bows appeared on the scene before I had the chance to even think about following up my attack.

'What the hell is going on?' demanded one of them.

They saw the other man rolling around on the floor with his hands covering his bloodstained face. Then they looked at me. Paddy was quick to intervene and told them that he was a witness and that the man on the floor had had too much to drink and was becoming abusive and pushing everybody around. I told them that I had only pushed him away from me to defend myself and that he had fallen flat on his face.

They paused for a moment and looked at each other. Then one of them nodded his head in agreement with our version of events. Both of the doormen raised the injured man back onto his feet and led him to the exit door. Paddy and I laughed and clashed our beer glasses together to celebrate our success in flooring the man, who was quite obviously a sailor, and having him thrown out of the club.

Later, we left and started to walk the few miles back to base. Paddy was his usual self and laughed and joked on the way. It was late, but the night was warm and there wasn't a single cloud in the sky. After a mile or so, we passed a field full of sheep. A wooden fence ran down the edge of the field and we stopped and leaned against it. Paddy started to laugh loudly.

'What are you laughing at?' I asked curiously.

'You know how we're always telling jokes about shagging sheep?' he giggled, with the usual big daft grin on his face.

'Er, yes. You mean like, the best place to shag one is on the edge of a cliff because they push back harder.'

'Yeah.'

I wasn't sure what Paddy was thinking because at times he was just unpredictable. 'What the hell are you on about? Are you going to kill one?' I continued.

He laughed again. 'No, I'm going to shag one.'

I burst into laughter and watched Paddy climb over the fence.

'Quiet, Steve, I need to catch one first.'

I couldn't stop laughing and had to hold my sides because my ribs were literally hurting. I watched Paddy as he chased and caught one of the sheep. He grabbed hold of it from behind and held its tail. It kicked and tried to get away and it bleated loudly. He then dropped his trousers and pants and pushed his erect penis into the back end of the sheep. I looked on in complete amazement as he started to shag it.

'Fucking hell, Paddy, that one looks a lot better than some of those tarts back at the nightclub.'

'Quiet, Steve, you're putting me off my stroke,' he laughed.

'She looks like she's enjoying it, or is it a he?'

'It's a she.' He laughed again and then withdrew before pulling his pants up and climbing back over the fence. The sheep ran off into the darkness and bleated loudly.

'Well, was she any good?' I asked.

'She was good, but I was better.'

We both laughed for quite some time and continued on our way.

An hour or so later we were back inside HMS Raleigh and walking towards our accommodation block. A window on the first floor of a neighbouring block opened and a male head peered out.

'Keep the fucking noise down,' he shouted.

'Fuck off and go to bed,' Paddy snapped.

The man continued to hurl abuse. We knew that the

accommodation block he was in was home to the Royal Marines band service (whose members were called 'bandies'). They weren't Marines, they were musicians, and were reputed to be some of the best military musicians in the world.

I didn't like his level of abuse and told Paddy that I had a large marrow, which was shaped like a caveman's club, in my locker.

'I'm going to get my marrow and pan his fucking head in,' I told Paddy in a serious manner.

'Yeah, let's do it,' replied Paddy. 'Let's pan the stupid bandy's fucking head in.'

We entered our room and I unlocked my locker to get the marrow. A loud knock on the door turned our attention towards the doorway. The door started to open slowly and creaked with the motion. A big tall man, wearing a white T-shirt, stood facing us.

'Remember me, do you?' he said sarcastically and had a smarmy look on his face. I recognised him as the tall sailor from the Harbour Lights nightclub whom I had been fighting with earlier. He had changed his clothes. His face was swollen and badly bruised and a first-aid plaster covered the bridge of his nose.

'What do you want?' demanded Paddy.

'Him,' he replied, and pointed at me.

I knew his intentions. He wanted revenge. I slowly and cautiously moved towards him and stopped out of arm's reach. He looked puzzled, unsure of when to make his move. I saw my chance and took it, once again knocking him down onto the floor with the same powerful head-butt. He fell backwards and into the corridor, where his head banged against the opposite wall. Blood splattered onto the wall and was all over his face and clothes. I stood above him, victorious once more, but was curious as to his identity.

'Who are you?' I asked him.

He looked up at me and realised I wasn't going to attack him further.

'I'm a leading seaman, and if you hit me any more I'm going to report you and you'll be in deep trouble. You might even get kicked out of the Marines,' he continued.

I didn't know what to think and wasn't totally sure what a leading seaman's rank was. I was still quite a young Marine and had little experience of working with the Navy. We never saw them when we worked in commando units unless we were using the Navy ships to deploy onto beaches. This was also the reason why I didn't know who the petty officer was a couple of weeks earlier. (A leading seaman was the Navy's equivalent rank to a Marine corporal, which made him senior in rank to me.)

I felt very confused. I was proud of being a Marine and didn't want to risk being kicked out. So I stood up and allowed him to return to his feet.

'If you let me hit you in return for what you've done to me, I'll go away and not report anything,' he suggested.

I didn't want to get into any further trouble, especially after I had just finished being punished for a previous incident.

'OK then, do it,' I agreed.

Paddy's face dropped. He couldn't believe his ears. The sailor didn't need to be told twice. He head-butted me twice in the face. My front teeth cracked and felt numb. My mouth filled with blood, and blood also trickled from a cut in my lip. I rubbed my tongue over my teeth and felt that they were loose.

'Are you done?' I asked the sailor.

He looked at me briefly before bolting down the corridor and disappearing through a doorway. I turned and looked at Paddy. He looked shocked and concerned.

'Fucking hell, why did you let him do that?' he asked with a totally bewildered look on his face.

'I don't really know,' I replied.

I felt disorientated and even more confused than before. Did I do the right thing, I wondered. Paddy suggested that I should go to the guardroom and report that I had been assaulted. We never gave any thought as to what I had done to him and I just agreed with Paddy. Maybe if I reported the attack the sailor would have to face disciplinary action.

'What on earth has happened to you?' exclaimed the duty petty officer as I walked through the well-lit guardroom door. I told him that a tall sailor had assaulted me back in our accommodation block and that it was for no apparent reason. He acted quickly and detailed two naval policemen to search the block for the man I had described.

One of them returned about thirty minutes later and reported that they had found him. He had apparently barricaded himself in his room, just in case I decided to pay him a visit. The naval policeman said he had to remove the door from its hinges to gain access to him.

Moments later, the second naval policeman arrived and was accompanied by the tall sailor. I looked at him. Bollocks, I thought. His face was badly swollen, bruised and bloodstained. I realised I had foolishly forgotten about the mess I had made of him earlier.

The petty officer was astonished and made it very clear to both of us that we were in deep trouble and would have to answer to the commanding officer. We were both admitted into the sickbay (hospital) and placed in separate wards. I was examined by a doctor, who called out a dentist. The dentist looked at my loose teeth and then fastened them together with enamel. I was then escorted back to my bed, where I immediately went to sleep.

The following morning, the naval police interviewed us both separately. We had to make written statements to give our versions of events, which, of course, were different. I blamed him and he blamed me. The final judgement would be made by the commanding officer, who would try the case a couple of days later.

We were both asked who we wanted to represent us and present our case. The leading seaman opted for his departmental officer and, to everybody's surprise, I made an unusual request and asked to represent myself. At first, the naval policemen laughed at my request, but later it was granted.

Two days later, the case was tried by the commanding officer. I stood at ease outside his office, waiting to be told to march in. The door opened.

'Marine Preece, attention.' I rapidly slammed my heels together and stood to attention.

'Quick march . . . halt.'

The master-at-arms spoke sharply as he gave me my orders. I was brought to a halt about five paces from the captain's table. The commanding officer stood behind it. He was dressed in his naval officer's uniform and had a grey beard. He looked old and reminded me of Captain Birds Eye who used to appear on adverts for fish fingers.

The master-at-arms was the Navy's equivalent rank to a regimental sergeant-major. He addressed the commanding officer and told him my identity and the charges of which I had been accused. They were charging me with assaulting a senior rank.

The old man looked me directly in the eyes and frowned. I felt as if he had already decided that I was guilty and was going to come straight out with a punishment. Instead, a line of questioning began. I thought carefully as I answered the barrage of questions. They began with the incident in the nightclub. The leading seaman gave his explanation of how I had head-butted him and knocked him to the ground. He described my movement as being so fast that at first he did not know what had hit him. I laughed at his remark, but only in my mind. Inside, I felt great satisfaction at what he had said. It was quite a compliment. He was a lot bigger than I was and yet I had easily defeated him in a fight. I knew I could use our difference in height to my advantage and thought hard about how I would present this.

'Marine Preece,' said the commanding officer.

'Yes, sir,' I responded.

'Can you explain what the leading seaman has just told me?'

'Yes, sir . . . I know this might sound a bit silly to you, sir . . . but look at the size of him compared to me.'

His eyebrows rose and he stared at the leading seaman, who was now looking down at me.

'Yes, carry on,' ordered the commanding officer, nodding his head.

'Well, sir, he tried to head-butt me. But because of our height difference, he banged his face on my forehead.'

He looked long and deep into my eyes and his thick bushy eyebrows rose like a bird spanning its wings. Everybody in the room looked at each other. They were totally flabbergasted by my answer. For a few moments there was a total silence . . . .

'Well, Marine Preece, can you explain how he ended up on the floor?'

'Yes, sir. In defence against his attack, I pushed him away from me. He stumbled backwards and fell onto the floor,' I replied.

'Then what happened?' He was intrigued and wanted to hear the rest of my story.

'The doormen came over and threw him out, sir,' I answered swiftly.

The commanding officer wanted to check and discuss my version of events with the master-at-arms, so we were both separately marched out of the room.

The sailor frowned in total disbelief at my fabricated explanation. I was the total opposite and felt very pleased with the pack of lies I was able to conjure up to explain the reasons for my actions.

His defending officer, who accompanied him, reassured him that it was not over yet. However, it soon came to light that I had won round one of the hearing.

The captain's table took on board the judgement of the nightclub's doormen and the fact that they had removed the leading seaman from the premises and not me. They continued that, although my explanation of the reason for the head-butt was debatable, it was in fact quite possible. A statement from Paddy also backed up my version of events; fortunately, it was taken after I had the chance to speak to him the day after the incident.

One down and one to go, I thought. It was time for round two: the events in the accommodation block. Back under the pressure of intensive questioning once more, I used the same explanation and tactic. I said that he had come to my room to try to attack me once more and tried to head-butt me in the same manner as before, and that once again he had failed to connect properly with his intended target and banged his face hard against my forehead. I knew I was pushing my luck, but it was the only thing I could think of at the time. Again, there was a total silence . . .

It worked. The commanding officer concluded that, if the leading seaman had misjudged his first attempt at head-butting me, then he could have easily misjudged his second attempt. However, the commanding officer was still curious about another matter. He shook his head slowly and rubbed his chin with his fingers.

'If this man threatened you with severe disciplinary action in the event of you hitting him back when he attacked you . . . why did you just stand there and let him do it?'

The answers were already waiting to flow out of my mouth, like a bird singing on a rooftop. I felt confident and ready to provide the right answers to any other questions he wanted me to answer.

'Well, sir, if given the choice of taking a beating or being disgracefully discharged from the Royal Marine Corps, I would always take the beating. After all, sir, physically inflicted wounds heal, whereas mental wounds to my pride and honour may not,' I concluded.

'Hhhmmmmm,' he replied and then nodded to the master-at-arms.

We were once again both marched out of the room until a decision was made as to the results of the case. Outside in the corridor, the leading hand was talking to his defending officer. He was shaking his head and pointing in my direction. I could overhear him saying words like, I don't believe it, where did he get that from, that's impossible, he's lying, etc.

Approximately thirty minutes later, the door opened and we were marched back in. The commanding officer spoke abruptly.

'Marine Preece.'

'Yes, sir,' I replied sharply.

'Of the charge brought against you of assaulting a senior rank, I find you not guilty.'

'Yes, sir, thank you, sir.'

I was then instructed to do an about turn and march out of the room. The leading seaman had to stay behind to answer the charges brought against him. As I marched past him I smiled and winked at him. He frowned and shook his head.

I later heard that he was found guilty of assaulting me on both occasions. His consequent penalty was forty-eight days' detention in Portsmouth Naval Detention Quarters and he was also stripped of his leading seaman rank.

The specialist training course was over a week after this. Paddy and I had now totally finished all the phases of the training we'd been forced to do under the quota system, and we left HMS Raleigh along with the other course delegates. We were all off to our newly appointed commando units.

Paddy patted me hard on the back and laughed loudly as we drove out of the main gate. 'I'll tell you what, Steve, if you fell into a bucket of shit, I'm sure you would come out smelling of roses,' he laughed.

CHAPTER TEN

THE COMMANDO LOGISTIC REGIMENT

It was a dark rainy night when I arrived at my newly assigned commando unit, the Commando Logistic Regiment at Seaton Barracks in Plymouth. The role of this unit was to supply logistics (food rations, weapons and equipment) to the forward commando units, who fought on the front line.

Owing to my specialist training, I was employed in technical administration in the main headquarters, and worked with the then new computers. I was once again in the position of joining a new unit and not knowing anybody.

Unfortunately, Paddy had been posted to a different commando unit somewhere else, up north. Oh well, I thought, at least this time I'm not just a new piece of skin. However, I still needed to settle in and make new friends.

My new colleagues were easy to get along with and were mature, experienced Marines who had also served in the front-line commando units prior to being posted here. The accommodation blocks were similar to those at Commando Training Centre and a vast improvement on those back at Condor Barracks in Arbroath. I was put in a four-man room and shared it with one other Marine. It had two spare bed spaces and lockers, which we shared to store our kit.

My roommate was called Sam Olsen. He was a huge figure of a man with bulging eyes and brown wavy hair. He was also the proud owner of a pair of shoulders that stretched the width of a pool table. When I first met him he instantly reminded me of Desperate Dan from *The Dandy*.

The regiment was in a state of preparation for a forthcoming three-month winter deployment to Norway, so for the next couple of weeks it was all work and no play, and this meant very little socialising. Christmas leave soon came around, so all of us, except the usual rear party (skeleton crew), headed home.

During my leave periods, which were about six weeks a year, I teamed up with my brother Peter and went out drinking around the town every night. On this occasion, Peter and I had been out drinking all day and had thoroughly enjoyed the Christmas atmosphere. We drank around ten pints of beer on a lunch-time session and another ten pints during the evening.

We returned home late and staggered in through the front door. We were absolutely plastered and headed straight upstairs and got into our beds. We still slept in bunk beds and I always insisted on taking the top bunk because Peter still tended to wet the bed even though he was now an adult. We bid each other goodnight and were soon sound asleep.

Water splashed and trickled down my face. Bloody rain, I thought, and opened my eyes. I looked into the darkness, but didn't see the clouds I expected to see and instead was staring at a light-blue lampshade and a ceiling. The water continued to splash on my chest so I quickly sat up and realised that I was still at home in bed.

The window curtains were next to my bed so I pushed them

to one side to let some of the outside moonlight into the room. I looked around and saw Peter stood below me at the side of his bed. He still looked as if he was asleep and yet had his penis held firmly in his hand, pointing it upwards towards me.

Urine continued to gush out like a fountain of water and splash around in my general direction.

'Peter,' I shouted.

He didn't answer.

'Peter!' I yelled slightly louder, trying not to wake up our parents. 'Look at what you're doing.'

'It's all right, Steve, I'm on the toilet,' he replied in a drowsy state.

'No, you aren't,' I replied and jumped down off my bunk.

I grabbed hold of him by his shirt and pushed him hard down the hallway and into the toilet. He turned towards me, still in a semi-conscious state and urinated on to my chest.

'You dirty bastard,' I shouted and punched him hard in the face.

He moaned and was then fully conscious. His left eye began to swell as a result of the blow and he looked confused, unsure of why I had hit him.

My body smelt strongly of stale urine so I went into the bathroom and washed it all off. I heard Peter groan as he walked back to the bedroom and got back into bed. I knew there was no point in me going back to bed as my bedclothes and mattress were soaking wet with urine, so I acquired myself some spare bedding and slept downstairs on the sofa.

A couple of hours later, my mother came down and entered the room. She saw that I was lying on the sofa and started shouting at me.

'You horrible bully. Just who the hell do you think you are, some sort of big shot?'

'But, Mother, I . . .'

'What are you trying to prove, hitting your brother like that?' she continued.

'But . . . but . . .'

'Don't bother,' she interrupted and left the room.

I don't believe it, I thought. How can she blame me after what he did?

She soon returned. She wasn't finished yet.

'And another thing, you dirty bugger.'

'Bloody hell, what next?' I asked.

'You've wet your bed. A grown man and you've wet your bed.'

I didn't bother trying to explain. She wouldn't listen and refused to speak to me for the remainder of my leave. Peter didn't help matters as he told me he couldn't remember a thing.

Such is life, I thought, as I later made the long train journey back to Plymouth.

The time had now come for my new troop's posting to Norway, so off we went. A cold wind gushed across the deck of the ship as it neared the city of Oslo. Sam and I stood on the upper deck to admire the view and we watched with admiration as we cruised along the fjords past the snow-covered mountains.

'Bloody cold, isn't it?' said Sam.

'Yes, it bloody is,' I replied. 'About minus thirty degrees Celsius. How was your leave, Sam?'

'Oh, the usual.'

I smiled at him. 'What's the usual?'

'You know, the usual. Lots to drink, plenty to eat and a couple of fights.'

'Oh, the usual,' I replied. He nodded.

We leaned against a railing and looked over the side of the ship. Large sheets of ice cracked and gave way under the immense force and weight of the ship's bow. The distant lights of Oslo got brighter as we neared its port. We went back below decks to get our kit ready. It was nearing time to disembark for the journey to SOR Gardermoen camp.

SOR Gardermoen camp was a derelict Territorial Army (TA) camp. The Norwegian TA used it during the summer months and the Royal Marines during the winter. It was made up of several large wooden buildings which we turned into accommodation blocks, a working headquarters, a main dining hall, a sickbay and a makeshift bar.

The bar was our main source of entertainment and was plentiful with duty-free booze. The alcohol was so inexpensive that most Marines purchased pints of spirits, pints of wine or a crate of Pils lager to save revisiting the bar to buy round after round. Alcohol abuse was far from uncommon.

On weekends, we had the privilege of a liberty wagon, which was made available for transport into Jessheim, the local town. The venue there was a beer keller, which had a discothèque and a small pizza restaurant. It also had a good reputation for loose women. The only pitfall was that the local beer was far more expensive than a typical pint of beer back home in the UK. However, to combat this we drank as much duty-free booze in the camp bar as we could and climbed aboard the liberty wagon for our free lift into town.

The local Norwegians resented us using their beer keller. We had a bad reputation for stealing their beer and taking their women, so brawls consequently took place on a regular basis.

One Saturday night, the camp bar was crowded with Marines and various members of the Army. The Army ranks were attached to the Logistic Regiment for the duration of the winter deployment. A crate of Pils lager lay at my feet. Sam grinned with pleasure as he removed a jagged bottle top with his teeth and greedily gulped down his first bottle of the night. I grinned too as I watched him do it.

'Here's to the Marine Corps,' I shouted, and raised my beer bottle into the air.

A mass of hands rose into the air as other soldiers held up their drinks to acknowledge my proposed toast.

At the start of the evening, most people talked about their experiences in the mountains and the subject of arctic warfare training. However, later in the evening it changed to the more common subjects that gave pleasure to the Marines, such as drinking, fucking and fighting. In other words, how much, how many and how tough?

'Have you ever been to Manchester?' Sam asked me.

'No, I haven't.'

'I have,' a voice called out from behind us.

We turned and saw a puny middle-aged man stood behind us. He was wearing a pair of jeans and a sweatshirt with a Royal Corps of Transport badge on it.

'I have,' he repeated. 'I've been there twice.'

We ignored his remark and carried on talking between ourselves. We didn't have a great deal of respect for normal Army ranks. They were referred to as crap hats because their berets were issued on joining up and they did not have to be earned in the way that Marines, Paras and the SAS regiment had to earn theirs. To make matters worse, he was a part-time soldier from the TA.

The puny man was bad-mannered and continued trying to butt in to our conversation. Sam's patience was running thin.

'Who the fuck is he?' he growled.

'I don't know,' I replied. 'Some driver in the RCT, I think. He's beginning to get on my nerves.'

We both stared in the direction of the driver. 'Why don't you fuck off?' snarled Sam.

The driver quickly realised that we were not impressed with his rude and impudent manner and promptly left the room. A short while later, I left the bar to visit the toilet. My consumption of beer had taken its effect and I needed to empty the contents of my bladder. The toilets were located in an adjoining corridor. When I entered I saw that there was a queue of several other men who wanted to relieve themselves and use the urinals. The rude driver was stood in front of me, as he was waiting too. He turned around and looked at me.

'You're a bad-mannered cunt, aren't you?' I said to him.

'What do you mean?' he answered, and looked me directly in the eyes.

I felt confronted, so I didn't answer his question. Instead, I head-butted him on the side of his head. I held back an amount of force and only used enough to warn him to back off.

Suddenly, several of the men in the toilet were onto me like a shot and held my arms back in an effort to calm me down and stop me fighting with the driver.

'Calm down, Steve, calm down. He's gone,' said one of the other Marines. I could feel the anger leaving my body and once again I felt relaxed. The Marines holding my arms back released their grip when I told them that I still wanted to relieve myself.

The bar wasn't as crowded when I returned. A lot of men had gone into town via the liberty wagon. Sam was stood by the bar. He grinned and passed me a glass of beer.

'Did you stick the nut on him?' he asked.

'Yes.'

He laughed. 'Good. He's over there.' He indicated the location of the driver by nodding his head. Several men stood together in a group. They weren't Marines; they were all Army lads from the Royal Ordnance Squadron. I could hear the driver's voice coming from somewhere amongst them, telling the group about his encounter with me earlier in the toilets.

'I couldn't get angry with him,' I heard him say. 'He's only a young bit of skin.'

I heard his remark and knew he was referring to me. Consequently, I flew into a rage and barged my way into the crowd before throwing several hard punches at his face. The blows knocked him backwards against a wall. The group of men reacted quickly to restrain me and once again I found myself being pinned down. The beaten driver took his chance to escape and bolted through the nearest exit and out of the building.

Sam quickly commanded the men holding me down to get off me. They released their arm locks and dispersed.

'Cheers, Sam,' I said.

'Do him, Steve. Go and smash his fucking head in,' Sam replied.

I was angry, very angry, and didn't need any further encouragement. The snow crunched under my feet as I headed for the Army ranks' accommodation block. It was cold outside and I could feel my face freezing up during the short journey.

When I reached the block I kicked the snow from my boots and entered the building. Inside, there were two long corridors: one to the left and one to the right. There were about six rooms on either side and all the doors were shut. I walked down the right-hand corridor and stopped at the first door. Bollocks, I thought. If I have to search the whole building to get my hands on him then so be it. I knocked three times on the door and pushed it open. Two strangers, who were sat up in bed, turned towards me.

'Excuse me, lads, do you know which room the TA Royal Corps of Transport drivers are in?' I asked them politely.

They looked startled and then there was a short silence. A third man appeared from an open locker door. It was the driver I was looking for.

'What do you want?' he smirked.

My temper shot through the roof and I immediately started shouting at him.

'You can't get angry with me,' he said.

'Well I am fucking angry with you and I'm going to smash your stupid fucking head in.'

I surged forward and struck him in the face with my fist, then quickly followed up with several further blows. Furniture clattered across the room as I threw him around like a rag doll. He tried to put up a fight but I was too strong for him. The two other men disappeared beneath their sheets, probably hoping I was a bad dream and that I would go away. I knocked the driver down to the floor and he fell onto his back. He lay motionless and had given up the struggle. He looked at me and his smirk was gone. I pressed my right boot down onto his head.

'I'm angry . . . I'm fucking angry,' I growled at the top of my voice.

He curled up into a ball and offered no resistance to a possible further attack. I looked at him and panted for breath.

The door behind me creaked. I turned around and felt a cold gust of wind rush into the room. It whistled in through the corridor and I could hear the main exit doors swinging and realised that the other two men had made themselves scarce.

I looked down at the defenceless piece of shit lying on the floor and then made my exit from the building. I felt fatigued and just wanted to go back to my room and climb into bed.

The following morning, I was awoken by Sam's voice.

'Steve . . . Steve, it's seven o'clock, time to get up,' he called from his bed at the other side of the room.

I opened my eyes and could see that he had switched the room light on. I looked out of a nearby window and saw that it was still dark. Snowflakes quietly tapped against the many small window panes. My clock showed five minutes past seven. Dark mornings were a common sight in a country that had only four hours of daylight at this time of the year.

My body ached. I had a huge hangover and my right hand ached. I pulled it from beneath the blankets and saw that it was swollen and badly bruised. The previous night's events came into my mind and I remembered what I had done. Sam passed me a cup of coffee.

'Did you give him a good beating then?' he asked.

'Yeah, a good beating.'

Sam laughed. 'Good. I hate them fucking stabs.' (Stupid TA bastards – a term used widely across Britain's military forces.)

I finished my coffee and took a shower. I took several deep breaths to cope with the hangover. Also, my hand throbbed and ached when I moved my fingers. I then dressed and made my way to the sickbay to ask for some anti-inflammatory pills.

The sickbay was similar to the other blocks, with a middle exit door and two corridors running off in different directions. I saw a sign which said 'CASUALTY' and had an arrow on it that pointed to the right-hand corridor. I walked down it and took a seat in the waiting room, which was half full of people waiting to see the doctor.

I sat and stared at my hand. It still ached a lot but I knew it would be worse later when the effects of the alcohol had worn off. I felt curious as to who else was waiting to see the doctor and looked at the person sat on my right-hand side.

A uniformed man with a very badly swollen face looked at

me for a moment and then looked at the ground. Fucking hell, I thought. It's him, the TA fucking driver. That's what I did to him last night.

I looked at my hand. Suddenly it didn't seem to matter any more. I could picture the driver going into the doctor's room before me. The doctor would probably ask him what had happened and he would point at me. I decided to leave with my now minor injury. We were going out into the mountains for a couple of weeks. It was a welcome move, as I was getting sick of drinking beer.

CHAPTER ELEVEN

THE BEER KELLER

Fumes belched out of the exhaust pipe of the four-ton liberty wagon as it left Gardermoen camp destined for the beer keller in Jessheim. It was freezing cold in the back of the wagon, but our clothing was enough to keep us warm for the twenty-minute journey.

After several weeks of working in the mountains, we were ready to let off some steam, and keen to try to get fixed up with some of the Norwegian women. When we arrived, we joined a small queue of people waiting to get inside the beer keller. It was absolutely freezing outside, but thankfully the wait was short and we were soon inside.

We found that the bar was downstairs and that the upstairs area consisted of an extortionate pizza restaurant. We paid a small fee to have our coats hung in the club's cloakroom and then made our way to the bar.

The bar area was well lit and had several sets of tables and chairs dotted around three corners of the room. The other corner was home to a wooden dance floor with a discothèque and a DJ to operate it. The place was quite busy and lots of loose women were sitting around waiting to be asked to dance.

We all bought a beer each, as it was far too expensive to buy a round. Because of this, we had all had a good skinful of the duty-free liquor back at our base, prior to departure. Some Marines also smuggled small bottles or hip flasks of alcoholic spirits into the club and just bought orange juice to mix with it. Others would mine-sweep other people's beer, which caused a bit of friction from time to time.

Halfway through the night, a group of Norwegian men sat staring at us. They had been watching our behaviour during the evening and seemed unimpressed. We had noticed them watching us but initially paid no attention. However, much later, one of the Norwegians from the group approached me. Here we go, I thought. He's obviously built up enough Dutch courage to let me know what's on his mind.

He stopped directly in front of me and looked straight into my eyes. He was well built across the shoulders and had short thick blond hair.

'I am from Oslo,' he said in broken English.

'So what?' I replied.

'There is much bad feeling amongst us. We hate you Englishmen.'

I raised my eyebrows. 'Why?'

He paused for a moment. His eyes flickered and he looked as if he was searching his mind for an answer to the quick question I threw at him.

'You steal our beer . . . take our women and you fight with us.' His efforts at speaking English had much improved.

Before I could reply to his comments, a huge fist smashed into his face, knocking him to the floor. Sam stood beside me. He had overheard the conversation between us and reacted swiftly to resolve the situation. The other members of the

Norwegian group began to shout abuse at us, but quickly dispersed when I threw my empty beer glass at the wall above their heads. It instantly smashed into lots of pieces and showered the area.

Two Norwegian doormen appeared and stood between the angry group and us. Both men were about 6 ft 6 in. tall and built like brick shit-houses. One of them spoke to his fellow countryman in their native tongue and unfortunately we couldn't understand what was being said. When he had finished, he did not attempt to ask for our side of the story and pointed to the exit door at the top of the stairs.

'Get out, Englishmen,' he ordered.

'Come on then, you big fat bastard.' I also pointed to the exit door. 'Let's go outside and fight about it.'

He frowned and I then beckoned them both to follow Sam and myself as we made our way up the stairs. At the top, one of the doormen stood staring at me. He looked like a giant and had huge muscular arms, which were bursting out of his tight white shirt. He looked confused.

'You want to fight with me?' he asked in a big deep voice. His huge frame towered over me.

'Yes, and my mate wants to fight your colleague,' I answered.

He nodded his head and pointed to the open door. We walked out into the snow-filled area outside and turned, ready to do battle with them. However, to our surprise we saw the door close and both men remained inside. One of them looked through a small window on the door and smiled.

'Goodnight, Englishmen,' he said, smiling and waving his hand before moving out of sight.

Sam and I looked at each other.

'Fuck it . . . they would have pulverised us,' said Sam. 'Those guys must have muscles in their piss.'

'Yeah, you're right, Sam, let's go home.'

A few minutes later, a military police wagon pulled up across the other side of the road. The sole driver wound his window down and shouted across to us. He asked if we wanted a lift back to Gardermoen camp. And obviously we didn't hesitate to accept his most kind offer.

'Get in the back, lads, and be careful of the dog – it bites,' said the military policeman.

We opened the doors at the rear of the van and saw a huge Alsatian dog. It growled at us and snapped its sharp white teeth. Fortunately, it was restrained by a leash, which was attached to something in the back of the wagon. The leash was a short one and restrained the dog enough for us to be able to climb aboard and sit in the van without it being able to reach us.

During the journey back, the dog continued to growl and bark at us. It looked fierce and snapped its jaws, exposing its big canine teeth. Sam scratched his head and the dog went wild at the movement of his arm. Then Sam boldly stood on its paw and bit it hard on one of its ears.

The dog yelped and raced away from him into the back end of the wagon. As it ran, its leash snapped and it launched itself over the passenger seat and sat beside the driver.

'What's up with you, boy?' we heard the driver say. 'Are you bored with trying to frighten our passengers?' The dog sighed and put its head down and just groaned . . .

The following night I returned to the beer keller, accompanied by another Marine called Richie. The doormen held no grudges about the previous evening and allowed us to enter the club without any problems. One of them joked about me wanting to fight him. I think he couldn't actually believe that a man half his size was so keen to take him on. The bar was quite busy and had a warm, friendly atmosphere, unlike the previous evening.

Richie and I were keen to get ourselves a woman and tried our luck with a couple of Norwegian girls who were sat at a nearby table. They were both good looking and bright and cheerful. One was called Jane. She was tall and skinny with short blonde bushy hair and a sizeable chest. The other was called Ingrid. She was slightly shorter with long blonde hair and an average-sized chest.

Neither of us wasted any time in getting them up to dance. After a couple of jigs and a bit of laughter I was grappling with Ingrid in a slow smooch. We went straight for the lip lock and started swapping spit with a bit of French kissing. I could see Richie already deep into the process and he was rubbing his hands around Jane's buttocks.

A couple of drinks later, they invited us back to Ingrid's house, so we collected our coats from the cloakroom and left. Jane had come in her small dark blue car. I didn't know what model it was because it was foreign to me, but I thought that it resembled a British Ford Fiesta. Richie climbed into the passenger seat beside Jane and I got into the back with Ingrid. En route I was all over Ingrid and we snogged continuously. I had my hand down her trousers and she had her hand down mine. I could feel her excitement as she tried to push her tongue so far down my throat that it tickled my tonsils.

Ingrid's house was detached and almost completely made of wood. This was common practice for the Norwegians, as wood is a good insulator from the cold. Inside, it was warm and cosy. The floors were polished wood with a scattering of rugs and carpets. The heat came from a couple of electric heaters, which were left running to pump hot hair around the building.

After a hot cup of coffee, Ingrid took me by the hand and led me into her bedroom. Jane giggled in the background as she went into a different bedroom with Richie. Ingrid and I tore each other's clothes off and were soon locked in a passionate embrace. What followed was not so much making love as shagging like there was no tomorrow. It felt terrific. I recalled my joke earlier in the night, when I told Richie that if I didn't get to screw something soon my scrotum sack was going to burst from the pressure.

We lay there puffing and panting and smiling at each other. I had drunk a lot of beer during the evening and felt drowsy. At this point I must have fallen asleep. The next thing I knew I could hear a voice. It seemed distant but was getting louder.

'Rich . . . Richie. Steve has fallen out of bed,' shouted Ingrid.

Richie, who was still busy in another room with Jane, heard Ingrid calling him and entered the room. I was semi-conscious and could just about hear Richie coming in. I heard him laugh.

'Steve. Steve, you're lying naked on the floor. Come on, get back into bed,' he said.

For a moment, I felt more conscious and realised that Richie was helping to lift me back into bed. Then there was darkness as I drifted back into unconsciousness.

Again I could hear Ingrid shouting, 'Richie . . . Richie . . . Richie.'

I could hear Richie walk back into the room once again. I looked towards the door and saw that he was laughing hysterically.

'What are you laughing at?' I asked him.

He held his ribs as if they were hurting and laughed even louder. He pointed in my direction.

'Look what you're doing, Steve. Look at what you're doing,' he answered.

I then realised that I was not lying in bed like I thought, but standing beside it. I could feel myself slowly coming round and then I heard Ingrid shouting at me.

'Why . . . why are you pissing on me?' she shrieked.

I looked at her and saw a stream of urine splashing all over her face and body. I then noticed that I was holding my penis in my hand and that the urine was coming from me. For a few moments, I thought I was dreaming, as it all seemed to be happening in slow motion.

'Stop pissing on me. Stop,' she screamed.

'Er, yeah, sorry,' I replied. Richie continued to laugh, which made Ingrid even angrier.

'Get out . . . get out of my house. Get out . . . get out of my house,' she repeated continuously.

Pots, pans ornaments and whatever else she could lay her hands on were hurled at me as I searched for my clothing. A few things hit me but I ignored them and rapidly got dressed.

'Come on, Steve, let's get the fuck out of here,' shouted Richie, who had already got dressed. I fastened the laces on my boots and rushed out of the door, which was then slammed shut behind us. Richie kept bursting spontaneously into laughter as we walked along the snow-covered road back to SOR Gardermoen camp. It was a long and very cold walk back to base, but we didn't care, we'd had our fun . . .

CHAPTER TWELVE

RIVALRY

At eight o'clock one evening, I sat in the camp bar along with several other Marines. They were the usual familiar faces who came into the bar for a heavy drinking session within the first half hour or even few minutes of the bar opening. Generally, if we'd been out in the field most of us were waiting for the bar door to open at seven o'clock.

We bought the usual crate of Pils lager each and downed several bottles quickly to quench our thirst. I was sat with a guy called Zac, who was a Geordie and had a centre-parting. Both Zac and myself were renowned for telling jokes, and we kept the banter going throughout the evening. Later, a chef called Geoff joined our company. He was a tall, greasy-looking man with grey hair and a grey moustache. He was accompanied by a woman who was a signaller in the Women's Royal Army Corps. She was attached to the regiment for the winter deployment. Her name was Judy and she strongly resembled the Hunchback of Notre-Dame (Quasimodo). It was strongly rumoured that Geoff had her knickers up and down like a yo-yo, but he laughed at such comments and joked that you don't look at the fireplace when you're poking the fire.

Midway through the night, Zac suggested we should have a piss-drinking competition. Everybody thought it was a good idea and started to fill up pint glasses with steaming hot urine. Laughter roared around the bar when Judy stood up and dropped her trousers and knickers, before grabbing hold of a pint glass, placing it between her legs and topping it up with piss.

A large number of pint glasses filled the table. It was cold in the bar and you could see the steam rising from them. Everybody looked on. They were all enthralled with watching the contenders preparing themselves to start the competition. There were seven of us in all, including Judy. The rules were that you had to drink the entire contents of the glass in two efforts, without throwing up. After we had all had two full glasses, there was only Judy and myself left. Everybody else had thrown up all over the floor. This entertained the rest of the bar's drinkers, who gave a rapturous round of applause after every attempt.

It was my turn again and I had to down a third glass. My stomach felt bloated and I felt sick. I could feel and taste the hot urine in and around the area of my throat and the stench ran around inside my nostrils. Judy smiled at me as I put my hand around the next glass and took a deep breath.

'Cheers, Quasi,' I said, and gulped the third pint down.

I drank three-quarters of the pint and then gargled with the remainder. The other Marines roared with laughter and clapped until their hands hurt. Judy looked at me. Her smile was gone. Then she looked at the glasses of urine and took hold of her third pint.

'Here's to you, Royal,' she toasted. She drank it in one go and slammed the empty glass onto the table.

'Come on, Royal, it's your turn,' she smiled.

The crowd were silent and absolutely flabbergasted at her mega performance.

'Bloody hell, Judy,' I frowned. 'You might be one hell of an ugly motherfucker but from here you're looking good.'

I grabbed hold of my fourth and final pint and started drinking it straight away. Unfortunately, this time my body had had enough and my insides erupted without control. To make the most of the situation, I aimed the fountain of piss and vomit at Judy. It spurted like a heavy waterfall all over her head and face. When I stopped, my insides were empty but my throat continued to force me to retch as I coughed up the residue of lumps and stomach bile.

Geoff patted me on the back and gave me a fresh bottle of Pils lager to cleanse my mouth of the horrible substance. Everybody cheered.

'Three cheers for Steve's efforts,' Zac shouted. Three loud cheers followed.

After the last cheer, Judy interrupted. 'Just a minute, Royals, I haven't finished yet.'

Everybody stopped and looked at her. Spew and piss were dripping down her face and hair and her clothes were soaking wet. She looked like something that had just stepped out of a horror movie. She wiped the fluid from her face as if it was sweat and gulped down her fourth pint. She drank the lot and raised her glass into the air.

'You beauty,' I yelled. 'That's fucking mega.'

She laughed and drank a bottle of Pils lager handed to her by Geoff.

'Good on you, girl,' he said. 'Go and get showered.'

'OK,' she acknowledged and instantly threw up all over Geoff. It splashed off his chest and trouser legs.

'Fuck it,' he laughed. 'Let's both go and get showered.'

Everybody cheered and applauded as Geoff and Judy left the bar, arm in arm.

Two of the Marines who were working as barmen appeared with mops and brushes and quickly cleaned up the resulting mess from the floor and tables. This left a strong smell of disinfectant, but it was much better than the stench that had filled the cold air minutes before.

After half an hour or so, the banter died down. A lot of the Marines who were in the bar during the piss-drinking competition had gone ashore (into town) and were destined for the beer keller. I looked at Zac and saw a startled look on his face.

'Fuck me,' Zac exclaimed in his broad Geordie accent. 'It's the Paras.'

All the Marines in the bar turned and looked towards the door. I looked too and saw a group of men enter the bar. They were dressed in jeans and burgundy sweatshirts which bore the Parachute Regiment's insignia badge and the words '2 PARA'.

The room went so silent that you could have heard a pin drop. It was common knowledge that the Parachute Regiment were the greatest rivals of the Royal Marines as they were a similar type of soldier. For some reason, they hated each other, yet they respected each other. The thing that they had in common was that they were both elite fighting groups and both had to earn the right to wear their beret.

The silence didn't bother the Paratroopers. They boldly walked across the room and ordered vast amounts of beer, before sitting down around two spare tables at the far end of the room. People started talking again, but you could feel the tension between the groups.

'Fucking necky bastards,' said Zac.

I burst into song. 'Dead Paras in the ssskkkyyy.'

This was a take-off of a song called 'Ghost Riders in the Sky', except the Marines changed the words. Also, an expression that the Marines used to use was that only two things fell from the sky, bird shit and Paratroopers. Nevertheless, in return I'm sure the Paras had more than their fair share of names and expressions for the Marines.

One of the Marines shouted comments in the direction of the Paras. 'What a bunch of cunts you lot turned out to be. Shot your boss in the back.'

A lot of people, excluding the Paras, burst into laughter. The comments were damning remarks referring to Colonel H. Jones, the commanding officer of the 2nd Parachute Regiment in 1982. He was fatally shot in the back during an assault on Goose Green in the Falklands War in 1982, and the Marines liked to contend that, contrary to the official reports, his own men had done it.

A few Marines, including myself, did not find the remarks very funny and thought they were below the belt and uncalled for. The expressions on the Paras' faces said it all and they looked uneasy. Consequently, a few Marines including myself purchased a couple of cases of beer and joined their company to apologise for their reception and to smooth things over.

We managed to mix in quite well with our rivals and joked together. This was the first time their regiment had been to the Arctic and they told us how difficult they were finding it. We sympathised with them, as we all had memories of our first three-month deployment, which was usually the most difficult due to lack of experience. The conversing seemed to be well received and the tension between us seemed to ease, with both sides being more receptive.

The Paras all wore their burgundy sweatshirts, complete with badge, as if it were a military-type uniform. Most of us found this quite amusing, as it was the sort of thing we did in basic training. However, some of the Marines saw this as an opportunity to take the piss. Zac made several sets of cardboard wings and Marine-type badges with RM written on them and passed them around. We all laughed and pinned them onto our T-shirts. The winged badge was the regimental badge of the Parachute Regiment and was also a sign used by parachute-trained Marines. Passing the training for the right to wear this badge was called getting your wings. Both the Marines and the Paratroopers wore this badge on the right arms of their military uniforms.

One of the guys made a wet suit and oxygen tank out of black plastic bin liners and a roll mat. He made imitation flippers out of the cardboard Zac had left over and fastened these to his feet. He looked like a frogman and repeatedly rolled off a table in front of the Paras as if he were scuba diving.

I wasn't sure what the angle was with this one, as he was taking off our own Special Boat Squadron (SBS). Whatever his intentions were, it was funny, and everybody, including our rivals, laughed together. The horseplay was taken in jest and we all mingled a lot more closely.

Later in the night, when we were all well under the influence of drink, I was talking to one of the Paratroopers about my previous tour of Northern Ireland. He was about the same age and build as me and we seemed to have a lot in common. We laughed and joked together about the piss-taking and the way Zac had made some cardboard wings to mimic the badges on their sweatshirts. Then, all of a sudden, this guy's face went all serious and he stared me in the eyes. His smile had dropped and he looked angry. I knew this expression and the fact that this was a pride thing.

'What's that RN for, Royal Navy?' he asked in a serious

voice and pointed to the cardboard badge on my chest. I knew this was his attempt to try to take the piss out of me so I rapidly went on the defensive.

'No, mate. It's RM for Royal Marines, actually,' I replied. 'What's that, bird shit?' I asked sharply and pointed to his winged Para insignia badge.

He burst into laughter and obviously hadn't heard that expression before. As he laughed, he reached out and ripped the cardboard RM badge from my T-shirt. My smile turned to a frown, the joke was over. I reached out and grabbed him by the throat and gently squeezed his windpipe.

'Put it back, now,' I demanded in a deep and threatening voice.

He squawked and choked under the pressure of my grip. His faced turned purply-red and he tried to speak, but words failed to come from his mouth. He then placed the cardboard badge back onto my T-shirt, so I released my grip. I watched him as he coughed and spluttered and sucked in big mouthfuls of oxygen.

His colleagues looked on and you could have cut the atmosphere with a knife. Animosity once again filled the air. One of the other Paratroopers started shouting and pushed his way towards me through the crowd that had formed around us. He was clearly very angry and was showing his teeth like a wild animal that wanted to eat me. He stopped a few inches away from me and stared deep into my eyes. I felt threatened and could feel his breath on my face.

'If you want to fight . . . fight me,' he snarled.

His approach reminded me of a cowboy film I had once seen, with John Wayne preparing to indulge in a gunfight. My only form of defence was attack, and I moved in. By now, it was a common sight for my colleagues to see my head connect swiftly with an opponent's face. Surprise was my advantage: his nose crunched under the force of the blow and blood spurted into the air. I speedily followed up my attack with a couple of punches to his jaw and knocked him backwards onto the floor. Everybody looked on and then the Marines started to chant.

'Here we go, here we go, here we go . . . here we go, here we go, here we go-ohh.'

Adrenalin pumped through their bodies; they were excited.

An older Marine, who was in charge of running the bar, rushed towards me.

'Steve, for fuck's sake get out now or you're barred out,' he shouted anxiously.

I looked at him and saw the desperation on his face. I knew he wanted to avoid further trouble and nodded my head to acknowledge that I would leave. Behind me, the tension and bad feeling between the Marines and the Paras still hung in the air, but I didn't care. If I didn't leave then I would be barred from using the bar. For me, there was no choice.

The following day, I expected to hear about a huge brawl that had taken place when I left the bar, as it had seemed imminent. Instead, I heard that the older and more experienced Paratroopers had beaten up their younger subordinates for being involved in trouble with the Marines in the first place. We admired them for the way in which they disciplined and punished their younger soldiers and later felt a level of respect as we watched them leave Gardermoen camp.

CHAPTER THIRTEEN

CONFUSION

After the winter deployment, we headed back to the UK and wasted no time getting out and about in the city of Plymouth's nightlife scene. The main high street was called Union Street and was about two miles long. It was a very busy place and home to a countless number of public bars and clubs. Generally, if one of the pubs or clubs we frequented wasn't in Union Street, it was certainly fairly close to it.

One of my favourite haunts was a club called Cascades. It was a nightclub, just off the beaten track of the main high street and was tucked away on the opposite side of a two-storey car park. This was quite popular with a lot of Marine and Army personnel and definitely not a place for the faint-hearted. The inside was quite dark and a large wooden dance floor dominated the main room, with the bar at the far end of it. The dance floor wasn't huge, exactly, it was just big in comparison to the rest of the room. This area was most popular within the last ten minutes of each evening when the Marines would direct their undivided attention towards the female of the species.

There was a bar opposite the doorway, which housed some stairs that led down to another couple of rooms and bars. The decoration was shabby and your feet generally stuck to the floor as you walked around the place. However, the shabby decoration was of little or no concern to those who frequented the club. Its wild atmosphere was a magnetic attraction. All sorts of antics happened in there, but nothing ever seemed out of place. Fights occurred on a regular basis, but nobody was too bothered as long as their beer wasn't spilled. There were always plenty of loose women in this club, who usually came to mix with the Marines, so getting fixed up was never a problem.

One night I met a girl called Diane. She was around twenty years old with a nice figure and long black hair which was tied up in a bun. She lived in Plymouth, but originally came from Manchester to work in one of the local hospitals. To my delight, she invited me back to her place for the night.

After the arduous three-month deployment to the wastes of the Arctic I needed a woman, but not until the club's bar was closed. I was very drunk by the time we left and had been drinking bottles of very strong lager virtually all day. Thankfully, we didn't have far to go as her home was roughly a mile away; it was a bedsit on the first floor of a three-storey house. I was pleased to find a toilet at the end of the first flight of stairs to relieve myself before climbing the second flight of stairs to Diane's room. Her room was quite small, but very tidy. Its biggest asset, which immediately caught my attention, was a huge bed with a thick flowery quilt on top of it.

We didn't waste any time with coffee-drinking or even conversation. Instead, we tore each other's clothes off and were soon locked in a passionate embrace. Our writhing bodies slammed away at each other like steam trains, hammering down a track. It was a good hard shag, after which I instantly fell asleep.

Later, I opened my eyes and watched the ceiling spin around in the dark. My bladder was full and needed relieving, so I got up and went to the toilet. I was still very drunk and quite drowsy, which made the toilet a hard target to hit whilst draining my bladder. My head ached and throbbed with numbness as I climbed back into the big double bed. My side of it felt cold, which seemed strange, as I had only been away for a short time. Once again, I was soon fast asleep, but only for a moment. Someone was shouting at me. My eyelids were heavy and opened slowly.

'Hey, wake up. What are you doing in my bed?' a strange voice shouted.

A young man had jumped out of the bed. He had blond spiky hair, shaped like a Mohican. The sight of him confused me. Bloody hell, she's changed, I thought. Thinking that this person didn't look like the woman whom I had climbed into bed with, I sat up and looked around, and then realised I was no longer in the same room I had gone to sleep in.

'What are you doing in my bed?' he asked again.

I couldn't find the words to answer him. What am I doing in his bed, I thought. I didn't know. I stood up and faced him, before realising we were both completely naked. I tried to gather my thoughts to ease my confusion. Bloody hell. What have I done? Why am I in bed with a man?!!!!

Meanwhile, I watched the strange man race around the room in search of his underwear to cover his manhood. I looked at him and felt deeply shocked with the situation. He picked up a pair of underpants and put them on to cover himself up.

'Who are you with?' he frowned.

I was still completely lost for words. I had no idea who I was with. I repeatedly opened my mouth to answer, but nothing came out.

'Are you from Germany?' he continued, with the same frown on his face.

For a moment, I wasn't sure if I was from Germany or not. I didn't know what to think.

'Yar, yar,' I answered and nodded my head.

'Who are you with?'

I shook my head. I had no recollection of whom I was with, where I was or how I had gotten there.

'Are you with Diane?'

Then the penny dropped. I realised what I had done and whom I was with. I felt elated.

'Fucking hell, mate,' I shouted. 'I'm with Diane. I've obviously come into the wrong room and got into the wrong bed. Fucking hell.'

I quickly walked out of the room. Outside, I stood in a hallway and saw that I was at the foot of the stairs, which I recognised. I took a couple of big deep breaths and released a huge sigh of relief as I walked up the stairs and smiled as I passed the toilet halfway up. I nodded my head, agreeing with myself that I must have gotten up in the middle of the night for a piss, used the toilet and gone down the stairs instead of up them, and into the wrong room and the wrong bed.

I pushed open the door to Diane's room and saw her lying sound asleep under her flowery quilt. I climbed back into bed beside her and pulled the quilt up to my chin. Having realised what I had done, I wondered how I must have woken him up. I smiled to myself and shook my head slowly. Diane put her arm around me. Her eyes opened slightly.

'You're freezing,' she said. 'Have you been to the toilet?'

'I certainly have,' I replied.

Then we both went back to sleep.

CHAPTER FOURTEEN

LET'S PARTY

Loose women and wild sex were commonplace in my social life. I nearly always managed to pull a woman when I went out. I wasn't fussy, though. I generally made my mind up on the figure of a woman, or even just her availability, rather than how good-looking she was. Our general philosophy was, if you were having problems getting fixed up with a decent-looking woman, try the older and fatter ones, as they were easier prey.

If we'd been away on deployment in the Arctic, Cyprus or Northern Ireland then our opportunities to sleep with women would have been limited owing to full-time operational commitment, which could be as long as six months at a time. So, when the chance arose I literally took the bull by the horns and made up for lost time.

Parties were regularly organised, especially on Sunday afternoons as the pubs didn't open all day at that time and it was a good way of carrying on from a Sunday lunch-time drinking session. By this time, I'd made a lot of new friends in the unit. I moved into a new room, which I shared with another Marine, called Briggs. He was a tall broad-shouldered man from Manchester. He had black hair and a thick black moustache. I could tell straight away that we were going to get on, as he told me he'd drank 20 pints the night before and had just put in his best-ever performance in training that day.

Briggs and I became very good friends and were regularly in the gym together to maintain our high level of physical fitness. There was never a dull moment with him. He worked hard at his fitness and even harder at his soldiering skills, when we were out on exercise in the field or on active duty. Socially, he drank heavily and played hard. He was always wearing fancy dress and would do almost anything for a laugh. We even boxed together and both did quite well in the Marine Corps boxing championships.

One Sunday afternoon, Briggs, myself and a chubby-faced Marine called Billy were invited to another Marine's house for a party. He was called Smithy. Smithy was in his late twenties and very well built with a physique similar to a bodybuilder. He had a very dry sense of humour, which could be a frightening experience for those who didn't know him. Generally, if he didn't like someone, he had a nasty habit of letting them know.

Our shopping bags were heavy with booze. It was our way of showing our gratitude for the invite to the party. We all stood close together on the snow-filled driveway of Smithy's house and he greeted us at the door.

'Come on in, lads. You're all very welcome,' he said. He looked really pleased to see us and had a big warm smile on his face.

The front room was quite big and roomy with a warm gas fire. We saw several people sat huddled together on a huge red couch, around the fire. A large wooden table stood at the opposite side of the room and had several plates filled with a wide variety of food.

The mood of the people already in the room was quiet, and soft music was playing in the background. Briggs disliked the choice of music and changed the tape. He played 'Sunday Bloody Sunday' by U2. This is a song about the Troubles in Northern Ireland. He turned up the volume and it blasted out of the two large black speakers situated on separate sides of the room. The huddled group were a lot more reserved than we were and watched with surprise as the three of us began to pogo and jump into the air in time with the music. Everybody laughed and joined in the fun. Smithy's face was filled with delight; this was his kind of party. We played numerous party games together: generally a game or competition where the loser had to drink a certain amount of beer, either standing upside down or through a pair of sweaty socks or knickers.

After a while, Smithy suggested that we tuck into the food, which was still neatly spread on the table. We each pulled up a seat and tucked one of the available paper napkins into the top of our T-shirts. It must have looked like a monkeys' tea party. Billy threw a peanut at me, and it bounced off my nose. Briggs laughed as a biscuit thrown by me hit him on the head. He too got in on the act and launched a custard pie at Billy, which splattered in his face. He laughed hysterically. Then . . . uproar. We hurled plates of food and glasses of beer at each other. The room was in turmoil. Food dishes, plates, cups and saucers clattered and smashed all around the place. Eggs, tomatoes and various sandwiches splattered on the walls. The other group took cover behind the couch. There was only one way to escape the flying objects, so I bolted for the front door. Briggs and Billy quickly followed. We were all covered from head to toe in various foodstuffs and had facial bruises caused by the flying china.

The diesel engine of a black cab rattled on the other side of the road. Briggs whistled to catch the driver's attention, who signalled to say he was for hire.

'Union Street, please,' said Billy to the driver.

We howled with laughter, it had been one hell of a party. At the time, we didn't give a passing thought to the shambles and mess we had created and left behind.

Later in the evening, I got fixed up with a big fat ginger-haired lass in Cascades nightclub. I chatted her up as I was leaving the club in the early hours of the morning. She asked me if I would like to go back to her flat for a coffee and I agreed. But I also insisted that she should cook me some beans on toast because I felt ravenous. The request for beans on toast sketch was becoming a bit of a habit of mine, and some women used to invite me back to their place for beans on toast instead of a coffee.

After I had finished eating, I climbed into bed with her and immediately fell unconscious. She expressed her disappointment when she awoke me at four o'clock in the morning and asked me to leave because I was snoring too loudly. I got dressed and caught a taxi back to Seaton Barracks.

'Briggs . . . Briggsy,' I shouted when I awoke the next morning.

His head poked out of his bed sheets.

'What do you want, Steve?'

'Good day yesterday, wasn't it?'

'Yes. That was one hell of a party. We must have left Smithy's place in one hell of a mess.'

'Yeah, I know. Do you think we should go and get Billy and call round to Smithy's house to apologise?'

'Yeah. I suppose he'll be a bit pissed off.'

We got washed and dressed before finding Billy. He too felt

that we should apologise for our behaviour, so we went to Smithy's house. Our heads were bowed down in shame as the door creaked open. Smithy stood in the doorway. He looked surprised and curious.

'Smithy. We've come to apologise for our behaviour yesterday and also for the mess and damage that we caused.'

Smithy looked startled. He laughed very loudly. 'Are you guys kidding? That was one hell of a paaaarrttttyy.'

CHAPTER FIFTEEN

LIVING BY THE SWORD

By 1985, I'd been in for just over two years and toured several parts of the world on deployments with the commando units I had been posted to. Amongst the Marines there was always the same code of practice: don't gob off unless you can back it up with your fists, and always maintain the high soldiering standards required of a Marine or expect to be beaten up.

Generally, I held my own. There were a lot of other Marines who were a lot tougher than I was, but I could give as good as I got. At one stage, I was involved in a fight every time I went ashore (into town). I couldn't help it. My temper was so fiery that I would explode even if someone stared at me in a way I did not like. The jeans I wore from day to day were covered in various blood groups from people I'd been fighting with, and yet none of them were mine. I tended to talk and openly boast about fighting as I had accepted it as part of being a Marine. I wasn't the only one, there were many like me. We were fearless.

I often used to think to myself that if I was killed in combat I would like to have a military funeral with full military honours. I could picture other Marines in their best Blues uniforms with their rifles pointed into the air firing shots over my gravestone, and also the sound of the Royal Marines bugler sounding the 'Last Post'. Yeah, that would be OK, I thought.

One year, on another arctic deployment, we set up a bar back at Gardermoen camp in Norway. As usual, we drank heavily when we weren't in the field and fought viciously amongst ourselves. One of the Marines serving with me was nicknamed Masher. He was a big broad lad with a thick walrus moustache. His fitness was impeccable. We were all very fit, but Masher had the ability to go home on leave for several weeks and not do any physical training, yet still perform at peak level against everybody who had not stopped training. His goal was to join the SBS (Special Boat Squadron), known as the counterparts of the SAS.

We were good friends and very much alike in a lot of ways, especially with our reputation for fighting in our makeshift bar. The walls in the bar had bloodstains from the numerous nightly fights that took place. The military police were never called as we contained what happened in the bar amongst ourselves. If you got beat up, you got beat up, and that was the end of that.

One night, I was lying in bed with a hangover from the previous evening. Everybody who shared my room had gone out, and the room was filled with darkness. I stared at the ceiling and listened to the periods of laughter and violence that came from our bar next door. Then I drifted off to sleep.

It was late when the sound of the room's door opening awoke me. A tall dark figure of a man entered.

'Steve, are you awake?' he called out, in a whisper. His face became clear in the darkness. It was Masher.

'Yes, Masher. What do you want?'

'Which room are the Army signallers in?'

Members of the Army Signals Regiment were often attached to this unit on military tours abroad.

'Why?' I asked curiously.

'A couple of them were mouthing off at me earlier in the bar. I'm going to teach them a lesson.'

'Fair one,' I replied. 'I've got a pickaxe handle and a torch, if you want to use them.'

He sniggered at my offer. 'Yes, cheers Steve, good idea.'

'What about a balaclava to hide your face?'

'Yes,' he sniggered again. He put on the balaclava. 'OK, I'm ready. Where are they?' he asked again.

'Next door.'

Masher grinned before pulling the balaclava down over his face. He switched on the torch and quietly left the room, with the pickaxe handle held firmly in his right hand. I heard several thuds, followed by screams of pain coming from the neighbouring room. Then silence . . .

The door opened and a torch beam dazzled me as it shone in my face. Masher was back. His hand cupped his mouth to dim the noise from his laughter. He was pleased with his performance.

'It sounded good,' I whispered.

'Yes . . . it was good.'

A wicked grin covered his face, but was soon hidden when he pulled the balaclava back over it again.

'I'm going to do it again,' he said as he hurried out of the room.

More thuds and screams came from next door. This time they were louder and the thuds were more frequent. Then another silence . . .

The door opened once again and Masher re-entered. He removed the balaclava and thanked me for loaning it to him.

He was still grinning as he bid me goodnight before leaving my room.

The next day, we learned the true extent of the damage. He had beaten up three of the signallers with the pickaxe handle. Two suffered broken legs and one had a broken collarbone and a broken jaw.

Several days later, the Royal Marines police arrived and wasted very little time in commencing their enquiries. They were not quite sure who they were looking for, but they must have had some idea because Masher was amongst those whom they had chosen to question. However, everybody remained tight-lipped. The enquiry continued for the whole of the following week. Still nothing . . .

The Commando Logistic Regiment began its preparations to leave Gardermoen camp and to load its troops onto a waiting ship. It was part of the final phase of the arctic warfare deployment, to board ship and head north for the final exercise. The ship rocked steadily on the rising tide as we headed out into the open sea. Looking out of my cabin's porthole, I could see the sun rising. Sunrays reflected off the surface of the sea and covered its vast area like a blanket. I felt warm and relaxed as I lay back on my bunk and enjoyed the peaceful view. A knock on the door interrupted my drifting thoughts.

'Come in,' I shouted.

A short, stocky man with a baldy head, dressed in uniform entered. His bright-red MP armband immediately alerted me to his identity.

'Are you Marine Preece?' he asked.

'Yes . . . why?'

'I'm Corporal Jones from the Royal Marines police. We are carrying out an investigation into an alleged assault and would like to ask you some questions.'

Oh fuck, I thought. 'Yes, OK. Right.'

'Put something on your feet and come with me,' he ordered.

Other Marines stared at me as I followed the policeman along the corridor. Their faces displayed their open curiosity. Some winked or nodded their heads as a good-luck gesture. Then the police corporal came to a halt and knocked on a cabin door, which rattled under his fist.

'Come in,' a voice called from inside.

'Wait here, Marine Preece,' he commanded.

I stood at ease with my back to the opposite wall and watched him disappear into the cabin. I could hear several muffled voices coming from inside. I knew they were preparing to interview me, but I didn't feel nervous. I felt quite lethargic and leaned against the wall behind me to support my body weight. The door opened and the corporal re-appeared.

'Get off that fucking wall and stand to attention,' he screamed.

I immediately burst into life and sprang to attention. I slammed the heels of my boots together, pushed my chest out and put the back of my neck tightly into the back of my shirt collar.

'Marine Preece. Quick march . . . halt!' he ordered.

Inside, two other men were facing me. Both were Royal Marines policemen. One was a sergeant and the other was a lance-corporal. The sergeant introduced himself.

'I'm Sergeant Cooper of the Royal Marines police and this other gentleman is Lance-Corporal Smith, also of the Royal Marines police.'

The lance-corporal nodded to acknowledge his introduction.

'Sit down, Preece,' shouted the sergeant in an aggressive manner, and he pointed to a light-coloured wooden chair in front of the desk they were both now sitting at. I looked him straight in the eyes and wondered how he would begin his approach.

'Right, I suppose you are wondering why you are here?' he shouted.

Before I could answer, he continued: 'Well, I'll tell you. We are carrying out an investigation into an alleged aggravated assault concerning another Marine and three soldiers from the Royal Signals Regiment. We believe that you may be able to help us with our enquiries.'

I frowned and remained calm. 'I'm sorry, sergeant, I don't know what you are talking about.'

He snapped straight back at me. 'Listen, you smarmy little bastard, you know why you're here. I don't want to waste your time and I don't want you to waste mine. So start from the beginning and tell me all about it.' Both men were staring straight at me and were waiting for my response. Careful, Steve, careful, I thought.

'You tell me why I'm here and I'll tell you what I want to tell you,' I replied.

The sergeant's eyebrows rose. His face turned bright red and then his temper raged. 'You cheeky little bastard. Who the hell do you think you are talking to? I've got a good mind to kick your fucking head in.'

For a moment I was frightened. I could feel his aggression. The tone of his voice was ear piercing. He was angry, really angry.

'Are you threatening me?' I asked in a calm but sure voice.

His frown lifted and then he calmed down. It was like a lull after a storm. Then he started again on a new tack. 'Do you have a girlfriend at home?'

I frowned and looked at them both. I was confused. 'Yes.'

'What's she like?'

'She wears white socks and has piss stains in her knickers.'

He put on a false smile and pretended to be amused at my cheeky reply. 'When was the last time you saw her?'

'About three months ago.'

'About three months ago,' he shouted back at me. 'Before we came on deployment to Norway.'

'Yes,' I replied, realising the tactful angle he was taking to his approach.

His facial expression changed and he started to scream and shout once again. 'Well, what would she think if she never saw you for another three months, whilst you're sat banged up in Colchester military nick for withholding information?'

He waited for an answer. I knew he was trying to scare me but I declined to succumb to his tactics. 'Well, sergeant, she hasn't missed me for the last three months, so I don't think another three will bother her.'

His temper erupted again and he grabbed me by the scruff of the neck. 'One of these days,' he screamed, 'I'm going to get you. One of these dark nights, you'll have had too much to drink and will be lying face down in the gutter. When this happens I'll either kick you or fucking nick you.'

Silence filled the room. They both waited without success for a reply.

'Do you know what they call me?' he asked calmly.

I shook my head.

'They call me the Mountie, because I always get my man. I'll get the Marine who carried out this assault and sooner or later I'll get you. Get out of my fucking sight.' He pointed to the door.

I swiftly left and closed the door behind me. I breathed a huge sigh of relief which helped ease the nerves and tension that had built up inside my body. Then I saw Masher stood at ease in the corridor along with the corporal who had earlier escorted me. I winked at him as a signal of reassurance that I had said nothing. He grinned in response.

Several hours later I heard that he had confessed under questioning and admitted assaulting the signallers. Luckily, he had declined to reveal where he had obtained the torch, pickaxe handle and balaclava.

After the final NATO exercise on Britain's Northern Flank, Masher was sentenced to sixty days' imprisonment in the Royal Navy's detention quarters in Portsmouth. Apparently, he enjoyed every minute of it and used the extra physical training which was dished out to punish prisoners to enhance his personal physical fitness in readiness to attempt the gruelling selection trials of the SBS. He now serves with this Special Service.

CHAPTER SIXTEEN

PRETEND IT'S YOURS

Some time later, back in Plymouth, I met a local girl called Suzie. She was a good-looking blonde bombshell with long straight hair and a slim petite figure. Her personality was warm and friendly. I met her in Cascades nightclub one night when I was staggering out of the front door in an absolutely polatic drunken state. I literally fell on her and landed with my arms around her neck. She just laughed and helped me into a waiting taxi.

I met her frequently and she told me that her boyfriend, who served with the Royal Navy, had recently dumped her. I was sympathetic towards her, as she seemed genuinely upset. She told me that she thought I was a very nice fellow, whose only fault was the nasty people whom I chose to associate with. Maybe she's extremely naive or just plain stupid, I thought.

She knew a Marine's wage wasn't very attractive and continually insisted that she should pay for all the drinks. I thought I was in heaven and couldn't believe my luck. Here I was with a woman who wanted to pick me up outside the barracks each night and drive the car whilst I got drunk. At the end of each night, she conveniently dropped me off at the barracks, gave me a kiss and watched me stagger in through the main gate. I was so enthralled by my luck and good fortune that for the first couple of weeks I never even thought about having sex with her. I was too busy enjoying my free chauffeur-driven taxi and booze-up.

Eventually, it was her who mentioned having sex. She still lived with her mother, so she suggested using the car as our playpen. A quiet lane on the edge of Dartmoor was the venue and proved to be a fitting end to our nights out. Sometimes, it was hard to find somewhere completely remote, as quite often other couples had the same idea. I found it very amusing, their windows were always steamed up and their cars rocked away in the darkness. Suzie enjoyed having sex in the back of her car and laughed when she saw the soles of her feet in the car's wing mirrors. After a few weeks, other Marines began to get jealous of my new-found lifestyle – as I was soon to find out.

One night in town, we went into The Tube disco pub down Union Street in Plymouth. The Tube was a new posh wine bar with tons of flashing lights and mega loud music. I was slightly drunk and stood alone at the bar, awaiting Suzie's return from the toilet. I felt someone poke me hard in the back with their finger.

'Hey, you,' a voice shouted behind me.

I turned around to see who it was. Two men, roughly my age, stood facing me. I knew they were Marines from their short hairstyle and the way they were dressed. I wasn't nervous and just smiled at them.

'Yes, lads, what do you want?' I asked cautiously.

'What are you doing with Suzie?' answered one of them.

'She's my wife,' I quickly replied.

'No she's not,' he snapped back.

I smiled again as I wasn't frightened of these two. 'OK then . . . she's my sister'.

'She is not,' he shouted, and grabbed hold of my jumper.

He twisted the cloth and pulled me towards him. His grip tightened and he snarled at me, baring his teeth like an animal. Without hesitation, I leapt forward and head-butted him hard on the bridge of his nose. I could feel it crunch under the force of the blow. His legs buckled and blood spurted across his face as he fell down onto the floor. His friend moved in, but quickly joined him when I carried out an action replay of the first head-butt. Then I felt hands clawing at my face from behind and they dug deep into my cheeks. My elbow was my only weapon, so I turned and rammed it hard into the face of the attacker. A loud scream filled my ears and then I realised it was a woman. All three of them rolled around on the floor with their bloodied faces held in their hands.

I didn't care when I saw it was a woman. She had attacked me and I had to defend myself. I felt a little unhappy, though, as she was quite tasty. But tough shit, I thought.

Two huge bouncers appeared on the scene. They were dressed in the usual black tuxedos and dickey bows with cummerbunds and white shirts. They saw the three people on the floor and me stood above them and aggressively slammed me against the nearby wall.

'It wasn't my fault. It wasn't my fault,' I pleaded.

They looked at the three people on the floor and then stared at each other with puzzled looks on their faces. They finally released their grip when, fortunately for me, a barmaid came over and backed up my story. This changed their aggressive attitude towards me and they both apologised.

When Suzie returned from the toilet, she saw the three blood-covered assailants being evicted from the pub and was startled when she saw the deep scratches on my face.

'Steve . . . what happened . . . are you OK?' she asked.

'It wasn't my fault . . . come on, let's go,' I insisted.

We linked arms and left the pub. As we made our exit, we walked past the three assailants. They just put their heads down and looked the other way. The car vroomed as Suzie accelerated and we headed for our quiet spot on Dartmoor.

Some time after this, early one Tuesday morning, I was sat at my desk in the headquarters office. My head ached; the previous night had been a heavy one out on the town. Then the telephone rang. I hesitated and let it ring several more times before I picked up the receiver.

'Hello, headquarters, Marine Preece speaking, sir.'

'Hello . . . is that you Steve?' It was Suzie.

'Hello, Suzie. What are you ringing me at work for?' I asked curiously.

'I want to talk to you. It's something important.'

She sounded distressed, so I felt concerned for her.

'What is it? What's the matter?'

'I don't want to tell you over the telephone.'

'It's OK, there's nobody listening.'

She began to cry and then there was a short silence. 'I'm pregnant,' she cried out.

Shit, I thought. A horrible chill ran down my spine. I couldn't believe what I was hearing. Maybe it's not mine, I thought.

'Steve . . . Steve . . . are you still there?' she cried.

'Yes . . . How many weeks' pregnant are you?'

'Seven.'

I looked at a year planner chart situated on an opposite wall and made a quick calculation of dates. 'But I've only been seeing you for six weeks and I never had sex with you for the first two.'

'I know,' she cried. 'It's my ex-fiancé's . . . but I want to marry you. I love you.'

'No . . . I'm sorry, Suzie, it won't work.'

'It will . . . it will,' she continued to cry.

I frowned. 'Why don't you have an abortion?' I suggested.

'No, that would be murdering it.'

Sweat trickled down my forehead as I searched my mind about the situation.

'Steve . . . I want to marry you.'

I almost fell off my chair. 'What . . . and end up with somebody else's baby? No way.'

'But Steve,' Suzie quickly and anxiously replied. 'Can't you pretend it's yours?'

I closed my eyes and shook my head. Bloody hell, I thought. This is just some tart I've been shagging. Now she wants me to marry her and father some bloody sailor's baby. Bollocks. Suzie interrupted my thoughts.

'Steve . . . can you? Can you pretend it's yours?'

'No I bloody can't,' I snapped back.

'Oh Steve, please, please, I love you Steve. I want to marry you.'

'No, I'm sorry, Suzie, I can't and I won't do this.'

'Please, please, Steve. I love you, I really do,' she sobbed.

I went cold. 'No, I'm sorry, I'll have to go.'

I put down the phone and inhaled deeply. Then I breathed a huge sigh of relief. Fuck me, I thought. That was a bit close for comfort. (Suzie did go on to have the baby some time later, but I had cut all ties with her and only met her one more time after the phone call.)

Shortly afterwards, I was deployed on a three-month tour on active service in Cyprus with one of the other commando units. Active tours of duty meant all work and no play. However, when I returned to my parent commando unit in Plymouth it was antics as usual.

I had decided to play a joke on one of my Marine colleagues who was working in the Signal and Communications Centre. I telephoned the centre and recognised his voice straight away. I wanted to just say hello to him as he was one of my socialising colleagues and I hadn't seen him for the past three months. But, he had played a few tricks on me in my time so I thought I'd make the most of it. That is, of course, if he fell for the joke.

'Hello, COMCEN [Communications Centre], Marine Jones speaking, sir,' he answered in a disciplined voice.

I put my best Northern Irish accent on and spoke into the telephone receiver. 'Don't panic, there's a bomb in the building and it's set to go off in ten minutes.'

There was a silence as I put down the receiver. I paused for a few moments and picked up the telephone again.

My friend's voice came over the receiver again. 'Hello, COMCEN, Marine Jones speaking, sir.'

'Hello, mate, it's Steve.'

'Hello, Steve, how the fuck are you?' he said excitedly. 'Have you just got back from Cyprus? When are we going on the piss?' He didn't sound worried about his previous call. 'Have you had any strange phone calls today?' I asked curiously.

'No, mate, nothing too major. I'll see you tonight and we'll go out and get drunk.'

'Yeah, OK,' I smiled and put down the receiver.

The bastard didn't bite on my little joke, I thought. Never mind, I'll try another time. Then the telephone rang and I answered it. 'Hello, Marine Preece speaking, sir.'

'Hello, Steve, I heard you were back,' said a familiar voice.

I recognised it instantly. It was Nosey Parker, another

Marine mate of mine from Blackpool. Nosey was a nickname for any serviceman who had the surname of Parker.

'Yes, mate, I got back today.'

'Have you just telephoned Jonesey in the COMCEN, pretending you were an Irishman and had planted a bomb?'

'Yes,' I laughed. 'But he didn't take the bait.'

'Oh yes he did,' Nosey laughed. 'They've evacuated the COMCEN and administrative buildings and there's hundreds of them outside.'

'You're bullshitting me,' I said in astonishment.

'No I'm not, Steve. All the senior-ranking officers are there as well. Go and tell them it was you winding your mate up and that it was a harmless hoax.'

'Fuck that, Nosey mate, they'll lock me up and throw away the key.'

'Yeah, you're probably right. We'd better keep it quiet.'

We agreed that the joke had worked, but that it would be best to keep things quiet. I bid Nosey goodbye, but not before arranging to meet him in the NAAFI at 7 p.m. that evening.

The evening promised to be great as not only would we have a reunion to celebrate but also, for some reason or other, there was a function on in the bar and the beer was to be on the house – free.

In the mid-afternoon, the RSM summoned me. I had butterflies in my stomach when I marched into his office, as I felt that word must have got out somehow and he was going to reprimand me for the hoax telephone call. How wrong I was. When I spoke to him he immediately shook my hand and welcomed me back from my active service tour of duty in Cyprus. He then told me that most people had been kept out of the communications centre all day by a bomb-hoax phone call and that there was nobody left around to burn the residual confidential signal papers. He told me that I was available to cover the task and to get on with it immediately.

'Yes, sir, will do, sir,' I said, feeling relief that he didn't know it was me, rather than being totally fed up that I was missing the free beer in the NAAFI bar. At 7.05 p.m., I stood alone next to the small brick-built incinerator. I had several large boxes of signal papers and knew it would take hours to burn them all. I rubbed my chin and tried to think of another solution. I saw a large metal refuse skip a few yards away.

That's it, I thought. I'll dowse the insides of the boxes with some petrol and set fire to them before throwing them into the metal refuse skip. This seemed like a great idea at the time so I didn't hang around wasting my free-beer time. I put a small amount of petrol onto the boxes and hurled them up into the air and into the skip. Twenty minutes later, I arrived at the NAAFI and celebrated my reunion with my friends.

When Nosey saw me, though, he immediately asked me how I'd managed to complete the task so quickly.

'You don't want to know,' I laughed.

The following morning, when I returned to work, I was summoned once again by the regimental sergeant-major. On the way to his office I guessed why. I saw what was left of the metal refuse skip and it looked all buckled and fire-burnt. What I hadn't known the previous night was that the skip was full of partially empty paint tins and white spirits, which are highly flammable. Fortunately, the skip contained the fire and nothing else was damaged.

When I entered the RSM's room, he sat looking at me with a face like thunder. 'Preece.'

'Yes, sir.'

'I thought I told you to burn the confidential signals material in the brick-built incinerator.'

'Yes, sir, I did,' I responded quickly, trying my best to look puzzled.

'The incinerator is bloody spotless, lad. You would find it hard to believe that lots of material was burnt in there last night.'

'Yes, sir, spotless, thank you, sir.'

He looked at me with his eyebrows raised high. 'Have you seen the state of that refuse skip outside?'

'Yes, sir, I have. It's a mess. I heard it was full of paint tins and stuff like that.'

'Hhhmmm,' he smiled. 'And you have no idea how it was ignited?'

'No, sir,' I squinted.

'Hhhmm. OK, make yourself scarce, lad.'

'Yes, sir, will do, sir,' I replied, and smartly marched out of the room.

I knew he knew it was me. I knew he knew there was free beer laid on in the NAAFI. I knew he knew that there had been no material burnt in the incinerator the evening before. But I also knew he knew that he could never prove it.

CHAPTER SEVENTEEN

A THIEF AMONGST THE RANKS

'Hey, Steve,' shouted Briggs across the room.

'What?' I answered and opened my eyes.

'What time is it?'

I looked at my bedside clock. 'It's ten o'clock, mate.'

'Heavy night last night, wasn't it?'

'Yeah, I can't even remember coming back to barracks.'

'Neither can I,' replied Briggs before we both nodded back off to sleep.

Our room was on the first floor of a two-floor accommodation block. It was a fairly big room which was meant to house four men. However, only the two of us shared it and we had plenty of space. The room had a brown carpet on the floor, cream-coloured walls, four beds, four bedside lockers, four kit lockers and a table and chair tucked into one of the corners.

'Hey, Steve.'

'Ten past ten,' I answered, anticipating that he was going to ask me the time again.

'No . . . my wallet has gone. Someone must have stolen it.'

I lifted my head from beneath my bedclothes, and sat up

and looked at him. A frown covered his face as he searched frantically through his trouser and coat pockets.

'Don't be silly, Briggs, no one would do that.'

I couldn't accept that another Marine would steal our money because we all generally respected our own kind who wore the coveted Green Beret.

'Look, your wallet is on the table over there.' He frowned and pointed to a small table in the far corner of the room. My wallet was the sole item on its white surface and was lying open. Briggs picked it up and looked through it.

'Its empty, Steve.'

'Yeah, it probably is. We must have spent all our money on drink last night.'

'Hhhhmmmmm,' Briggs rubbed his rugged unshaven chin.

'Yeah, you're probably right, I've either lost it or spent all my cash and thrown the wallet away.'

I was still tired and had a heavy hangover so I settled back down and went back to sleep.

The following weekend, on a Sunday afternoon, I was sat on my bed writing a letter to my mother. The door creaked open and a head peered in.

'Hello, Steve, it's Pete.'

Pete was a lance-corporal who worked in the unit's administration block. He was around thirty years old and spoke with a broad Scottish accent. He had been a sergeant a few years before, but got caught stealing unit funds and subsequently had his stripes removed. He had apparently stolen thousands of pounds but they could only prove a sum of a few hundred.

'All right, Pete, how are you?'

'I'm fine thanks, I want to ask you a favour. Nigel and I have been out for a few beers. Can you give us a shake [wake them up] around six-thirty this evening?'

'Yes, no problem. Six-thirty.'

'Cheers, Steve,' he smiled and closed the door behind him.

Pete and Nigel shared a room in a different wing of the block. I could tell from his slurred speech and glazed eyes that they had been out drinking during lunch-time. They wanted to sleep off the effects of their drinking session before going out again on the night.

After I finished writing my letter, I switched on the television and watched some football. Around 6.25 p.m., I switched off the television and headed for Pete's and Nigel's room to wake them up. I knocked on the door and pushed it open. The air inside smelt strongly of stale alcohol and the room was in desperate need of airing. Both men were still asleep and snoring loudly. I opened two windows to let in the fresh air.

'Come on, lads, it's time to wake up,' I shouted in a sharp voice.

The snoring stopped. 'Oh . . . yeah, thanks, Steve,' answered Pete.

'Yes, me too,' murmured Nigel.

I left the room for a few minutes to relieve myself in an adjacent toilet. When I returned I saw Nigel with a concerned look on his face. He seemed to be upset about something.

'What's the matter, Nigel?' I asked curiously.

'My wallet has gone.'

'Yes, and so has mine,' joined in Pete. 'Someone must have stolen them.'

I smiled and shook my head slowly. 'No, don't be silly, no one would do that.'

As soon as I spoke, I realised that these were the same words I had said to Briggs during the previous week. My smile changed to a frown. 'Wait a minute, I've said this before. The same thing happened to Briggs and me last week.' We sat down and put our heads together.

During the afternoon, Pete and Nigel had returned from town with two other Marines. One was a black guy called Ashley, and the other was a Scotsman called Jock Biggle. Ashley was a tall, muscular man who didn't drink a lot but generally got along with everyone. However, Jock had recently been caught red-handed breaking into a slot machine in the galley (dining hall) with a sledgehammer. We all agreed that it had to be him. Nigel quickly dressed and led the way to Jock's room.

'The thieving Scotch bastard is going to pay for this,' growled Nigel.

'Yeah, let's go and kick the fucking shit out of him,' I replied. Both Pete and Nigel nodded in agreement.

When we reached Jock's room, we didn't bother knocking and literally thrust the door open. Jock was lying face down on his bed and was snoring heavily. We noticed his wallet lying open on the floor. Pete picked it up and looked through it. It was totally empty.

'Look . . . he's been robbed too,' said Pete.

We left without waking him and debated our suspicions. We decided with very little thought that it couldn't possibly be Ashley as he lived in a separate accommodation block. The case was closed. We didn't have a clue who it was.

Three weeks later, it was Briggs' twenty-fourth birthday. Myself and another Marine called Nick took him for a night on the town to celebrate. Nick was roughly the same age as Briggs and came from Alnwick in north-east England. We went to Plymouth's wildest nightspot, Union Street. Throughout the evening, both Nick and myself stayed reasonably sober. This was because we were both still suffering from the side effects of the previous night's social activities.

This didn't deter Briggs from enjoying himself. He drank

copious amounts of drinks bought by other Marines who knew it was his birthday. One of these people was Ashley. He bought Briggs an extra large vodka. This surprised us as it was unlike him to buy anybody a drink, let alone an extra large one. Even so, Briggs took full advantage of his offer.

At the end of the evening, all three of us headed back to Seaton Barracks. Briggs was in one hell of a drunken state and unsteady on his feet. Both Nick and I had to work very hard to support him, as he was really close to passing out.

'I hope you had a good night, lads,' said Ashley as he walked past us on the street. He had a big mischievous grin on his face.

'Yeah . . . fucking brilliant,' slurred Briggs.

Soon after this, we arrived back at the barracks and put Briggs to bed. He was unconscious before his head hit the pillow and he started to snore loudly. I thanked Nick for helping me to look after Briggs and bid him goodnight.

'Goodnight, Briggsy,' shouted Nick.

I smiled at Nick as we both knew quite well that Briggs wouldn't answer. Nick then went off to his own room, which was next door. Briggs continued to snore loudly from beneath his bedclothes. I smiled to myself and then drifted into a deep sleep. A couple of hours later, I was suddenly awoken by a loud banging noise on our room door. I opened my eyes and looked at my digital alarm clock on the bedside cabinet. It was 3.30 a.m.

'Steve, Steve, it's Nick.' The door rattled under his fist. It was locked. Ninety-nine times out of a hundred it would have been open, but on this occasion I had locked it without even thinking about it.

'Steve, it's Nick, wake up and let me in.'

Something's up, I thought. 'Hold on, Nick, I'll open the door.'

As soon as I turned the key in the lock, Nick pushed the door open and entered the room. He looked annoyed.

'What's the matter, mate?' I asked him.

'I've just caught Ashley going through my pockets.'

'Hold on a minute. Sit down, Nick, and start from the beginning.'

Nick sat down and started to explain what had happened. 'About fifteen minutes ago, I was lying awake in bed. My door opened and I saw Ashley come into my room. Because it was dark, he didn't notice that I was awake. Then he started rifling through my trouser pockets.'

'Did you stop him?' I asked curiously.

'No. He realised that I wasn't asleep and dropped the trousers before rushing out of the room. I got out of bed and switched on the light and then looked into the corridor. There was nobody there.'

'Is that everything?'

'No. I sat down to think about it as I wasn't sure if I had been dreaming. Then the door opened again and Ashley was stood there. He asked me if I knew which room Ginge Worrall lived in. I told him that I saw him going through my pockets and that I knew he was now trying to cover his tracks.'

'What did he say? Did he deny it?'

'No, he just left without saying anything and then I woke you.'

I paused for thought. It all added up now. It must have been Ashley who had been stealing our wallets over the previous weeks.

Briggs continued to snore loudly, totally oblivious as to what was happening.

'OK, Nick, I've got a crowbar in my locker. I'll get it and we'll go and sort the thieving bastard out. I'm going to smash his fucking face in.'

Nick looked startled. 'Oh, I don't know, Steve.'

I held the strong steel crowbar in my hand. 'Yes, come on, let's do it. He's the bastard who's been ripping us all off.'

'No, let's get the military police involved,' Nick insisted. 'We'll get him kicked out of the corps,' he continued.

I paused. I was angry and really wanted to beat him with my crowbar.

'OK, Nick,' I reluctantly agreed. 'Let's do it your way.'

Nick reported the incident to the Royal Marines police, who spent the next few days interviewing Ashley. A couple of days later, I was working in the headquarters' squadron office. The phone rang and I answered it.

'Hello, HQ squadron office, Marine Preece speaking, sir.'

'Hello, Steve, it's Ashley,' the caller replied.

My face dropped. 'What the fuck do you want?'

'I need to ask you a favour.'

I was startled. 'Favour, what fucking favour?'

'The military police have found a coat in my locker with your name on it. I stole it from you, Steve, and I'm sorry about that.'

'Yeah, of course you are, Ashley,' I snapped sarcastically. 'So what's this favour?'

There was a moment's silence during which I could hear his breathing on the other side of the line. I waited for his answer.

'I want you to tell them you lent it to me.'

On hearing this, I first felt like smashing the receiver of the telephone into the desk on which it sat. I couldn't believe my ears. Anger surged through my body and I felt like I was going to explode.

'I'll tell you what, Ashley.' He didn't reply, but listened for what I was going to say. 'I've got a fucking big heavy crowbar in my locker which has got your name on it, and when I get the chance I'm going to wrap it around your fucking neck. So fuck off and stay away from me.'

The phone went dead. He had hung up.

Following the Royal Marines police investigation, we heard that they had found several kit lockers full of stolen goods in Ashley's room. He had apparently been ripping other Marines off for a long time, destroying the trust we held amongst us for all who wore the coveted Green Beret. One of the thefts he admitted brought to light that he had gone as far as abseiling down a couple of floors from the roof of an accommodation block and climbing in through an open window. He carried out his theft and then abseiled down to the ground floor.

Later, to our dismay and amazement, we learnt that Ashley had claimed he had carried out the thefts because he had been subjected to racial prejudice from other Marines and saw his acts as a way of getting his own back. Unfortunately, the military police accepted his claim as part of mitigating circumstances against the charges brought against him and the majority of these were later dropped. A lot of the other Marines were furious because they knew that the racism claims were totally untrue. Colour prejudice amongst the Marines was virtually unheard of. Once you had made the grade to wear the Green Beret, the colour of your skin never really came into it.

Unlike the MPs, we knew he was lying and felt very angry towards him. He was later given a swift posting to the Commachio Group Unit to work in offshore protection on the oilfields of Scotland. This was for his own safety and probably the best thing they could have done for him, as you could literally feel the tension amongst the Marines when they spoke of him.

CHAPTER EIGHTEEN

BOXING SQUAD

Fights down Union Street were always a common sight. The numerous servicemen that socialised there practically guaranteed trouble. I personally fought on a regular basis and became quite confident when it came to using my fists. Having now been in the Marines for nearly three and a half years, I decided to try my hand at boxing. If you volunteered to box in the Marines you were given special leave from duty to take part in the training. This sounded like a good idea, so both Briggs and myself enlisted onto the squad.

The boxing squad consisted of about fifteen Marines in total, covering a variety of different boxing weights and sizes. Although we all had a very high level of personal physical fitness, we found the physical part of the boxing training very hard work. Each day we would start with at least a ten- or twelve-mile run and then be relentlessly pushed through circuit training in the gym. We sparred with each other at the end of the day when we were completely knackered, the idea being that we would be fast, powerful and furious when we boxed in the Marine Corps championships in a couple of months' time.

After the first two weeks, our level of fitness seemed to grow stronger and stronger by the day. Our boxing coach pushed us hard, but never gave us any level of exercise that he could not personally achieve himself.

The coach was nicknamed Batsy, and was called this by literally everyone who knew him, although I never really found out why. He worked as a driver and we often wondered how he had passed his test because he was completely reckless when he let loose on the road. He tried very hard to look good when he drove past people but this seemed to make him less conscious of what he was driving into.

A week before the Marine Corps boxing championships were due to take place, we were stood on the weighing scales to check what weight we would be boxing at. A few of us were too heavy so Batsy wanted us to shed a few more pounds of body weight. He selected a few of us to carry out more circuit training, which took place inside the unit's sauna.

The sauna was a big wooden box with the usual hot coals fire and a few levels of shelving to sit on and experience different levels of heat. We were pushed hard and had to step up and down the shelves carrying dumb-bell weights in our hands. We were soaking wet with sweat. After a while, I felt weak and found it hard to breathe. Batsy pushed us harder and harder. Then he told us to stop and go outside and stand by the weighing scales. If you had lost the weight he had wanted you to lose you could stop training and go and get changed. If you hadn't you had to go back into the sauna and carry on with the circuit training.

One of the hardest parts of the training was meal times. The super heavyweight boxers could eat as much as they liked and piled their plates high with food. The amount of food they placed on their plates was amazing. The biggest guy in the squad was a blond-haired lad whom we called Scouse because he came from Liverpool. He was a good, strong and experienced boxer and boxed southpaw (left-handed). This was something that I always found confusing when I sparred with him. Boxing with a right-handed boxer was easy because he was throwing and blocking the punches in the same fashion as me. However, with the southpaws everything was the total opposite and therefore confusing. Scouse could eat for England and looked as if he did.

My boxing weight was classed as light middleweight, so I could have half a plate of light food. At first this pissed me off, but when I saw what the flyweights had to eat, I felt much better. I'm sure they found staring at my half-full plate of food just as agonising as I found the super heavyweights' plates, because their plates looked like something you would give to a rabbit.

The Marine Corps boxing championships were soon upon us and the big event was held at the Commando Training Centre in Lympstone, Devon. It always felt strange returning there as we had all done our basic training there several years before. However, once you arrived through the main gates you always felt like you had never left. The memories of basic training came flooding back as if it had happened only yesterday.

That morning, we all had to attend a weigh-in, where our fighting weights would be checked to confirm our level of entry into the championships. Thankfully, my weight was OK, as some poor individuals had to use a skipping rope to lose a few more ounces.

As for the rest of us, we had several hours before the tournament started and were now free to eat as much food as we liked. It felt like we hadn't seen food for months and we stuffed as much as possible into our mouths until we could eat no more.

The early fights were the preliminary fights and were held in the smaller of two available gyms. The fights were called bouts, and to get into the finals you had to win three bouts. Each bout consisted of three rounds and each round lasted two minutes. This might not seem like a lot, but believe me, when you were in the boxing ring it seemed to last forever. There were four boxing rings in total and all were occupied by prospective Rocky-style champions. The preliminary rounds were fought over one day and concluded with only the finalists remaining to fight in the big event, held in the big gym on the following day.

My first fight was against a Marine called Taff Jones; he was a Welshman from 40 Commando Unit based in Taunton, Somerset. We knew each other fairly well as we had served together a year or so ago when I had been attached to 40 Commando for a three-month deployment to Cyprus. Although we never hung around together socially, he knew I was a handful as he had seen me on several occasions scrapping in the local pubs. He looked nervous.

Inside, I felt good. I felt, fit, strong and confident, and was keen to get on with my first boxing bout in the Marine Corps championships.

'Round one,' a voice called out.

Immediately, we rushed towards each other in the middle of the ring and exchanged a number of sharp jabs and a few big right-hand punches. Although points were scored with jab punches, the jab was more of a distance feeler of how far away your opponent was or alternatively used to block and parry away punches like a shield.

By the end of the second round I felt like I was in control. I was throwing lots of accurate punches and receiving very little from Taff. I finally finished him with what we called a postman's knock. That is, I pretended to throw a left jab and then pulled it back sharply and threw a big right. This was repeated in quick succession and was a very powerful technique.

My second fight came as a bit of a surprise. I was drawn against a Marine Jackson: the same Marine Jackson (or 'Jacko') who was one of the bad guys in Yankee Company, 45 Commando, when I first arrived there about two and a half years before.

At first, I felt nervous as I stared at him across the ring. I watched him staring at me. He didn't recognise me. To him, I was just another opponent. I looked at him. His wonky battle-scarred nose reminded me of the times back in Arbroath. Yes, I said to myself. This is my opportunity to get my own back. I'm going to fucking hammer the bastard.

Before the first bell, we met in the middle of the ring to touch gloves. This is a boxer's way of shaking hands and wishing his opponent good luck. As we stared at each other, I could see the hate in his eyes. He was a warhorse and was keen to knock down anything that stood in his way. I knew this, but by this time in my career, so was I.

We stared deeply into each other's eyes, psyching each other out.

'You're going down,' said Jacko in a calm voice.

'Fuck you,' I swiftly replied as we banged gloves.

We both walked back to our corners without taking our eyes off our opponent. DING DING. The bell rang. 'Round one,' a voice shouted.

We rapidly exchanged a flurry of blows. It was as if we wanted to kill each other, and as quickly as possible. We both displayed a good level of skill and determination, both in our attacking blows and our skilful defensive boxing. The crowd around the other boxing rings saw the aggression on display in our bout and came over to watch. Their chants sounded loud at first, but started to sound distant as we continued to fight.

The second round was very much the same. As soon as the bell rang, Jacko shouted, 'You're going down.' To which I replied, 'Fuck you.' We both had bloodstained faces and shirts, and splashes of our blood covered the canvas of the ring. The intensity of the fight had not lessened and we were both determined to win.

As the third and final round commenced, Jacko shouted, 'Third time lucky for you. You're going down, fucking down.'

'Fuck you, you piece of shit,' I snapped back. 'I'm going to put you down for all the shit you gave me when I was a piece of skin in Yankee Company.'

He looked at me. He raised his eyebrows and looked puzzled. This was probably because he treated all the new young Marines like shit and their faces never really registered.

'You're still going down,' he snarled.

'Fuck you,' I replied, to which he returned a faint smile.

The third round was fiercer than the first two. I was getting tired but my anger drove me on. I had no intention of losing this bout or even drawing it to Jacko. I hated him and wanted to put him down on the canvas.

Then he surged forward. I saw his shoulders hunch and knew immediately that he intended to use his head to head-butt me. I continued to throw jabs to push him off and could feel his anger as he entered the immediate space around me. Then he lunged forward, his forehead hurtling into the area of my face. I sensed this and moved back at what felt like the same speed and timing he came at me. This caused him to lose his balance and his momentum threw him forward with his head down. I saw my opportunity and threw a flurry of left and right hooks to both sides of his head. He groaned as each blow banged heavily into his skull. He knew I was taking control and moving in for the kill, so he stepped back to move out of my reach. However, I moved with him and saw his chin rise to see where I was. I threw a sharp uppercut punch with as much strength as I could muster and the effect was devastating for Jacko. The blow lifted him off his feet and backwards onto the canvas of the ring floor. I stood over him as the referee counted out the time. His arms moved as if he wanted to get up, but could not. He had nothing left. The referee counted him out and raised my right arm into the air. A huge cheer sounded out from the mass of spectators. My victory against the well-known Jacko was well received.

Thankfully, I had a bit of a break before my next bout and went over to one of the other rings to see how Scouse was getting on. He had already won his first two bouts and needed to win his third and final bout to get into the final.

Super heavyweight boxing was different from the lighter classes. The boxers were a hell of a lot bigger and more cumbersome with their movements. However, they were more powerful and one blow from them would be like being hit by a sledgehammer. During our preparation training, Scouse used to boast about his preferred boxing technique. At some time during his bouts he would drop down on a bent knee and throw a big left-handed punch to his opponent's stomach, followed by a fast jab as he rose up higher and then a good hard jab to the head. He also claimed that he could hypnotise his opponents by holding his glove out in front of him and making small circles with his hand in front of their faces. He had apparently used the stomach and head technique during his first two bouts and knocked both opponents clean out. Then I watched him make short work of his third opponent in the second round as he delivered his powerful three sharp and effective blows. His opponent seemed to lift off the floor each time he hit him and then a loud thundering noise filled the gym as he fell backwards onto the canvas.

Briggs patted me on the back. 'All right, Steve, I hear you're doing well.'

'Yeah, I'm doing OK, but I'm shattered now and I've got another fight in a few minutes.'

'I know, mate,' he smiled. 'I'm not surprised you're knackered. That Jacko is a fucking hard bastard. You done well to beat him. He thinks you're a tough cookie and said he doesn't mind getting beat by somebody who can box like that.'

'Hhhhmmm,' I nodded and walked over to the ring for my final bout.

My last fight was against an Irish guy called Brian. He had short black hair, which was receding at the front, and was of similar height and build to myself. He was quite fit and held a black belt in judo. We both knew I was the better boxer but, unfortunately for me, Brian had got a bye into this round without having to fight a single bout (there had been nobody left to fight him in the first bout, and his would-be opponent in the second bout was withdrawn due to injury). This meant that he was fresh and would be a more worthy opponent.

I stood quietly next to Batsy in my corner of the ring. I ached all over from my fight with Jacko and was absolutely shattered. My eight-ounce gloves felt more like heavy weights pulling my hands down towards the floor. I knew this wasn't going to be easy.

Come on, Steve, you can put Brian on his arse, you've done it enough times before, I thought to myself.

DING DING. The bell rang out and the round started. I began well but my gloves seemed to be getting heavier and heavier. I felt distant and had to struggle to defend myself against Brian's attacking blows. I worked hard and managed to contain his attack for the remainder of the first round, but I could feel a lot of strength and power in his blows. Back in my corner, I looked at Batsy.

'I've had it here, Batsy. I can hardly get my gloves up, they seem to weigh a ton.'

'You're tired, Steve, you've had a hard day,' he frowned.

'Keep your head, Steve,' shouted Briggs. 'Use your head.'

DING DING, the bell rang for the second round and I slowly walked towards Brian. My guard was low and my strength sapped. I struggled to lift my gloves up to protect myself. Brian saw my weakness and rained a number of heavy blows hard into my face. Then I head-butted him right on the nose. I felt like it was the only way I could stop his onslaught. Blood spurted out of his nose and he fell back onto the canvas.

Briggs jumped quickly into the ring and raised my arm into the air. I looked towards Brian, who was now rolling around on the floor holding his nose.

'Yyeeeeeesssss!' Briggs shouted.

'No,' interrupted the referee, bluntly. 'He's disqualified.'

I wasn't bothered who won. I felt drained and dizzy. When Briggs originally shouted 'use your head' at the start of the second round, he meant think about what you need to do. However, I hadn't thought about it and spontaneously used my head to defend myself.

The following day was the finals of all the preliminary bouts. They were held in the big gym with no expense spared. There was a single boxing ring in the centre of the gym with its ropes and corner posts painted in the colours of red, white and blue. Hundreds of seats surrounded it and the Royal Marines band played military music softly in the far corner. Huge trophies sat on a nearby table awaiting the winners of each bout.

All the Marine officers wore white jackets, black shirts and trousers and white dickey bows, and all their female partners were dressed in posh evening gowns. The rest of us were dressed in jeans, T-shirts and training shoes.

Our boxing squad's support was now with Scouse and we waited patiently for his entrance. His mother, father and girlfriend sat in the front row. They looked as excited as we were. Then the buglers from the band burst into the theme music from *Rocky*. The audience sat up in their seats and focused on the well-lit boxing ring. The atmosphere felt electric.

Scouse made his entrance and waved both his gloves in the air. A rapturous round of applause echoed around the gymnasium from the many people who knew him. He proudly climbed into the ring and stood facing the blue corner, where he held the ropes and bounced up and down a few times before repeatedly banging his gloves together. He looked fierce. He waved to acknowledge the presence of his mother, father and his very stunning girlfriend, who were sat amongst the crowd.

The *Rocky* theme music started again and Scouse's opponent entered the ring. There was a small round of applause from a few of the spectators. This puzzled me at first, but then I realised why. The opposing boxer was a recruit who was still in basic training. He had not yet earned the coveted Green Beret and was therefore not yet a Marine.

He looked about eighteen years old, was six foot tall and, like Scouse, was built like a brick shit-house. His head was shaven in true recruit fashion and he looked very nervous as he gently bounced up and down in the red corner.

DING DING. The bell rang and the first round began. The opponents approached each other and met in the middle of the ring. Then we watched the whole of the first round with total amazement. Each time Scouse moved towards his opponent, he started his hypnosis technique and made a circular motion with his right glove. The recruit seemed to respond to this as he never threw a single punch and just bounced around the ring, moving towards Scouse's glove and then away from it. Amazingly enough, when the first round had finished they hadn't actually exchanged a single blow.

The second round was very similar, except three punches were thrown: two jabs from Scouse and one from his opponent. Everybody looked around the gym at each other as if they couldn't believe what they were seeing in this Marine Corps super heavyweight final.

Before the bell rang for the third round, Briggs stood up and shouted, 'For fuck's sake, Scouse, fucking box will you?'

Scouse was looking down at the canvas in his corner. Then he raised his head and looked towards us and shouted, 'Right, this is it. I'm going to fucking kill him.'

His voice echoed and you could feel the aggression in his huge frame. Then he slammed his gloves together causing a huge thunderous banging sound that seemed to fill the gym and then echo around it.

Everybody looked at each other. A few nodded and you could hear the words being repeated. He's going to fucking kill him. He'd convinced most of us that he meant what he said.

DING DING. The bell rang for the third round. Scouse rushed to meet his opponent in the middle of the ring and danced around from side to side with swift movements similar to the speed of the lighter weight boxers. Unlike Scouse, the recruit slowly walked forward with a huge frown on his face.

'COME ON,' shouted Scouse as he beckoned his opponent to move towards him with his leading glove. The response was amazing. The recruit threw a big right-handed punch, which hit Scouse hard on the chin. A thunder sounded its mighty power, followed by an almost deafening booming noise as Scouse hit the canvas. We watched him try to get up, but no matter how hard he tried he could not find the strength to manage it. Then he lay down on his back, like a true knocked-out boxer. A big grin covered his face as he lay there staring at the ceiling. He knew he was out and couldn't do anything about it.

His corner man threw a towel into the middle of the ring and the referee raised the right arm of the triumphant recruit to mark his victory. Two members of our boxing squad climbed into the ring and helped Scouse onto his feet. They both threw one of Scouse's arms over their shoulders and literally carried him back to the blue corner. Even then as he stood against the ropes he fought to stay on his feet. The big grin still covered his face as he stared at us in disbelief. The whole tournament had been one hell of an experience.

CHAPTER NINETEEN

SUMMER LEAVE 1986

By the summer of 1986, I had completed three three-month tours of the Arctic as part of the Cold War deployments, one three-month tour of Northern Ireland and one three-month tour of Cyprus. I served these duties with 45 Commando Unit, the Commando Logistic Regiment and via detached duties to other commando units, which were requests I had been lucky enough to get granted while on the quota system, which was still ongoing.

When I was on active service deployments I usually kept myself out of trouble and focused on my work. After the deployments had finished, my lifestyle inevitably became repetitive. I would go out on the town, get drunk, get myself a woman and have a fight or two. This also seemed to be a way of life for a lot of Marines whom I served with. I suppose it was a Marine's way of letting off steam.

Following the tour of Cyprus, we were granted a spot of home leave. I felt quite excited as I sat on the train heading north and bounced up and down on the springs of my seat as the carriages rattled along the track.

My eldest brother, Martin, was getting married after a courtship of about ten years. He was marrying Janine, his childhood sweetheart, and he had honoured me by asking me to be his best man, which of course I accepted.

When the train neared my stop, I started to grin. I felt good inside and proud of the work I did. I had been away for three months doing the job I used to dream about when I was a child. I was looking forward to seeing my mum and dad and telling them all about it.

As I sat there daydreaming, I heard a whistle sound on the platform. I looked out of the carriage window and saw that it was my stop. The train was moving slowly, but not stopping at its usual place. Fuck me, I thought, it's not going to stop. I jumped up and grabbed my heavy backpack and slung its shoulder straps over my shoulders. I looked down at the platform. The train was starting to pick up speed. Bollocks, I can do this, I thought and proceeded to open the door to jump down onto the platform.

'What are you doing?' shouted a train guard from the opposite end of the carriage.

I smiled and waved at him. I was already in motion and on my way out of the door.

'You'll kill yourself,' he screamed.

When I hit the platform, I felt the sheer speed of the train. My legs were pumping away like mad, but I quickly took control and slowed down well before the end of it. Another guard appeared. It was the platform guard, dressed in his British Rail uniform. He was puffing and panting heavily when he reached me and struggled for breath. He put his hands on his hips. 'You could have killed yourself,' he gasped, and fought to regain his breath.

'Not today,' I smiled. 'I've got too much to live for.'

Outside the station, I caught a bus to cover the last few

miles of my journey home. It was late when it pulled up at my stop, so I headed straight for a nearby pub. My dad smiled when I walked through the doors of the bar. He had been expecting me and checked the time on his watch. He was stood leaning against the long wooden bar, conversing with a middle-aged spotty barmaid who looked cock-eyed. A coal fire blazed away, inset on the far wall, and soft music played quietly in the background. A group of locals sat in one corner playing cards, and another two played pool on the blue pool table.

'What would you like to drink, son?' he smiled.

'What time does the bar shut, Dad?'

'In one hour.'

'I'll have five pints of Guinness please.'

'Coming up,' he grinned. 'Would you like a rum and peppermint as well?'

'Yeah.'

He purchased the beer and we sat down at an empty table next to the bar.

'Cheers, Dad,' I gestured, and raised my glass.

I downed the first three pints in as many minutes and the fourth a short time later. Then I noticed the locals pointing at my empty glasses and sneering behind their playing cards. I pretended not to notice. I'd been a Marine for three and a half years now and had grown apart from these people I'd known in my childhood. As an adult, they didn't really know me, or vice versa. My home leave cycle was a mere six weeks a year and I didn't always come home to spend it. I chatted happily with my father and sipped from my fifth pint of Guinness. We spoke quietly about my experiences in Northern Ireland and Cyprus and I brought him up to date with the realities of war.

'You must have plenty of money,' a voice called out from the crowd of card players.

I looked up. All four of the card players were sat looking towards me and also both of the pool players. I was unsure which one of them had made the comment so I aimed my answer at all of them.

'I earn what I spend and really that's none of your business,' I snarled.

There was a silence and then I could hear the coal fire burning away above the sound of the quiet soft music.

'Ignore them and enjoy your beer, son,' whispered my father.

'Hhhhhmmmm,' I replied and nodded. I felt angry and my temper was brewing inside.

'We pay our taxes and therefore all the wages for the armed forces,' the same voice as before called out.

I looked over at the card players and saw that it was a man called Vinny. He was a couple of years older than me and scruffy in appearance. He had long brown hair, tied back in a ponytail, and a face covered in acne.

'That means we've paid for your beer,' he continued in a cocky manner.

'Fuck off, wanker,' I snarled.

My father finished his drink and stood up. He looked nervous, but also disappointed with my reception from the locals.

'Come on, son, let's go home,' he whispered, and pulled on his coat.

'Hhhhhhmmm,' I answered and swilled down the remainder of my fifth pint.

As I placed the empty glass on the table, one of the pool players grabbed hold of me from behind with both arms and put mild choking pressure on my throat.

'Do they teach you unarmed combat, then, soldier boy?' he laughed.

At this, I burst into action and stood up, taking hold of the grip he had on my throat. I dropped down low and thrust my buttocks into his body before leaning forward and throwing him over my head and over the bar. His body smashed into the mirror on the wall behind the bar and a high number of spirits bottles crashed around him and smashed, spilling their contents all over the floor.

By this time, I was very angry and turned to look at the group of startled locals. One of the pool players was stood next to me, with his wooden cue in his hand. I grabbed it and hit him in the gut with the heavy end. I then proceeded to beat the cue into Vinny's head and the crowd around him ran out of the nearby exit door.

He screamed with pain but I showed no mercy. I watched him cry like a baby.

'You don't pay my wages, fuckdust,' I screamed. 'I earn them fighting for good-for-nothing pieces of shit like you.'

'I'm sorry, I'm sorry, I'm sorry,' he whimpered.

I let go and pushed his head away from me. He sobbed heavily. Then I could hear the crackling of the coal fire again.

'Come on, son, let's go home,' my father whispered. 'We've got a wedding to go to tomorrow.'

'Hhhmmmm,' I sighed, and drank my remaining rum and peppermint before leaving for the short walk home.

The following morning I awoke around 5.45 a.m. My bedroom window was east-facing and the beams of the rising sun penetrated the cheap, thin blue curtains that covered it. I got out of bed and quickly got washed and changed into my shorts, T-shirt and training shoes. It was part of my routine when I came home to rise early and run along the coastline watching the picturesque sunrise. It gave me time to think and plan my day, and also helped to clear the previous night's beer out of my system.

Around 10.00 a.m., I saw my brother Martin. He was nervous about everything going right at his wedding, and whether his suit would arrive back from the cleaners on time. He was now twenty-seven years old, about 5 ft 7 in. tall and of stocky build. He had grown into a serious man, who always took things to heart. He was overly worried about people saying the wrong things about him, and quite different from the aggressive type of person he once was in his late teens and early twenties. He lacked confidence in himself, which was something I personally blamed on our upbringing.

Anyway, his suit arrived around 10.30 a.m., so I prepared my Blues military uniform and polished my boots and brasses that were part of my locket union (Marine belt buckle). As we prepared our clothes, we heard our other brother Peter come down the stairs and then enter the room.

'Morning,' he smiled.

'Morning,' replied Martin. 'You look like shit.'

'Yeah, I had a heavy night on the piss last night and have a head like a baby's pram.'

'Like a what?' I interrupted with a confused look on my face.

'Like a baby's pram,' he laughed. 'Full of shit and broken biscuits.'

I smiled at him. 'Have you bought a suit?' I questioned, because I knew he didn't have one.

'No, I haven't.'

I pointed at Martin who was now using the iron on his trousers. 'It's his fucking wedding,' I shouted. 'Where's your fucking suit?'

'Keep your hair on. I've bought a suit out of the catalogue especially for his fucking wedding. I'm not paying for it though. After the wedding, I'm going to send it back and tell them it's too small.'

Martin shook his head and continued to make a bodge job of ironing a straight line in his trouser legs. I took the iron off him and did the honours, as I was quite a dab hand with an iron.

'I heard about your arrival home last night, Steve,' said Peter as he drank a cup of coffee.

'Yeah, a few arseholes shooting their mouths off.'

'I heard you threw the pub landlord over the bar and smacked a couple of the regulars.'

'Was that the landlord? Oh well. I suppose you heard right.'

'Good, I didn't like either of the locals anyway. They think you're mental. The landlord has also said that you're barred out of the pub until the next time you come home on leave.'

'No sleep lost there. Let's go for a beer before the wedding.'

'Yeah, fuck it,' interrupted Martin. 'I'm as nervous as fuck, let's go and have a couple of beers.'

'Me and your mother are coming as well,' shouted Dad as we prepared to leave. We all left our house and headed for the local pub.

'Steve's barred out,' commented Peter as we walked out the door.

Our father shook his head. 'Fuck the landlord, he got what he asked for and that's that. When we go in son, just sit down and we'll get the beer in.'

'Hhhhmm,' I nodded.

Inside, the bar was empty. There were a few bloodstains on the floor and a load of sticky tape holding together what was left of the mirror that stood behind the bar. I sat down at a table and watched the same spotty barmaid from the previous night point at me.

'No, no, I'm sorry but that lunatic is not getting served,' she scowled. 'He shouldn't be allowed to walk among the public, he's dangerous.'

'Yes, but only if you upset him,' added Peter.

'Where's the landlord?' asked my father.

'He's in hospital having stitches put in his head and arms, because of him.'

'Look, just serve me with the beer and I'll square it with the landlord later. It was him who was out of order, not Steve.'

'Eeerrr, OK,' she agreed. 'But just one drink.'

She served him with a round of drinks and several more after that. I noticed he bought her a couple of beers as well to keep her sweet.

At 12.30 p.m., a couple of posh cars arrived to take us to the wedding. We drank up and climbed into the waiting cars along with some friends and relations. En route, our mother complained about the continuous breaking of wind and opened the window to let some fresh air into the car. Martin looked nervous and sat quietly in the back of the car, drinking a can of beer and staring out of the window.

After about twenty minutes, we arrived at the church. Inside, it was brightly lit, with lots of colourful floral decorations spread throughout. The vicar greeted us and informed us that the bride hadn't yet arrived. Peter lifted his leg and released a long, wet-sounding fart.

'Behave, you dirty bastard,' snarled Martin.

Peter did it again, but this time he bent forward to do it.

'Fucking behave, you dirty bastard,' snarled Martin again.

'Gentlemen, gentlemen, please,' interrupted the vicar. 'The bride has arrived.'

Janine entered the church. She looked fantastic and was escorted down the aisle by her father, as 'Here Comes the Bride' was played on the organ. The ceremony went fairly smoothly, and both Martin and Janine said their vows without error.

After the ceremony, we all walked casually out of the

church for a quick photograph session, prior to heading for the local working man's club for the reception. Peter carried on his wind-breaking antics as we walked out through the archways of the large wooden exit doors.

Later, we arrived at the reception in the working man's club. It was held in a big function room with bright red wallpaper, lots of rows of seats and tables, a small dance floor and a small stage at the end of it, which housed a discothèque. One of the tables held hundreds of glasses of whisky. They were stacked on tin trays, each of which held about 20 glasses filled to the brim. These were to be used to toast the bride and groom later when everybody had arrived.

I sat down next to my mother and father and thought about what I was going to say in my best man's speech. I had nothing prepared as I just intended to cuff what I was going to say and hope it all came out all right. Then I heard somebody break wind and smiled to myself when I saw Peter stood next to the table where all the whiskies were placed and slyly helping himself to a couple of glasses. Hhhhmmmm, good idea, I thought, and calmly walked over to the table where Peter was stood. He smiled when he saw me and picked up another glass before releasing some more wind.

I laughed and then quickly downed four glasses of whisky. It tasted like fire-water and burned the back of my throat. My eyes started to water and my head got really warm. Peter laughed and then drank another, before lifting his right leg up and releasing another fart. We both burst into laughter and I proceeded to help myself to several more glasses of whisky. This continued until everybody had arrived and the tray I was taking the whisky glasses from had only one more full glass remaining.

When it was time for my speech I climbed up onto the stage. I still wasn't quite sure what I was going to say, so I picked up the nearby microphone and just gave Martin a good slagging about pissing the bed when he was a kid. Thankfully, this seemed to go down quite well with the guests.

Then came the boring part of reading out all the wedding cards. They seemed to go on forever, but I persevered and finished the pile I had stacked on one of the discothèque's loudspeakers.

'Well, thanks for the cards, everybody,' I said, and went to propose a toast to the bride and groom.

'No, Steve,' Janine politely interrupted, with another pile of wedding cards in her hand. 'There's all these as well.'

Oh fuck, I thought, I'm sick of reading the fucking cards. I grabbed the pile of cards from her and she smiled as I turned towards the guests, a lot of whom were waiting to have their cards read out.

'Like I said, thanks for the cards,' I shouted, and then threw them all into the air. I laughed as they scattered around the dance floor and into the crowd. Then there was a total silence. Everybody was stood or sat staring straight at me and none of them looked very impressed with my card-throwing antic.

'Eeeeeh, he's thrown my card onto the floor,' complained one of the female guests.

'I know, he's thrown mine too and I paid £2.50 for it,' snapped another, who then asked one of the many young children stood next to the dance floor to pick it up and give it to Janine. Then others did the same. Whispers of disgust were passed between the guests and they didn't seem very happy.

I pressed my mouth up against the microphone and sighed. 'Well, if you don't like my sense of humour, there's the exit door. You can all take it and fuck off. I don't care, the bar's open and I'm happy.'

They all looked at each other. Then I saw the old man who lived next door to my mother smile and start to clap. Then everybody started to clap and out of the sunken atmosphere there rose a rapturous round of applause. This was a great relief, so I stood down from the stage and went to drink some more whisky. Peter was still stood by what was left of the full whisky glasses and lifted his leg before releasing yet another blast of his bad wind.

I stayed late in the club bar and left well after all the other members of my family. When I exited the club I flagged down a taxi and climbed into the passenger seat. I slurred heavily as I made a couple of attempts to give the taxi driver my address. He responded by giving me a pen and paper and got me to write it down because no matter how hard I tried, I just couldn't string the words together. Then I fell back against the seat as he sped off down the road. My head felt very hot and heavy and I slipped into a semi-conscious state. Ten minutes later, we pulled up outside my mother's house.

'We're here, mate,' said the taxi driver.

I could hear him, but he sounded a long way off.

'We're here, mate,' he repeated. 'Wake up.'

'Uhh. Oh yeah,' I answered, and rubbed my eyes.

The short sleep had made me feel a lot better and my slurring had almost completely worn off.

'How much is that?' I asked the driver.

'Just ten pounds.'

I pulled out my wallet and looked inside. I still had plenty of money, but something didn't seem right.

'How much?' I exclaimed anxiously.

'Ten pounds to you,' he smirked.

'Ten pounds!' I snapped. 'You can fuck off, it's not ten pounds.'

'Yes it is,' he frowned.

'No it's fucking not.'

'It is, mate, it is,' he insisted.

It wasn't right, I knew it wasn't. I looked at him. 'I'll tell you what, mate. Get your boss on the radio and ask him to give you a price of how much that journey should cost.'

'What for?' he questioned.

'Just fucking do it, now,' I shouted aggressively.

He looked startled and unsure of what to do. 'Oh shit. My meter's not working, I've got the price wrong.' He shook his head. 'It's only five quid, not ten.'

'You robbing bastard,' I screamed. 'At least Dick Turpin had the fucking decency to wear a mask when he robbed people. Here, here's two pounds and think yourself fucking lucky I haven't smashed your fucking skull in.'

I threw two pounds into his lap and climbed out of the car, before slamming the door shut. It then did a U-turn and sped off in the opposite direction. Fucking twat, I thought to myself, and pushed my key into the front door lock, which slowly creaked open. It was about one o'clock in the morning and I found the front room light had been left on.

That's strange, I thought, as I entered. Then I could smell and see smoke coming from the door to the kitchen. Oh shit, I thought. The fucking house is on fire. I ran into the kitchen, which was full of smoke and steam. I fell over something bulky on the floor. Then I realised it was the family dog. The fumes had got the better of him.

I could feel a fair amount of heat, but could not see any flames. The light was still on in the kitchen, but the visibility was very poor. When I got back onto my feet I was stood next to the gas cooker. I saw a pan smouldering away. The steam had been produced from water that must have been in the pan, and now the burning smell was coming from smoke from its melted base and a melted plastic handle. I turned off the gas and opened the back door to let some air in and the smoke and steam out. I grabbed hold of the dog with both arms and carried him into the garden to check if he was still alive. He was still breathing and slowly came around after a few minutes of fresh air. I patted him and he pushed his head against me and licked my hand with his dry tongue.

After about fifteen minutes a lot of the smoke had cleared from the kitchen. I could see the far wall through the smog, and what was left of the pan and gas cooker rings. Then I saw Peter. He was sat unconscious on a chair. Oh shit, I thought, and quickly ran back inside to check his breathing.

When I reached him I could hear him snoring heavily. I then put two and two together and got four. He must have come home and put a pan of food on the gas cooker and then fallen asleep. I felt fairly certain, because this wasn't the first time he had done this.

There was still a fair amount of smoke so I decided to frighten Peter back to his senses. I grabbed hold of his jumper and shook him wildly.

'Peter, Peter,' I shouted. 'The house is on fire. The house is on fire.'

'Uh, what?' he said as his eyes struggled to open.

'The fucking house is on fire!' I shouted louder.

He slowly reached for his pocket and retrieved matches and a cigarette. I watched him light the match and puff from the cigarette. Then he lifted his leg and farted. His eyes were now open. 'Uh, fire, yeah. Good night, wasn't it?'

I shook my head slowly. 'Give me one of those cigarettes,' I demanded. I didn't smoke, but I certainly felt like I needed one.

CHAPTER TWENTY

A LUCKY ESCAPE

'Hey, Steve,' a familiar voice called out as I walked in through the main gates of Seaton Barracks on my return from home leave. I looked up and saw Briggs. He had a big grin on his face and looked like he had something good to tell me.

'Hello, Briggsy,' I answered amiably. 'What's happening?'

'Go to the registry (unit records office).'

'Why?'

'Your posting has come through. You've got a draft to the NATO Allied Command Channel, HMS Warrior near Watford.'

'Brilliant,' I shouted happily. This was a posting I had put in for some time ago, and it was known as a difficult one to get accepted on. HMS Warrior was one of the main NATO bases for Europe. It was nicknamed the Hole, as a lot of it was situated deep underground. It was manned around the clock and ran a schedule of home leave cycles. This meant that one third of the ranks would be on leave at any one time, one third would be at work and the remaining third would be sleeping off a day or a night shift.

I was overjoyed with the great news and wasted very little

time in arranging a leaving celebration in the barracks' NAAFI bar a few days later. The bar was nothing special and, although the beer was cheap, very few Marines used it to socialise. Instead they generally headed into Plymouth city centre. The interior was quite spacious, but dimly lit. The walls were dressed with horrible-looking red and white wallpaper and the floor was deep red and highly polished. There were groups of seats, and chairs which were made of solid wood and had red studded canvas on the backrests and seating areas. The landlord was an ex-sailor called Dougie. He was a short stocky Scotsman, about fifty-five years old with thick black curly hair and dark plastic square-rimmed glasses. He had a personality that could turn even the dullest of bars into an exciting and entertaining venue. Also, he had great pride in his Scottish heritage and always, always wore some form of tartan.

To help me celebrate my new posting I invited about ten other Marines, all of whom were waiting patiently for the doors to open around seven o'clock. There was a range of ages and sizes amongst us, and I was the youngest and also the smallest in build. The biggest, oldest and most experienced Marine was a guy called Pete Cawthorn. Pete was absolutely huge. He was about 6½ ft tall and 16 st. heavy, bulky in appearance, with short, spiky ginger hair. He looked mean and aggressive and usually justified this with his actions when somebody annoyed him.

As we sipped our first pint, Pete, who was sat in the middle of our group, proposed a toast and everybody wished me all the very best of luck with my new posting. Then he unzipped his trouser fly to reveal yet another huge asset, his penis. Then he urinated onto the table and onto anybody within striking distance.

'Put that monster away, Pete,' shouted Dougie. 'You'll frighten away our customers.'

'Yeah, put that dangerous weapon away and I'll put some music on the jukebox,' added Briggs.

A few minutes later, Dean Martin sang out from the rundown old jukebox in the nearby corner.

'"Little Old Wine Drinker." This is for you, Steve,' grinned Briggs.

I smiled back. 'Cheers, mate, let's play spoof.'

Spoof was a popular game with the Marines. It was also a great way of getting drunk at somebody else's expense, providing you were cunning or lucky enough. To play the game, every participant needed three coins of any value. You kept your left hand behind your back and selected either three, two, one or no coins to hold out in your right hand, without telling or showing anyone the choice you'd made. The objective of the game was to guess how many coins were being held in the whole group's right hands. If you got it right you were out of the game, and play went on without you. As people successfully went out of the game, you would guess smaller and smaller amounts, because the fewer players there were the fewer coins there could be. It was never easy, and the only hard and fast rule was that you could not make impossible calls. This meant that if there were three players left in the game, with a possible total of nine coins, you could not call any number over nine, or any number which you knew to be impossible from the coins you were holding in your hand. If you did this, you had to buy everybody a drink. This got especially interesting when you were down to the last two players, and each was trying to bluff and second-guess the other. The loser had to buy everybody a drink, which was usually a spirit because they got you pissed quicker. At any point in the game you could call out the word 'spoof'. This meant you were guessing that everyone who was left in the game had no coins in their hand. If you were right, then all of these players had to buy you a double spirit drink. If you were wrong, then you had to buy all of them a single spirit drink.

We played continually throughout the evening and always managed to keep the normal drinking rounds going as well. As each round was bought, the Marine who purchased the drinks shouted out a toast in my honour and the drinks were downed in one gulp.

Late in the evening, we were all stood in a group near the bar, laughing and joking with Dougie, who was reeling off his war stories about the time he served in the Royal Navy. I cannot remember exactly why I did what was to follow, but it must have been down to drinking too much beer and getting too big for my boots, and to being in the bad habit of wanting to fight every time I got drunk.

I was stood next to Pete near the bar. I could feel a warm hot flush around my face and was, I would say, quite merry. I sized him up and, without warning, thrust my forehead as hard as I could clean into his face. This had become quite a trademark for me over the years and I had floored literally hundreds of people with this blow.

However, to my total astonishment, he didn't flinch and just stood there as solid as a rock, staring at me. The room went silent, except for the voice of Dean Martin sounding out from the jukebox in the background. A huge wicked grin covered Pete's face and his eyes bore deep into the growing fear that was steadily gripping me.

Fucking hell, I thought. That was my best shot and he hasn't moved an inch. His grin grew bigger and blood trickled out of his nose onto his bright white teeth. He looked excited, but at the same time insane. I turned and ran as fast as my legs could carry me. As I hurtled around the corners to the exit door I could hear him running close behind me. My heart pounded rapidly and a huge feeling of dread filled the area of my diaphragm. I was bewildered, and just couldn't believe that for the first time ever, one of the most powerful knockout blows I had ever used had had absolutely no effect apart from superficial wounds on its target.

Pete was catching me and I breathed heavily as I sprinted the short distance left to the exit door. BANG! The sound of me hitting the door with both hands echoed in the corridor. It was locked.

'Fucking bollocks!' I shouted as loud as I could.

It was late now and Dougie must have locked the door as we were drinking after the time allowed under military law. I heard Pete stop behind me. He was panting heavily, but at the same time I could hear him laughing under his heavy breath. I looked straight ahead and faced the door. I watched his shadow grow bigger on the wall above the door.

This is it, I thought. I'm going to fucking get it now and if my best shot didn't put him away then I deserve all I get. I turned around and looked at Pete. His huge figure was stood a couple of feet away from me. His eyes looked deep like the ocean and black in colour and the same big grin covered his face, which exposed his bloodstained teeth.

I tried to smile and held up my arms with my palms facing upwards. I knew he was now going to beat the shit out of me so it was my way of letting him know I was ready to accept my fate. He just stood there, grinning.

'What are you grinning for, Pete?' I asked curiously, in a state of confusion.

He shook his head. 'You stupid little bastard,' he smiled. He wiped the blood from his chin with his hand and then licked it with his tongue. Then he laughed loudly.

Now I was more confused than ever. 'Are you going to hit me then, Pete, or what?'

He shook his head. 'No, you stupid little bastard. You're a good Marine and I like you. Now go back to the bar and get the beers in.'

'Shit, Pete, I don't know why I did it.'

'You're a Marine, Steve, it's in your blood. Now get to the bar and get the fucking beers in.'

We went back into the bar arm-in-arm and everybody laughed. Dougie laughed the loudest and then started playing a tune on a set of bagpipes he produced from somewhere. Then he filled our beer glasses. 'He's a tough one, Steve, not the type you can pick on,' he said.

'Fucking hell, Dougie. Don't I know it?'

CHAPTER TWENTY-ONE

HMS WARRIOR

'Can I see some identification, please?' asked the Marine sentry who was on guard outside HMS Warrior's main gate.

'Yes, of course. I'm Marine Preece. I'm joining the Marine security detachment.'

'OK, mate,' he responded. 'The guardroom is over there.'

He pointed to the guardroom opposite. It had one-way glass panes fitted, which meant the occupants could see out, but no one could see in. HMS Warrior was one of Britain's top-secret NATO bases, and because of the important nature and purpose of this establishment, and in the interests of Britain's security, I do not wish to disclose any information that may be damaging to maintaining its role and integrity.

The Marines were there as an armed security detachment, with vicious guard dogs and an untold amount of weapons. Our role was to guard the establishment against terrorists and spies, ensure the safety of its occupants and also to protect the integrity of all the 'TOP SECRET' and above documents that were kept there.

The main body of service personnel that worked in the

place were part of the Royal Navy and the Royal Air Force. Much to my delight, nearly six hundred of them were females. This place was very different from life in the commando units, in that the duties revolved purely around security guard duties instead of the usual rugged soldiering that we were all professionally trained and well rehearsed in.

One of the guardroom windows slid open. 'Hello, Steve, welcome to Warrior,' a familiar voice called out. I looked at the face peering out at me. It was Adam Rogers, another Marine with whom I had served at my previous unit.

'Hello, Adam, can you tell me where I can find the sergeant-major's office please?'

'I'll do better than that, mate, I'll show you around the place.'

Adam showed me around and explained in detail the way things worked here. The security was airtight, but to the Marines it seemed fairly relaxed as we literally ruled the place. We had a great deal of power and authority that came with the role of the security detachment. We could literally stop and search anybody, have their cars stripped down to their frameworks if we suspected something was concealed or have the most senior of officers reprimanded if we found any breach in their personal security or handling of secret material.

The Marines had their own separate accommodation block. It was brick-built and very new in appearance. It had clean cream-painted walls and fitted carpets in all the corridors and rooms. The block was made up of a series of one- and four-man rooms and I was fortunate enough to get my own room.

I finished unpacking my bags and Adam continued to show me around. We went down to the Galaxy bar. This was the NAAFI bar that most establishments had and was the venue for the social activities of the lower ranks. Inside, it was unlike other NAAFI bars I had been in. It had bright wallpaper, lots of scenic pictures, two bars, a discothèque and a dance floor with coloured lights underneath, which reminded me of the '70s dance floor in *Saturday Night Fever*. Adam showed me a corner of one of the bars and told me that it was nicknamed the bootneck corner and only Marines were allowed in it. If anyone else dared to stand in that area they would be quickly removed, threatened or even assaulted. Disco nights were held regularly on Tuesdays, Thursdays and Sundays, and occasionally on other nights too. I felt absolutely flabbergasted when I saw the vast numbers of servicewomen in the bar and spent the first few weeks falling in love every five minutes.

I settled into my new job quite well and, after a few arguments and short scuffles, soon became a popular member of the Marine detachment. I wasn't the toughest guy around, but I held my ground and that's what was important. My social life increased dramatically and was at its busiest point of my life. I took every opportunity to frequent the NAAFI bar. The women outnumbered the men by at least five to one and for people like me it was heaven.

There was, however, one thing I didn't like. The bar was run by a committee, which was made up of several Navy and Air Force ranks. None of the Marines were interested in being part of it and unfortunately this was not always in our interests. The committee were responsible for opening and closing the bar and were personally responsible for reporting any incidents that occurred in their presence. They were like fascists and enjoyed their job to the full, taking great satisfaction in reporting the usual incidents of Marines fighting or causing a disturbance. This usually resulted in disciplinary action against any Marine involved. Unofficially, in the eyes of the Navy, a Marine involved in any trouble was presumed guilty until proven innocent. It wasn't fair, but that's the way it was.

After a while, I got into a routine. My duties involved working from 8.30 a.m. until 5 p.m. At 5.15 p.m., I worked out in the gymnasium and usually went for a four- or five-mile run. At 6.40 p.m., I would eat my evening meal and by 7 p.m. I would enter the NAAFI bar. I made several new friends from the detachment, most of whom were reprobates like me. They were always fighting, threatening people or shagging the willing servicewomen.

It didn't take us too long to learn how to avoid getting reprimanded for our antics. We became tactful in our approach and soon had the NAAFI bar committee in our pockets. We didn't pay them for their silence, but threatened to beat them up, which seemed to do the trick.

CHAPTER TWENTY-TWO

IT'S DETENTION QUARTERS FOR YOU

Outside of work, my social life was fantastic. A lot of service-people lived in houses away from the establishment and quite often held parties. I started to get on very well with a lot of Wrens (naval women) and WAFs (our name for Air Force women, although they were officially called WRAFs (Women's RAF)) who seemed to enjoy my company. They said I was unpredictable and they never knew what I was going to do next. Although they knew I was aggressive and troublesome, for some reason or other their attraction to me seemed to be quite strong. Indeed, sexually I had satisfied quite a few of them.

One night, a special function was being held in the NAAFI bar, as a leaving present for one of the Wrens. Several Marines, including myself, were kindly invited to attend. However, it wasn't scheduled to start until 8.30 p.m., so we all arranged to meet in a nearby pub in Northwood Hills.

Inside, a huge log fire heated the pub. The decor was bright and luxurious and the atmosphere felt warm and friendly. We bought a round of drinks and joined the company of several

Wrens who had arrived before us. We chatted amiably and kept them entertained with our endless string of crap jokes. I felt someone tap me gently on the back, so I turned around to see who it was.

'Hi, Steve,' whispered Claudia in her usual soft voice.

She was a very small and delicate young lady, in her early twenties, with a shapely figure and a pretty face. Her pleasant personality made me feel quite warm and relaxed when I conversed with her.

'Hello, Claudia,' I smiled. 'How are you?'

'I'm fine, Steve, thank you very much,' she smiled and fluttered her eyelashes before joining another group of Wrens sat at a nearby table.

A hideous laugh came from the opposite end of the bar. A tall, thin man with short brown hair stood with a mixed group of Wrens and sailors. He laughed again and it sounded like a high-pitched scream. I wondered who he was, because he was beginning to get on my nerves. At first I thought he must be another Marine, because he looked like one. But then I looked at his clothes. He was wearing long baggy trousers, a multi-coloured shirt and a bright red dickey bow. He must be in the RAF, I thought, with a sense of contentment.

One of the other Marines saw me observing this man and came over to give me the low-down on him. The other Marine was called Diz. He was a big, tall guy with a thick bushy moustache. I'd got to know him quite well and we had become good friends. I knew him from our recruit training at the commando training centre, where he'd started his basic training two weeks before me. Diz leaned forward and spoke to me quietly with a disappointed frown on his face.

'Believe it or not, he's a corporal in the Marines.'

'Is he?' I answered in astonishment.

'Yes. But he's not part of the detachment. He works for the

commander-in-chief.' (The highest ranking officer in the Royal Navy.)

I nodded. I felt glad he wasn't part of our detachment, but disappointed that he was a Marine.

'His name is Ken Phillips,' continued Diz. 'And guess what?'

He paused for my answer. 'What?' I asked.

'He's exactly how he looks. He's a fucking wanker.'

'A fucking wanker,' I agreed nodding my head.

'Yes. A fucking wanker,' finished Diz.

We both smiled and turned our attention back to the group of Wrens and continued with our crap jokes and frightening war stories. The Wrens rolled around in fits of laughter as Diz and I worked together like a comic double-act, spinning funny yarns and telling stupid jokes to keep them entertained. Meanwhile, Ken Phillips' hideous high-pitched laugh could be heard above the many conversations that were taking place. It seemed to grind away at you as if someone were dragging their fingernails down a blackboard.

I turned to watch what he was doing and to see who he was with. It was more than obvious that he made his own entertainment, as nobody seemed to want to talk to him. Nevertheless, to amuse himself he just pushed his way into other people's chat and made fun of what they were talking about. I then saw him walk towards little Claudia, who was wrestling with a tickly cough. A big grin covered his face as he slapped her hard on her back. This seemed to make her coughing worse and her face reddened as she struggled to contain it. He slapped her again, with a little bit more force than previously. He laughed again as she waved her hand and shook her head to show disapproval of his actions. Then her coughing bout started again and he moved in to give her another almighty wallop.

The force he used was far too much for her and her small, lightweight figure buckled under the pressure and hurtled head first over a small table a couple of feet in front of her. She landed face down but quickly got to her feet. I ran over to comfort her and check she was OK. She was dazed but clearly unimpressed with his behaviour.

Everybody looked at him and watched him laughing loudly. Some people covered their ears to block out the loud screeches that came out of his mouth.

'All good fun,' he shouted in an excited manner. 'Wrens are like turtles. When they're on their backs, they are fucked.'

He waved his hand in the air and walked towards the exit door. The occupants of the bar were almost silent. 'See you all later, back at the NAAFI bar,' he bellowed as he left.

Diz saw the angry look on my face. 'Leave it, Steve. I told you, he's a fucking wanker,' he whispered into my ear.

'You are right, Diz. He is a fucking wanker. He's also a bad excuse for a Marine.'

Diz nodded and tapped my beer glass with his. 'Fuck him, Steve, let's get drunk.'

'Hhhmmm, OK, mate, get the beers in,' I answered.

Much later, in the NAAFI bar, I saw Phillips conversing with a couple of sailors. He was stood just outside of the bootneck corner, near the edge of the dance floor. It was more than obvious that none of the Marine security detachment liked him. They all seemed to snub his attempts at talking to them and I noticed he never entered our corner.

I stared directly at him across the room and caught his eye within a few seconds. He smiled at me and waved his hand to beckon me to talk to him. He smiled again and walked towards me, stopping a few feet short of the area designated as the bootneck corner. What kind of man is this arsehole, I wondered? Picking on little Claudia like he did. He shouted some words to me but I couldn't hear because the disco music was very loud.

I moved towards him and saw him raise his hand to offer a handshake.

'All right, mate, I'm Ken, pleased to meet you,' he said in a loud and self-assured voice.

His wide grin dropped when I looked at him with a face like thunder and declined to accept his handshake. Instead I put my left arm across his shoulders and gently pulled him towards me so that our faces were very close when we spoke.

'What kind of Marine are you, picking on little Claudia?' I growled.

He looked puzzled and his face twisted with a frown. 'What do you mean?'

'Back in the pub in Northwood Hills.'

'Oh, that,' he smiled.

'Did you think it was funny?' I questioned.

The big grin returned to his face. 'Yes, yes I did.'

'Do you know what I think is funny?' I snarled.

'What?' he laughed.

'This,' I said softly.

Then I rapidly pulled him towards me and thrust my forehead hard into the bridge of his nose. Blood splashed into the air and he fell backwards and onto the floor. The crowded area cleared immediately as everybody in close proximity moved out of the way of the commotion. Some onlookers smiled as they watched him roll around on the floor in agony, with both his hands clasped over his face. He got onto his feet and blood leaked through the gaps where his fingers covered his face. Then he ran out of the bar.

For a few moments, nobody spoke and the only noise that could be heard was the disco music that was still playing. Diz patted me on the back and passed me a pint of beer.

'Good effort, Steve. He got what he deserved, he's a fucking wanker.'

'Hhhhhmmmm, I know,' I nodded. 'A fucking wanker.'

'Hey, Steve,' a familiar voice called from somewhere behind me. I turned around and saw that it was Rick Andrews, the duty guard commander (corporal of the duty base guard). He was a bodybuilder from Scarborough, about 5ft 11 in. tall, 16 to 17 st. heavy, with shoulders and a chest like a mountain. He had a great sense of humour and an immense strength from his enormous muscles. He was also a good friend of mine and hated Ken Phillips with a passion.

'You're not going to believe this, Steve,' he said in a broad Northern accent. 'But that wanker Ken Phillips has reported you for assaulting him. I'm afraid you have to come to the guardroom and speak to the naval police about it.'

At first, I didn't know whether or not to believe Rick as he was always winding people up and would generally go to great lengths to convince them that he wasn't.

'OK, Rick, I'll get my coat,' I frowned.

It was hanging over the back of a nearby chair, so I picked it up, pulled it on and fastened the buttons. When I looked up I couldn't see Rick anywhere. Maybe he was joking, I thought, and took off my coat.

Then another of the two duty guard commanders appeared. This one was called Jasper. He was a huge tall Scotsman who used to box for the Marines and also for Scotland. He was a big, horrible-looking fellow who, like Rick, was as hard as iron. Also like Rick, he had a very dry sense of humour. He had a girlfriend called Leanne, whom he used to call She-man because he thought it sounded better.

'Come on, Steve, let's go to the guardroom,' he said seriously. 'Where's Rick?'

'I don't know, I thought he was joking about arresting me.'

'No, he's not. You're in the shit.'

'Rick, come on,' shouted Jasper, when he saw Rick leaning over the bar chatting up the NAAFI barmaids.

Jasper was also a friend of mine and neither of the two were happy about having to escort me to the guardroom to be interviewed by the naval police. As we walked, we talked. Both Rick and Jasper spoke seriously during our conversation. Jasper rubbed his chin. 'I know he's a fucking wanker, Steve, but you shouldn't have hit him. At least not in front of all them witnesses.'

'The fucking wanker is pressing charges,' interrupted Rick. 'He wants you charged with assaulting a senior rank.'

'Oh fuck it, I'm not bothered,' I replied. 'I'll take what comes. Then smash his head in later.'

'Quiet,' whispered Jasper, as we walked into the guardroom where I was ordered to stand to attention in front of a waiting naval police petty officer (the Navy's equivalent rank to a Marine sergeant). Our interview was brief. I declined to make a statement and asked to wait until the following morning to discuss the case with the Marine sergeant-major. The guardroom cells were full, so he agreed to let me go unescorted back to my accommodation block and to report back to him at 8.30 the following morning.

I left the guardroom and made my way back to my room. Inside I found Diz sitting down patiently waiting for me.

'Don't worry, Steve, I'll say he hit you first and that you acted in self defence.'

'Oh, it's OK, Diz, but thanks anyway.'

'OK, mate,' he sighed as he got up and left. 'I'll see you in the morning.'

'Yeah, cheers, Diz, goodnight.'

The following morning, I awoke around 6.30 and got into my PT (physical training) kit before heading out for a four-mile run to clear my head. The sun shone brightly and flickered through the trees as I ran past wooded areas. I could hear the birds whistling and the odd dog barking here and there when I passed some of the mansion-type houses that were built in the area.

The morning exercise made me feel fresher and more awake to face the consequences of my actions from the previous evening. I showered and dressed and then made my way back to the guardroom. As I approached, several Marines looked at me through the open windows.

'Rocky, Rocky, Rocky, Rocky,' they chanted and started to applaud when I entered through the door. They had heard why I had assaulted Ken Phillips and were pleased that I had head-butted him. Rick offered me a seat and gave me a hot cup of tea, which I gladly accepted.

'What do you think, Rick?' I sighed.

He rubbed his broad chin. 'Hhhhmmm, just get your story sorted out before you see the naval police and take what comes.'

'Yes, OK, I will,' I said, and nodded my head to show my agreement.

At 8.15 a.m., I cautiously entered the sergeant-major's office. He was a tall, thinly built Irishman in his early forties with grey hair. He had about twenty-two years' service in the Marines behind him. His face was twisted with anger and disappointment and his dark authoritative eyes pierced into mine. He was seated for a moment and then he slapped the palm of his hand on his desk and stood up.

'Why . . . why did you assault Corporal Phillips?' he screamed angrily. 'He wants you charged with assaulting a senior rank and that could mean two years in prison for you. Well . . . what have you got to say for yourself?' I told him about little Claudia, whom he knew fairly well, and the events that took place leading up to when I assaulted him. Then I saw the anger drop from his face. His frown disappeared and he slowly rubbed his chin.

'Oh, bloody hell,' he murmured in a calmer manner. 'I'll speak to the naval police and also with Corporal Phillips. I still think this will mean forty-eight days in the Royal Naval detention quarters [military prison] for you. But it'll be a lot better than a possible two years.'

He said what he was most angry about was that Corporal Phillips had reported it to the naval police and not kept it internal to the Marine security detachment. At least that way he would have been able to sort it out himself without any pending prison terms. He left the room and returned around thirty minutes later. He told me that Corporal Phillips was willing to drop the charges if I apologised to him. Obviously, I accepted the offer and made my way to the Royal Navy police office, which was downstairs in the same building as the sergeant-major's office.

Ken Phillips stood at ease outside the police office when I arrived. He looked at me as I approached. He had a big red scuffmark across the bridge of his nose and his left eye was blackened and heavily swollen.

'Well,' he said and waited for my response.

'Ken, I'm very sorry. I had too much to drink and lost control of my senses.' I shook his hand and he smiled.

'Wait here,' he said softly, and pushed open the police office door and entered.

I waited patiently and smiled to myself. I wasn't really sorry, but a few words to please a geek like him would be a hell of a lot easier than forty-eight days in prison. A few minutes later the door opened and Ken came out. The door creaked heavily behind him and then it was slammed shut by somebody on the other side of it.

'That's it, I've dropped the charges,' he smiled.

'Thank you, but I still think you're a fucking wanker,' I answered quietly and started to walk away.

His smile disappeared and he shook his head and looked down at the floor before hurriedly leaving the building. I knew I had been lucky and I laughed out loud. The sound echoed around the empty hallway I was stood in.

CHAPTER TWENTY-THREE

IT'S EITHER HIM OR ME

The bootneck corner in the NAAFI bar was quite often the black spot for incidents. Most Marines upheld the rule that only their own kind were allowed in that area to the full. It was usually new joiners to the NATO base who unknowingly entered the forbidden corner. We repeatedly took great pleasure in removing the trickle of new Navy and Air Force personnel in one way or another. This included women, who generally got the same treatment.

It was a disco night when a Marine called Craig and myself were stood talking together in the bootneck corner over a pint of beer. The NAAFI bar was quiet and fairly empty as a lot of the usual faces were away on leave. Two men and two women who we didn't know entered the bar and came into the area classed as the bootneck corner. They all stood together and leaned against the bar looking for a barmaid to serve them. One of the men was well built and fit-looking with short black hair and the other was tall and skinny with short spiky blond hair. It was obvious which service they belonged to as they all wore T-shirts displaying RAF logos.

Craig looked at me and then moved towards them.

'Hey you lot, fuck off out of the corner now.'

A look of disbelief came over their faces as they looked at Craig.

'Move now,' Craig demanded, and pointed away from the area with his thumb.

'Why?' scowled the tall skinny man.

I grabbed an ice bucket off the bar and emptied its contents over his head. Craig stormed in and grabbed him by the throat. He squeezed a little against his windpipe and pushed him back against the wooden bar, before releasing his grip. The tall skinny man gasped for breath before the two men slowly and reluctantly made an exit and disappeared out of sight. The two women remained behind and were stood facing us with a look of disgust on their faces. One of them had long black hair, tied up at the back, and a shapely figure you would kill for. She was about twenty-three years old and very attractive. She looked us both up and down and began to shout at us.

'Pesky Marines, who the hell do you think you are?'

'Fuck off, you stupid little slut,' I replied.

'Don't you tell me to fuck off,' she snapped.

I picked up another ice bucket. 'If you don't fuck off, you'll get the ice bucket.'

'You wouldn't dare,' she snapped.

WHOOSH. The contents of the ice bucket splashed in her face. It was more water than ice as the ice cubes had melted. Her appearance rapidly changed from stunning to looking like a drowned rat. For a few moments, she stared at me. She looked angry, but surprisingly showed signs of breaking into a gentle smile. She turned and signalled her friend to follow her out of the exit door. As she walked away she smiled at me, which I found totally confusing.

'There's nothing as strange as women,' Craig laughed, and handed me a fresh pint of beer, bought by a few other Marines who had just joined our company. We told them what had just happened and they howled with laughter. They told us that they didn't know who the two men were but that the two women were WAFs. They knew the good-looking aggressive one and told me she was called Lucy. Apparently, she had a reputation for giving Marines a piece of her mind and usually looked down her nose at them.

I told them that I found her attractive and really fancied her. They told me she was from a very wealthy posh background and hated Marines with a vengeance, also that she hadn't had sex with a man for around eighteen months and that I had no chance of getting fixed up with her. We all laughed at these comments.

Later in the evening, to everybody's surprise, including mine, Lucy came back in the bar and walked straight over to me. Her hair was all neat and tidy again and must have been washed and blow-dried. She bought me a drink and told me that she hadn't met anyone like me before. She said she didn't want to argue with me because she liked me. This was my big chance to impress everybody and try to prove them wrong about getting fixed up with her.

'Do you fancy coming back to my room for a cup of coffee?' I asked her.

'Yes, why not?' she smiled.

All the Marines looked on in amazement as we left the bar area and held hands. We weren't allowed to have females in the Marines' block, but we sometimes got one of the dog handlers to tie one of the guard dogs to the bottom of the stairs. This was always effective enough to keep out unwelcome visitors. Back in my room we drank coffee and talked. She practically poured out her life story and confirmed the rumour that she hadn't been with a man for over eighteen months. I certainly believed her, because a few minutes later I got her into bed and made love to her. I don't know how many times she climaxed, but she just wanted more and more. Eventually I fell asleep, completely knackered.

We began to see a lot more of each other and started a steady relationship. It was more lust on both our parts than love. Her personality was totally different from mine and so was her background and family life. Her problem was, she was used to getting everything she wanted, and I guess I must have been her bit of rough. All her friends were in the RAF and usually found it hard to get along with me. I found their interests and conversation boring, as they were a totally different type of people to the Marines. One of them was even a trainspotter and used to listen to recorded tapes of trains running along a railway track. Sad bastard, I thought.

One night, after a NAAFI disco, I was leaving the bar in search of Lucy, who had gone to use a nearby toilet. I was very drunk and stepped out into the corridor, where I saw her talking to two men whom I didn't know. One of them looked straight at me.

'Who the fucking hell are you looking at?' I snarled.

He immediately jumped back and adopted what looked like some form of karate stance. He was just out of my reach and began to demonstrate his high level of karate kick techniques, kicking wildly into the air. Lucy looked at me and saw that my temper was about to blow.

'Don't, Steve, he'll kill you, he's the RAF karate champion,' she whimpered.

'I don't believe you're coming that shit with me,' I growled with anger and lifted up a nearby rubbish bin. I swung it over my head and hurled it straight at him, hitting him with it on his neck and right shoulder. The force and weight of the rubbish bin knocked him to the ground, but only for a moment as I then watched him and his friend bolt through the exit door behind them to escape into the darkness.

Lucy looked at me. 'Did you have to?' she scowled. 'They're friends of mine.'

I shrugged my shoulders and burped loudly. She frowned and shook her head before grabbing hold of my hand and pulling me out through the exit door. Back in my room she poured a coffee for us both. She was quiet and slowly rolled her eyes towards me. For a moment she reminded me of a tame pussycat.

'I've got something I want to tell,' she said in a quiet voice.

'What's that?' I asked curiously, but unconcerned.

'I come from a fairly wealthy background.'

'Yeah, and . . .?'

'Well . . . All my life I've had everything I've ever wanted. I've been treated well, with the greatest of respect.' She paused for a moment and stirred the two coffees before passing one of the cups to me.

'It that it?' I asked.

'No, no,' she continued. 'When I met you, you treated me like a piece of shit. And guess what?'

'What?' I frowned and felt unsure of what she was getting at.

'I absolutely love it,' she smiled and climbed into bed next to me.

As the weeks went by, Lucy and I got on very well. However, she unfortunately refused to change her attitude towards other Marines, whether they were friends of mine or not. In particular, she hated Diz and always looked down her nose at him or made sarcastic damning comments if he tried to speak to her. This annoyed both him and me, as he was now one of my best mates. Other Marines also detested her presence. One of them was another Liverpool man whom we called Scouse. He joined the Marines in the early '60s and fought in places like Aden and Cyprus in the early days. He was what we would call an old sweat (a highly experienced Marine, who had a lot of service behind him). He was quite open as to how much he hated Lucy and her attitude. He even asked me to have sex with her, shove my penis up her arse and pull her hair out during the process. He said he thought it was what she deserved. I just laughed at this as I practically agreed with him.

Soon, Lucy had to go away on a temporary detachment for a few weeks and I kissed her goodbye. Before she left, she told me to keep out of trouble and not to chat up any other women. I told her not to be silly and gave her a reassuring cuddle. That night and every night for the following three weeks I went down the NAAFI bar with Diz: except, of course, when either of us were on guard duty overnight. We drank loads of beer and threatened a few people and also inevitably got fixed up with numerous women.

Diz lived in the room on the floor directly above mine and often called into my room on his way to bed. If I had a woman, he used to rattle my door handle and bang hard on the door and laugh before shouting goodnight. One night, I was fed up with drinking and decided to stay in my room and go to bed early. Diz went into the NAAFI bar without me. Whilst he was there he spoke to one of the NAAFI barmaids who apparently fancied me. She was called Tracy and was short, fat, ugly and spotty. He told her that I felt the same about her and that I had asked him to tell her to come to my room when the bar closed because I wanted to have sex with her. He also told her that I wanted her to wear a basque with stockings and suspenders.

A giggling noise awoke me from a deep sleep. I looked at

my luminous clock, which was situated on my bedside cabinet. My room door, which wasn't locked, slowly closed shut and I could hear the person, who was obviously a female, standing next to my bed. I could just see the outline of her body through the darkness that filled the room.

'Who's that?' I asked.

'It's me, baby,' a vaguely familiar voice replied and lifted up my bedclothes.

I watched her as she started to shuffle into my bed and felt excited but, at the same time, curious, as I didn't know who it was. To satisfy my curiosity, I switched on the small light, which was housed on the wall above my bed. I saw it was Tracy and nearly jumped out of my skin as she puckered her lips for a kiss.

'Aaaaarrrrghhh,' I yowled and jumped out of bed. I rubbed my eyes with disbelief. She was stood there in front of me with lingerie on which was pulled tight around the rolls of fat that protruded through every available orifice. The ghastly sight, with her fat spotty face, made me burst into laughter. She laughed too.

'Come on,' she said. 'I want fucking.'

'I'm not fucking you, you ugly fat spotty bastard, so get your clothes on and fuck off.'

'I won't, I want fucking,' she demanded.

The door opened slowly and a head peered in. It was Diz and he was laughing wildly. I saw the gap through the door and bolted past him, which made him literally fall onto the floor outside, holding his ribs and laughing wildly. I ran down the corridor and Tracy chased after me. Every time she got close she smacked my bare buttocks with her hand and shouted, 'I want fucking.' A few other Marines were returning to their rooms and burst into laughter as I sprinted past them naked, with Tracy close behind.

Eventually, I had looped around the accommodation block corridors, through the shower blocks and back to my room. I was out of breath, but a minute or so ahead of my pursuer. Once back in my room, I grabbed her clothes off the floor and threw them outside into the corridor. Then I saw her hurtling towards me like a big naked rugby player so I ducked back inside and locked my door shut.

'I want fucking,' she shouted.

'FUCK OFF!' I screamed.

A few minutes later, I heard her leave and the doors in the corridor outside creaked shut. In the room above, I could hear Diz laughing wildly and slapping his hand against the wall.

A couple of days later, Lucy returned. She had enjoyed her trip away and told me she had missed me greatly. I told her I felt the same way and had had a quiet couple of weeks. She suggested it would be a good idea to go down to the NAAFI bar to celebrate her return, which I also thought was a good idea. After a few beers, she pestered me to go back to my room as she said she was feeling frisky. Reluctantly, because the bar was still open, I agreed and headed back to my room in Gurkha block.

We didn't bother with coffee, as she was more interested in having sex. During this I took her from behind, doggy style. She moaned with pleasure. Then I heard the doors creaking in the corridor outside. This could be Diz, I thought and I purposely hadn't bothered to lock the door. I could hear somebody casually whistling and heading towards my door. I smiled with excitement, but Lucy was totally oblivious to what was going on.

It has to be Diz, I thought, he's in for a big surprise when he comes in. I smiled to myself and thrust harder into Lucy, whose buttocks slapped with the movements. The door swung open and a drunken Diz staggered inside. His eyes lit up like candles and a huge grin covered his face. Lucy looked up and then burrowed her head beneath the pillow when she saw who it was. She was annoyed but also very embarrassed.

'What do you want?' I asked casually, with a grin all over my face and my hands on my hips.

He continued to grin and struggled to find some words.

'Eeeeeerrrrr, cup of tea, cup of tea. Would you both like a cup of tea?'

Diz and I laughed wildly, but Lucy kept her head beneath the pillows. He pushed me back and pulled the bedclothes off her to have a closer look at her naked body.

'Get out, Diz, bloody get out,' she screamed.

Diz turned around and left the room. Outside, his laughter echoed around in the corridor and seemed to get louder as he got further away.

'You bastard,' snapped Lucy. 'I bet you planned that. You know I don't like him.'

'Sorry, Lucy, I didn't expect it either and I forgot to lock the door.'

For the few weeks that followed, Lucy cursed any mention of Diz and made it perfectly clear that she couldn't stand the sight of him. I wasn't very pleased about her attitude towards him as I strongly valued his friendship.

On New Year's Eve, I was working in a nightclub as a doorman with Rick Andrews, the bodybuilder (certain types of moonlighting were allowed in the Marines, but we would never have been given permission for doorman work, so we simply didn't ask). He was a lot bigger than I was, but was keen to get the nightclub to employ me to work with him. He knew that no matter what happened, I would stick by him in the event of trouble. A few weeks prior to this night, we'd been joking about who was the toughest between us. I used to tell him that I was a fairly good boxer and would hit him ten times before he could hit me once. But his answer was always the same. He would smile and say, 'I've only got to hit you once, Steve.' This was always good banter between us and we remained strong friends. However, the events that happened this night really brought home the reality of how true his comments were.

The nightclub we worked in was called Castro's. It was located near the Brixton area of London. It had a reputation for trouble, but the money was good and we needed it to supplement our low Marine wage. We routinely used to put arm locks on people who caused trouble, throw them out of the exit doors and lock them out. This was different from some clubs, where the doormen would give the troublemakers a good kicking once they got them outside. On a few occasions, it was hard to avoid conflict as some people just came looking for trouble with us.

On this occasion, Rick and I walked together up the nightclub stairs towards the outside exit door. A tall, large-built man stood looking at us with his fists clenched. It was blatantly obvious that he was going to attack one of us when we got closer to him. I could feel his intentions and prepared myself to receive his attack when it came. At that point, Rick stopped and grasped my clenched fist.

'This one's mine,' he grinned.

'OK,' I nodded.

Rick moved a couple of steps in front of me and the tall man focused his aggressive look on him. He raised his fists, but Rick was already in motion and threw a sharp heavy right-hand punch. The blow hit the man in the chest and he seemed to fly backwards for about eight feet before his body made a cracking noise as it thwacked into the doors behind him. It looked like something off a comedy film where someone is dragged backwards by a hidden piece of elastic. I was flabbergasted at the power behind the blow and looked at Rick. His face showed an expression of shock that puzzled me.

'What's the matter?' I asked.

Rick shook his head slowly from side to side. 'I held back. When I hit him, I held back.'

'Fucking hell, Rick, now I know what you meant when you said you'd only have to hit me once.'

The remainder of the busy night went without incident and we returned to HMS Warrior. There was a party being held in the Marines' accommodation block. One of the four-man rooms had been emptied of furniture and a makeshift bar had been set up. There were plenty of women invited and everybody was dancing, laughing and generally having a good time.

Diz greeted me as we entered the room and gave me an ice-cold beer.

'I've got something to tell you, Steve,' he said casually.

'What's that, mate?' I smiled.

'I've been arguing with that girlfriend of yours. I don't like the way she keeps looking at me.'

I looked around the room at the vast number of loose women.

'Oh, bollocks to her, Diz, I'm sick of her as well.' We both laughed.

The door to the room opened and another Marine poked his head inside. 'Steve, there's a phone call for you. I think it's Lucy and she sounds upset.' He shouted so that I could hear him above the music.

'OK, mate, I'm coming, thanks,' I replied.

'I bet she's whingeing about me,' Diz frowned.

'She can whinge all she wants, but not to me. I'm sick of

her whingeing,' I replied. I went out into the corridor and picked up the hanging receiver from the telephone that was attached to the wall.

'Hello.'

'Hello, Steve, it's Lucy, I need to talk to you,' she sobbed.

'OK, calm down. I'll see you outside your accommodation block in two minutes,' I said and then replaced the receiver, before leaving Gurkha block to meet her.

The WAF accommodation block was a mere hundred or so yards away. As I got close I could see her stood in the doorway and could also hear her crying. Then I saw tears flowing down her cold, reddened cheeks. She put her arms around me and hugged me tightly, crying on my shoulder. For a moment she didn't speak, but instead made a lot out of her emotional state.

'What's the matter, Lucy?' I asked softly.

'It's that friend of yours, that Diz,' she scowled. 'He's been calling me names and I'm not happy about it. Go and sort him out,' she demanded.

'I will not, he's my mate,' I retorted.

She immediately stopped crying and looked me straight in the eyes. 'Well,' she growled and put her hands on her hips. 'It's either him or me, so sort it out.' She folded her arms to wait for my answer.

I paused for a few moments and looked her up and down. I remained calm and unflustered by her ultimatum. I also thought about the many loose women back in Gurkha block, who Diz was probably busy chatting up right at this moment. 'Well, fuck you.' I expressed my answer with little feeling and turned and walked away.

'Steve, Steve, Steve, Steve, Steve!' she shouted repeatedly, but I didn't answer. Then I heard her burst into tears once again and run back into her accommodation block. Back at the party, Diz laughed when I told him the outcome and passed me another ice-cold beer.

'There's plenty more fish in the sea, mate, especially here.'

'Yes, I know, Diz, let's get amongst them.'

We laughed together and joined the female company of the party.

CHAPTER TWENTY-FOUR

USMC – HE'S A NUTCASE

By September 1987, I'd been a Marine for about four and a half years and had served at HMS Warrior for exactly a year. I'd gained a bit of a reputation for being able to look after myself and not tolerating fools, and I was known to be a man of few words. I wasn't the toughest Marine walking the earth, but I certainly held my own. I had also been promoted to the dizzy heights of lance-corporal. This rank was only just graded above a Marine, but it gave me a bit more power and a few more perks.

Weekends were always quiet and boring in the NATO base. Most people who were not on weekend duty went home. The few that remained sat in the NAAFI bar drinking beer to pass away the evenings.

On this particular night, I was sat in the NAAFI bar with a Marine corporal called Bill Batey. He was in his late twenties and came from Sheffield. He'd served in the Marine Corps for around ten years. He was once ranked as a sergeant, a couple of years before, but had had the rank stripped from him because of an antic aboard a naval ship, where the Marines he was in charge of had stripped a duty officer naked and thrown him overboard because he had called last orders at the bar. The strange thing about Bill was that no matter how much beer he drank, he wibbled and wobbled but he never fell down. Also like the rest of us, no matter how much beer he drank, he would be ready to do his job the next day, whether it was a twenty-mile run or an arduous and dangerous patrol out in the field.

A small group of Wrens and a few more Marines joined us. No music played on the jukebox and the silence felt painful. Bill and myself racked our brains for a solution to the boredom. We tapped our fingers against our chins and looked around the room for something to trigger off an idea of what to do or where to go.

'Got it!' exclaimed Bill, as he snapped his fingers. 'Have you ever been to the United States Marine Corps [USMC] base in Eastcote?'

'Yeah,' I answered eagerly. 'They have a disco on a Saturday night.'

'What are we waiting for?' said Brian. 'Let's see if anyone else wants to come with us.'

We asked the few Marines and Wrens what they wanted to do and they all gladly accepted our invitation. Next, we needed transport and I suggested that Bill should ring the dog section where the duty dog handler had access to a van he used to do his security rounds. This had become a regular tactic, or resource, you might say, that I had begun to use instead of telephoning for a taxi. I knew the times when the dog handlers began their vehicle patrol rounds and got them to drop me off en route.

It was a tight squeeze to get around fifteen men and women into the van and an even tighter squeeze to get us all out of it at the other end. Like HMS Warrior, the USMC base had top-level security. It had high-level perimeter fences, guard dogs and British Ministry of Defence police guarding it. At the main gate a tall policeman shone a torch in Bill's face as we walked into a floodlit area towards the main gate. He was stood in front of a metal roadblock barrier, which was positioned across the base entrance.

'Fucking hell, mate, are you trying to blind me?' squinted Bill.

'Are you all service personnel?' he asked us in a deep, authoritative voice.

'Yes, all of us,' Bill sharply replied.

'Good. Can I see your ID cards please?'

He checked our ID cards and was happy apart from one of the females. She was a WAF and the policeman informed us that the United States Marine base would not accept her ID card, only those that were Navy or Royal Marines. Fortunately, he was happy for us to vouch for her and to let Bill, who was the most senior of our ranks present, sign her in.

Inside, the American disco bar was very similar to the one back in the commando units, with its highly polished red floors and dark wallpaper with miserable patterns on it. Only a few Yanks were present, as it appeared that their situation was similar to ours on a weekend (the Americans all had homes near their base which they could go back to on their weekends off).

I went to the bar to order some beer and stood next to a four star United States Marine Corps general, who was dressed in uniform and quietly drinking his beer. I rapidly put my heels together and acknowledged his high rank with respect. He smiled. 'Relax, son,' he said in a broad American accent. 'I'm off duty.' He then stood up and unbuckled his trouser belt, dropped his trousers and underwear, leaned forward and showed all of us his arsehole. 'Look. See, it's the same as yours when I'm off duty. Let's drink.'

The general bought us all a drink and shook our hands. We sat with him for a while, cracked some jokes and talked about war and the usual stuff that interested Marines. He was good company and he wished us all well when he left an hour or so later.

The Americans bought beer in three-pint jugs called pitchers, which they then poured into a glass. It was good-quality beer and really cheap, so your money was guaranteed to go a long way. The barman thought we were crazy as we just ordered the pitchers and drank straight from them. We swilled the beer wildly and downed a few pitchers each in a very short space of time. Later I stood propped against the bar. I was pissed out of my head. Bill started conversing a few feet away with a group of Englishmen whom I didn't recognise. I watched him slowly wobbling from side to side as he spoke. I couldn't hear what he was talking about, but his audience laughed wildly at whatever he had to say.

Then Bill turned and pointed to me and everybody looked over. Two of them broke from the small gathering and walked over towards me. They were both very tall and broad-shouldered. One of them, who had a thick bristly moustache, poked me in the chest with his index finger.

'Are you sociable?' he asked seriously.

I looked at him and frowned. Oh fuck, I thought, they're going to beat the shit out of me. 'Do you want a game of spoof?' I replied quickly.

Both of them instantly burst into laughter and then the remainder of the group joined our company. Bill had set me up. The group were all special patrol groups from the Metropolitan police force and the two who approached me were former Marines who had served with Bill during the Falklands War.

Several of the group, including Bill, joined me for a game of spoof. We changed the rules slightly so that, if you lost, you had to buy everybody a drink and also buy and drink a triple glass of Jack Daniels whiskey. No matter how hard the policemen tried, neither Bill nor myself lost a single game. Bill found this highly amusing, especially when two of the group collapsed on the floor in a heap as a result of drinking so much alcohol.

By the end of the night I was absolutely shiters (a Marine word for being drunk). I could hardly keep my eyes open. One of the Wrens, who was sat close by, took me by the arm and led me into the ladies' toilets where she splashed water over my face. This helped me a little, but I knew it was time to leave. I mentioned this to her and she agreed to help me get back to the NATO base.

The corridor outside the disco room was empty of people and I saw rows of pictures of American Marines, which filled the walls. One picture in particular caught my interest. It was of a United States Marine dressed in green camouflaged combat gear and had the word 'Marine' in blue and gold letters written across the bottom.

'Look at that, it's brilliant,' I whispered to the Wren.

'Why are you whispering?' she asked.

'Because I'm going to steal it,' I whispered back.

The picture came off the wall with very little effort or noise and I tucked it neatly under my arm. I smiled at the Wren and then we walked arm in arm out of the exit door. I felt quite pleased with myself and thought about how good the picture would look on my room wall back at HMS Warrior.

As we neared the exit gate, an MOD policeman looked at us through an open door of the well-lit guardroom. He then shone a bright torch onto both of us and zoomed in on the picture.

'What have you got there?' he bellowed.

In my drunken state, I struggled to find a reply. 'Er, it's just a picture,' I stammered.

'Who said you can have it?' he questioned.

'One of the US Marines whom I used to play rugby with,' I replied sharply.

'What's his name?' he frowned.

The speed of his reply threw me slightly. I became agitated and abuse was the only answer I could find. I felt really angry towards him.

'Why are you asking me these fucking questions?' I shouted. 'You daft cunt. I do the same job as you.'

His dark bushy eyebrows raised and he looked startled at my change in attitude. Another policeman joined him and was instructed to watch me, whilst he checked out my story.

I waited impatiently, and noticed the Wren who was with me had gone into the guardroom and was sat down talking to the policeman who was supposed to be watching me. A few minutes later, the other policeman returned, accompanied by an off-duty US Marine. I repeated my story to him and he bluntly refused to believe me. Consequently, we started to exchange some heated words and the US Marine snatched the picture from me. I made no resistance and gave up the picture without a struggle. He then insisted I leave the establishment, which I did, without waiting for anybody else. I didn't need telling twice as I knew I had been rumbled. Fair play, I thought, time to go. I staggered out of the gate and climbed into an empty taxi, which was fairly close by in a taxi rank.

Early the following morning, I was awoken by one of the Marines from the night shift and told to report to the guardroom as there were a couple of military policemen there who wanted to talk to me. I was still quite drunk, but immediately got out of bed and went into the shower room. I looked at myself in the mirror. My eyeballs looked like piss holes in the snow and the cheeks of my face were flushed bright red. I felt sick and violently vomited into a sink. This was made worse when I noticed lumps of bloodstained phlegm coming out of my mouth as I retched, coughed and spluttered.

Later, in the guardroom, I was interviewed by two special military police, who were the Ministry of Defence's equivalent of the civilian CID. All the people who were with me the previous night were present, apart from the Wren who was with me when I was stopped at the USMC base main gate. I didn't know the significance of this at the time. I was told to read the following statement, which was compiled by the two military policemen who'd been on duty:

MINISTRY OF DEFENCE POLICE OCCURRENCE REPORT
STATION: USMC EASTCOTE   DATE: 12   September 1987
SUBJECT: REMOVAL OF FRAMED RECRUITING POSTER FROM US MARINE BARRACKS

1. At 0055 hrs on Saturday 12 September 1987 whilst on duty in the main police office at USMC Eastcote I observed a person whom I now know to be Lance-Corporal [STEVEN PREECE], a member of the Royal Marines stationed at HMS WARRIOR, NORTHWOOD, leaving the Establishment and carrying under his arm a framed US Marine recruitment poster (armed US Marine in camouflage dress against a dark background, the word 'MARINE' in blue and gold letters across the bottom of the picture).

2. I challenged [PREECE] and asked him under whose authority he was taking the picture; he said that he had

been given the picture by the US Marines. When asked which Marine, he said he did not know his name but he plays rugby with him. He then said, 'Why are you asking me these fucking questions? I do the same job as you, you daft cunt.' [PREECE] was obviously under the influence of alcohol. He was unsteady on his feet and his speech was slurred. I told [PREECE] to remain outside the police office while I made further enquiries to verify his story. I contacted the duty Marine, [Sgt BOLLARD], who stated it was unlikely that anyone would give permission for any of the fittings to be removed from the barracks and said he would send someone down to the gate to help resolve the situation. When [PREECE] was informed about this he became increasingly agitated and abusive.

3. At 0105 hrs [Cpl GOFF], USMC, arrived at the north gate and had a conversation with [PREECE]. [PREECE] reiterated his claim that a US Marine had given him the picture. [GOFF] said this was impossible as he was the only member of the USMC remaining and he did not give permission for the picture to be removed. In reply to this [PREECE] said he had been given the picture earlier in the evening. A heated discussion then took place between [PREECE] and [GOFF]. It was not possible to substantiate [PREECE]'s claim as to how he came to be in possession of the picture as no other US Marines were present in the establishment. [GOFF] then took possession of the picture which was placed next to the police office wall and [PREECE] was requested to leave the establishment, which he did at 0115 hrs.

4. When [PREECE] was stopped initially, he was in company with a young woman whom I recognised as one of two members of the Wrens who arrived at

approximately 2046 hrs, shortly after the main body of a dozen or so Royal Marines from HMS WARRIOR to attend the Marines Enlisted Men's Club. During the discussions relating to the picture, the young woman remained in the background. On one occasion, I saw her standing on the step next to the door to the police office. The other constable on duty, Constable [JONES], was with me when the questioning was taking place. When the matter of the picture had been resolved, Constable [JONES] returned to the police office and I remained outside momentarily to unlock the gate for persons leaving the establishment. The Marines Club had been busy. Patrons were departing the station at frequent intervals and taxis were arriving regularly to make pickups. When I returned to the police office I saw that the young woman was sitting in the easy chair next to the door. A brief conversation took place between myself, the young woman and Constable [JONES] in which the young woman referred to [PREECE] as a 'nutcase', and she stated that he did not play rugby as he had claimed. The impression gained was that she did not believe that [PREECE] had permission to remove the picture from the station. At approximately 0120 hrs I left the police office and made my way to [the main headquarters block] to speak to the duty Marine concerning the incident. [. . .] I did not see the woman who was with [PREECE] again.

When I finished reading through the statement, I asked the policemen why they were they making such a big song and dance about a petty little recruitment poster and a bit of bad language. I also asked why they had sent such highly trained policemen to question me about it. Then all became clear. The

Wren who was accompanying me when I was leaving the USMC base had claimed that the two MOD policemen had tried to rape her when she had entered the guardroom. However, I had to inform them that I was so intoxicated that I couldn't remember what happened to her when I left the establishment. I did see her enter the police office, but not leave. I went on to explain that I didn't know why she referred to me as a nutcase and that it must have been because she had had too much to drink.

A day or so later, I was summoned in front of the commanding officer and told to explain the details of the statement. I stuck to my story. Her accusations of attempted rape carried more weight than the removal of the picture and my words to the policemen, so all the heat was taken away from me.

I never knew if her accusation was true or false, but it was never proven to be true. The last time I saw her she was a patient of a military psychiatrist, on a course of treatment which had been enforced by her superiors.

CHAPTER TWENTY-FIVE

THE ROYAL MARINE CORPS' BIRTHDAY

Rain lashed against my bedroom window at HMS Warrior as I opened my eyes on one cold winter's Saturday morning. It was 28 October 1987, the birthday of the inception of the Royal Marines, who were formed at approximately a quarter to three on 28 October 1664. This was always a very special day in the Royal Marines and always a cause for some sort of celebration.

I had a nice hot shower, which felt quite soothing as the spraying water bounced off my scalp. I'd been on duty until the very early hours of the morning and was still feeling fatigued. I didn't have to work that day, so I spent about one and a half hours in the gym pumping iron, before taking another shower and sitting down to relax and watch some television. Early in the afternoon, a knock rattled my room door and then it opened slowly. It was Taz, an RAF man with whom I had become acquainted. He was a couple of years younger than me and had longish straight mousy hair, which was combed in a parting from left to right. He was roughly the same height and build as I was and came from Cornwall.

'Hello, Steve mate, how's it going?' he smiled.

'Hi, Taz, good to see you. Come on in and have a cup of coffee.'

He entered the room and sat down. I made us both a cup of coffee and we talked for a while.

'I thought you'd be out pissing it up by now,' he said.

'What's that supposed to mean?' I frowned. 'I was on duty until the early hours of this morning and have no reason to go out on the piss yet.'

Taz grinned. 'I thought you Marines always celebrated your Marine Corps birthday, or something like that.'

'Oh, of course, it's the 28th, isn't it? Yes, us Marines do always celebrate it. However, a lot of the lads are still sleeping after a late night shift on duty or are away on home leave.'

'I'll come with you, if you want to go for a drink, Steve. I've always wanted to go for a few pints with you.'

'OK,' I quickly agreed. 'Let's go down the Iron Bridge [local pub] for a few pints of Guinness.'

The Iron Bridge was a small murky pub in Harrow. It had a cast-iron reputation for its excellent pint of Guinness. The pub landlord was an Irishman who took great pride in its quality and presentation. We enjoyed the Guinness and played pool on the vacant pool table. Throughout the afternoon, we joked constantly and were later joined by another Marine called Graeme. Graeme was a Scotsman who came from Glasgow. He was small in build and had chipped teeth. He had a bit of a reputation for being able to drink vast amounts of beer. We often joked that he must have hollow legs to store it in. In fact, when I first met him I was totally convinced that he must have been sneakily pouring it out and just pretending to drink it. To prove this, I got one of the other Marines to stay sober for the night and watch him as he drank. However, I was proved wrong and Graeme got my respect for being a good drinker.

Graeme was also celebrating the Marine Corps' birthday. He told me he had just got out of bed after working through the night and that a lot of the other Marines would join us in the NAAFI bar later on. That immediately set the venue for the evening session. By the time we made our way back to the NATO base we were quite merry. Diz, who was on duty and dressed in uniform, walked with us along the way to the NAAFI bar.

'Hello, Steve and Graeme. Are you going down the bar?' he smiled.

'Yeah, are any of the lads down there?' I asked eagerly.

'Yes, a few of them, they're waiting for you two.'

All of a sudden, and to my complete surprise, I felt a hard slap from someone's hand on the back of my neck. The blow was painful and I turned around to see who had delivered it. It was Taz. He was stood a few feet away with his fists clenched like a boxer.

'Come on, you daft cunt, I want to fight you,' he shouted.

He had a serious look on his face, but I assumed he was joking. This was because he used the words 'daft cunt', which were in the statement I had shown him from the incident at Eastcote. With this thought, I turned away and continued my conversation with Diz.

Taz attacked me again from behind, but this time he hit me a lot harder. The blow made a loud thwacking noise and hurt on contact. I turned once again and saw Taz beckon me towards him.

'Come on, hard man, fucking fight me,' he shouted aggressively.

My facial expression changed and then I heard Graeme say, 'Oh shit.'

For a few moments, I stood and looked at Taz. His cheeks were flushed bright red and his eyes were like piss holes in the snow. I felt disappointed with his actions, but didn't really want to hit him.

'Come on, Taz, stop this before you get hurt,' I said calmly.

'You're the one who's going to get hurt, you daft cunt,' he screamed in a more aggressive manner.

I didn't hesitate and moved in for the attack. I grabbed him by the throat with one hand and pulled his head back by his hair with the other. I then used my leg to sweep his feet away and forced him down hard onto the floor. He reacted quickly and threw a punch, which hit me hard in the face.

'Right, you little bastard, I'll fucking give you what you're looking for,' I screamed in a wild and aggressive fashion, before repeatedly slamming the heel of my shoe hard into his face and then jumping up and down on his head. A couple of seconds later, I stopped and there was a strange silence. I looked down and saw Taz's face covered in deep red blood.

'Fucking hell, he's unconscious,' said Graeme, and then both him and Diz started to laugh. I looked down at his bloodstained face and then pushed my fingers into his neck to check that he still had a pulse. He did and I could also feel his breath, which I checked with my cheek pushed up against his lips.

'It's OK, I've only knocked him out,' I said reassuringly to Diz and Graeme.

We all burst into fits of laughter and rolled around a bit, holding our ribs. What now, I thought, and looked at Graeme.

'Graeme, grab hold of his legs and help me throw him into these bushes,' I requested and pointed to the nearby clump of bushes.

'Are you serious?' he asked.

'Fucking right I am, get hold of his legs. He probably won't remember a thing when he wakes up.'

Graeme helped me to lift his unconscious body into the

bushes, where we covered him over with leaves. Diz rolled around, laughing wildly.

'Come on, Graeme, let's go, there's beer to be drunk,' I said, pointing to the NAAFI building. We moved off and Diz left to make his way to his place of duty. As he walked in the opposite direction we could hear him laughing to himself.

The NAAFI bar was pretty much exclusively populated by Marines when we arrived. Word had got around that the Marines would be celebrating in force this evening and a lot of people purposely stayed away. We joined some of our friends and stood in the bootneck corner. My Marine mate Craig had acquired a load of plastic buckets and gave one to all the Marines, except me, to fill with beer.

'Hey, Steve,' he smiled. 'Where have you been? We've been waiting for the pleasure of your company.'

'Hi, Craig, down the Iron Bridge,' I replied.

'Here, drink this, I've bought you a drink,' he smiled and passed me a bucket full of bitter. I laughed and grabbed the bucket from him. It was heavy to hold and held around twelve pints. To ease the burden of holding the heavy buckets we removed our socks, tied them together and then tied them to the buckets. We then used the socks like slings and held them around our necks.

After a while, everybody was quite merry and we started to sing numerous Marine songs. This made the atmosphere warm and friendly and other people started to enter the bar. I can remember seeing the bottom of my bucket as I swallowed the remaining dregs. By this time, my eyeballs felt heavy and I was very drunk and tired. I watched Craig finish off the remainder of his beer and looked at his eyes. They were almost shut and looked glazed and dilated. He saw me looking at him and tried to speak to me. His face sagged when he tried to smile and he opened his mouth to try to speak again. No matter how hard he tried, he couldn't string a coherent sentence together and shook his head. I tried to reply, only to hear my words sound just as distorted and incomprehensible.

I motioned to Craig to follow me out of the bar. It was time to leave and we were both close to unconsciousness. I pushed my way clumsily through a group of sailors who were harmlessly chatting together.

'You could say excuse me,' snapped one of them.

I couldn't find the energy to reply and pushed past them. Then I felt a hard blow in the middle of my back, which I knew was a punch from one of them. At first, I wasn't going to react, but then he punched me again. I turned and grabbed hold of his throat, similarly to how I had earlier grabbed Taz's throat. I pulled him towards me and punched him hard in the stomach. This made him fall against me, and I reacted by lifting him off the floor and over my head. I didn't feel like I had the strength to throw him over the bar so I just dropped him onto a nearby table, which made a loud crashing noise and fell on top of him as he spilled down onto the polished floor. Then I nodded to Craig and beckoned him to follow me out of the exit door. We quickly left the bar and all the commotion behind and staggered back to our accommodation block. I bid Craig goodnight and then staggered into my room, where I got undressed and fell asleep as soon as my head hit the pillow.

My bowels ached. I opened my eyes and looked into the darkness. My room spun around and around and the outline of objects that I could see in the dark seemed to become clear and then disappear. I was still very drunk and felt a dull ache in my stomach. I needed to go to the toilet for a crap: probably the reason I had woken up, I thought.

I pushed back my bed sheets and climbed out of bed onto

the floor. The room started to spin faster and I fell forward and banged my head against my clothes locker. I groaned with the numb pain that I could feel on my left cheek and struggled to stay upright. I wrestled with the door to my room and struggled with the key that was still in the lock. Then a turd started to exit from my buttocks and hung out of my arsehole like a turtle's head sticking out of its shell. Oh fuck, I thought, I'm going to crap myself. The key spun round in the lock and I made a sharp exit for the toilets, which were next door. The hanging turd dropped onto the floor just inside my room as I staggered out into the corridor. The corridor started to spin like my room did, except that it was well lit and I could see where I was going. I stumbled and fell against the toilet door and it creaked open. On stepping onto the cream-tiled floor I felt more turds falling from my buttocks. I tried in vain to pick them up and just slid over and over every time I tried to get up. My hands were covered in excrement and I fell against the row of white sinks, then against the mirrors, then against the wall and then into the shower area where I fell once again onto the floor. I moaned as my head banged off the tiled walls, and struggled to get to my feet. The turds were still coming out of my buttocks and a lump landed on a nearby small wooden stool. Eventually, I made it into one of the toilet cubicles and sat down on the toilet to finish the crap I had started. By this time, I had none left to deposit and looked at the crap, which was plastered all over my hands and feet.

Because of my drunken state, there was very little I could do about resolving the situation, so I pulled out the roll of toilet paper and wiped my hands, feet and, for what it was worth, my buttocks. Then I staggered back to my room, but not before slipping a few more times on the way out. Once back in my room, I fell onto my bed and immediately back into unconsciousness.

Later, I heard a knock on my door and then I heard it open. 'Steve, Steve, are you awake?' I heard Scouse call. I knew who it was because I had recognised his Liverpudlian accent straight away. I slid my head out from under my covers and groaned when I felt the many aches around my head and body. I could also smell something foul.

'Oooohhh. All right, Scouse,' I said in a weary voice. 'What day is it?'

'I don't know, Steve, I lose track sometimes when I'm working through the night.'

'Oh, what's up, mate?' I squinted.

'Have you been to the toilet this morning?'

I felt very puzzled at his strange question. 'What do you mean, Scouse? I don't understand what you mean.'

Scouse grinned. 'I've just been into the toilets and there's shit all over the floor, there's shit all over the mirrors, there's shit all over the sinks, there's shit all over the showers. There's even a small lump of shit on the wooden stool in there.'

I scratched my sore head and frowned. 'What's that got to do with me, Scouse?'

'Well, there's also shit all over the carpet in the corridor, there's shit on your door, there's shit all over your floor, all over your bed sheets, on your head and on your face.'

'Orr fucking hell, mate, I guess it must have been my fault,' I sighed.

Scouse grinned and shook his head. 'Get it cleaned up, Steve.'

'OK, Scouse, sorry mate.'

Then he left and I immediately got out of bed and started to clean up my unfortunate mess. I found the smell revolting and honestly felt like it was the hardest job I'd ever had to do in my whole life.

CHAPTER TWENTY-SIX

RAF HALTON – HOSPITAL

During a tour of Northern Ireland a few years earlier, I had acquired an injury to my right elbow, which was caused by flying glass as a result of being engaged in an exchange of hostile gunfire with a paramilitary group.

I always worked hard at maintaining a high level of physical fitness, but was starting to get problems with my elbow. Sharp pains ran up and down my arm like electric shocks and the discomfort was becoming unbearable. I had a huge hard lump, which protruded from my elbow joint. I'd put up with it for a long time now, but it was steadily getting worse, so I reported to the sickbay and asked for the doctor's opinion.

He told me that it looked nasty and that it would be best to get it X-rayed. The X-rays showed that a small fragment of glass was still lodged around the area of the joint. The only cure was to have it surgically removed, so I was quickly booked into the nearby Royal Air Force hospital, RAF Halton.

Once booked in, I was sat up in bed and the surgeon came round with his students and explained my medical condition and how he intended to remedy it. The following morning, after a night of starvation, I was injected by a young attractive nurse with something to put me to sleep. Things slowly became blurred and my eyelids weighed a ton. I could hear voices, which became unclear, then distant, then silent.

'Lance-Corporal Preece. Lance-Corporal Preece. Are you awake?' a soft female voice called out.

'Uh . . . what?' I opened my eyes.

'I've brought you a nice cup of tea,' she said. It was the nice young nurse again.

'Oh . . . yes, thank you. Ouch,' I replied.

My arm ached badly. It was heavily bandaged and supported by a sling, which hung down from an overhead stirrup. A plastic blood bag also hung over my head. It had a plastic tube attached to it which ran down to somewhere inside my bandaged arm. I felt dehydrated and was grateful for the cup of tea I had been given by the nurse.

'All right, mate,' a strange male voice called out.

I sipped my tea and then looked to my left to see who it was. There was a young man, roughly my age, looking at me from the opposite bed. One of his legs was heavily bandaged and supported with some form of pulley apparatus.

'I'm all right,' I replied. 'What happened to you?'

'I've done my knee in.'

'Looks bad,' I sighed.

'It's a lot better now. I'll be out in a few days. Are you a Marine?'

'Yes. My name's Steve. What's yours?'

'Jimmy,' he smiled. 'I'm in the Army. Pleased to meet you.'

The orthopaedic ward was mixed, with both male and female patients from all the branches of the armed forces, a lot of whom had very little to offer in the way of cheerfulness and a sense of humour. Thankfully, I got on well with Jimmy.

He seemed to be the only person close to being on my wavelength.

Most of the patients were suffering from leg problems and were consequently quite immobile. When the sister of the ward looked for the most able-bodied patient to be tea boy, then, I was unfortunately given the job, and several of the RAF patients joked that it was good to have a Marine acting as waiter. I wasn't very happy about their sarcastic comments but decided to have some fun whilst carrying out the tea-pouring tasks.

Tea was served at set times during the day, so I had to report to the small kitchen at the end of the ward to collect a waiting tea trolley. The trolley was heavily laden with two large pots of tea and one of coffee. There were also a few large plates of toasted bread, with butter and marmalade. My right arm ached as I pushed the trolley down the ward. One of the RAF men was sat up in the first bed that I approached. He clicked his fingers twice and shouted to me.

'I'll have toast and make it snappy.'

'One slice or two?' I asked.

'Two,' he grinned, pointing to the empty tray on his bed.

His big smirk quickly disappeared when I flung two pieces of toast at him, which bounced off his head.

'Tea or coffee?' I snarled.

'Er, no thank you,' he sighed.

He and most of the other patients buried their heads beneath the bedclothes. I laughed and so did Jimmy when I gave him one of the pots of tea and a plate full of toast. Next, I arrived at one of the more private side wards. These were usually reserved for higher ranking officers, and the one who occupied this one was an air vice-marshal in the Royal Air Force.

I knocked on the door and slowly entered. An old

gentleman with short grey hair greeted me. 'Good evening, young man,' he said in a very posh, upper-class type of voice.

'Good evening, sir,' I replied. 'Would you like some tea or coffee?'

'Yes. I would like a cup of rather strong coffee and make it rather sweet.'

'Right, sir, coming up.'

I went back to the trolley and filled a cup with coffee. I also added eight more spoonfuls from a spare jar of coffee and eight heaped spoonfuls of sugar, before topping it up with milk and water. It looked more like glue than coffee, but he said sweet and strong, so that's what he got.

'Here you are, sir. Rather sweet and rather strong,' I smiled and passed him the cup of coffee.

'Would you like any toast, sir?' I continued.

'No, young man. Put it on the table and close the door behind you.'

'Very good, sir. I hope you enjoy it.'

As I left and closed the door, I could hear the old man start to cough and splutter as he drank from the rancid cup I had given him. The remainder of the patients declined the refreshment I offered, so Jimmy and I tucked in. We laughed and joked together as the unhappy patients sat sulking whilst pretending to be occupied reading books or newspapers.

Later, I had to collect all the dirty pots and return them on the trolley back to the kitchen. This was an easy task as, apart from Jimmy and myself, only the air vice-marshal had accepted my offer of refreshment. I knocked on the old man's door and re-entered.

'Hello, young man,' he smiled.

'Hello, sir. Did you enjoy your coffee?' I asked, and then noticed a splashing of coffee stains on his white bed sheets.

'Oh yes, very nice,' he replied. Then I saw that one of the plant pots on a windowsill was full of coffee.

'Would you like another cup, sir?' I asked in a smarmy voice.

'No, no thank you,' he smiled, baring his false teeth like a Cheshire cat.

'Very good, sir,' I said and left the room.

Outside, I held my ribs with my good arm and laughed wildly. I found it hard to believe his cool manner after tasting what must have been the most horrid cup of coffee of his posh life.

The following day, to my delight, the ward sister told me that I was to be demoted from the position of tea boy and that it was owing to an unsatisfactory level of service. Oh good, I thought. I didn't like being made a tea boy, anyway.

The best part of the ward was the television room. It was less boring in there, as there was a good range of films to choose from. On a quiet Saturday afternoon, I sat alone watching the television when a middle-aged woman entered in a wheelchair. She briefly looked at me before pushing her wheels towards the television. She tapped her finger up and down the many channel buttons and changed the channel I was watching.

'Hey, what are you playing at?' I snapped.

'It's OK, I've been here longer than you,' she replied.

I laughed. I couldn't believe her cheek. 'So, it's like that is it?'

'Yes, it is.'

'Right, fine,' I said. 'There's a war film on at three o'clock tomorrow and I'm watching it.'

'We'll see about that,' she murmured in a sarcastic manner.

'Yes, we will,' I nodded and got up and left the room.

The next morning, she sat up in her bed and smiled at me.

I knew she was goading me, but I returned the smile anyway. Then I watched her scanning the television pages of her newspaper. She picked up a red clock from her bedside cabinet and went about setting the alarm.

'Hey, Marine,' she called over to me.

'What?' I asked seriously.

'I'm just going to have a nap. There's a Grand Prix race on at three o'clock. Er, it's the same time as that film you wanted to watch. That's a pity.'

I looked at her, but didn't respond to her remarks. She lay back on her bed and closed her eyes. I wasn't very impressed with her attitude and sat there looking at her clock. I could see the pointer on the clock that was used to set the alarm and realised that it was set to go off at around five minutes to three. I saw her wheelchair lying idle at the side of her bed. There were a few minutes left before the alarm went off, so I quickly put an idea into action.

I cautiously sneaked over and looked at her. She was sound asleep. Cool air hissed out of the valves of her wheelchair's tyres under the pressure of my finger. After a couple of minutes, both tyres were totally empty and spread flat over the cold, polished floor. I made my way into the television room and switched on the TV, as the film I wanted to watch was about to start. Then I heard the old girl's alarm clock go off loudly in the ward.

'Nurse, nurse,' she cried. 'Somebody has let my tyres down.'

I laughed loudly and then enjoyed the full length of the war film in peace, because she was unable to make it into the television room to join me.

At about eight o'clock that evening, Jimmy suggested that we challenge a couple of the RAF lads to a wheelchair race and that we use the quiet corridors as our racetrack. With a lot of persuasion, two of them finally accepted our challenge. We split into teams of two and prepared ourselves to begin the race. The handicaps were even. One of the RAF lads had his leg in plaster, similar to Jimmy, and the other had his arm strapped up in a similar fashion to mine.

'Go!' shouted Jimmy.

We all pushed hard on our wheels and sped off down the corridor. I found it hard to push with just one hand, but put as much effort into it as possible. The corridor was fairly dark and quite long and both Jimmy and myself reached the first corner around the same time and established a bit of a lead. We both screeched round the next corner almost on one wheel and my wheelchair veered out of control and smashed into a wall.

'Ouch, my bloody arm,' I squealed, in a fair amount of pain from the fall that followed my quick stop.

'Sssshhhit,' Jimmy shouted as he smashed straight through two glass-panelled doors. SSSSSMMMMMMMAAAAAASH, went the glass and Jimmy spilled out onto the floor.

'Aaaarrrrgh,' he screamed.

The two RAF lads pulled up behind me and looked unsure of what to do or say.

'Oh bollocks, let's pick him up,' I suggested.

Two nurses rapidly appeared on the scene and pulled back the wheelchair from the damaged door frames. They checked Jimmy to see if he was injured and then they sent us all to bed like four naughty children. Luckily, Jimmy didn't cut his leg on the glass due to the protection from his plaster pot. However, he was in a lot of pain as he had banged his leg hard when he fell down onto the floor. Later, when his pain had eased a little, he laughed about the race and said it had been the highlight of his stay in the hospital.

The following day, I was released from hospital. It was a couple of days earlier than planned, but I guess it was because I couldn't stay out of mischief. Jimmy bid me farewell and told me that he had enjoyed meeting me.

CHAPTER TWENTY-SEVEN

SICK LEAVE – A THOUGHT OF DEATH

The Marine detachment sergeant-major gave me an extra week's leave on top of the two weeks I had already been given by the hospital. I was quite pleased, as it would be the longest spell of home leave I would have had since joining the Marines nearly five years before.

Within an hour or so, I was sat on the train heading home. My arm was very sore from the operation and ached continuously. For the first couple of weeks at home, I didn't venture out but chose to stay in and watch the television while resting my arm. After this period of time, I was able to remove my bandages and sling and freely move my arm with very little discomfort. There was still a dull ache there, but my arm was well on the road to recovery.

My eldest brother Martin called me on the telephone to invite me out for a few beers. I didn't always see him when I was home on leave as he now lived in a flat on a different estate with his wife. Having been laid up for two weeks, I was only too glad to accept his invitation. The venue was one of the local working men's clubs, where the beer was good and inexpensive. Martin had been frequenting this type of place for some years now and his build reflected his heavy drinking habits. He had a heavy-set chest and shoulders and a bulging beer belly. Martin was quite aggressive by nature and very easy to upset. We had had our ups and downs over the years, which I believed was down to jealousy because his attempt to join the Marines some years before had failed and mine had succeeded. On previous visits home, he was always quick tempered during our conversations and often wanted to fight with me. I always declined to fight with him because he was my big brother and I loved him. Unfortunately, he only saw me during the few weeks a year I visited home and had no idea of the type of life I led in the Marines, or really of how violent I could be if I was pushed.

Nevertheless, this particular night he pushed me too far. We agreed to meet at the working man's club at seven o'clock that evening. I arrived at roughly five minutes to seven and entered through the large steel doors. Inside, there were two snooker tables and a handful of familiar local faces. The room was filled with smoke, and music played from a small radio that was housed on a shelf behind the small dingy bar. Martin was stood proudly against the bar and smiled broadly when he saw me arrive.

'All right, youngun?' he grinned.

'Hiya, Martin,' I responded, and we shook hands and sat down at a nearby table. We talked about various things and eventually we got around to talking about the Marines. Martin asked me numerous questions about the sort of life I led there, and I answered all his questions truthfully, yet he refused to believe anything I said.

'You're a liar,' he snarled. 'You're full of shit. I don't believe a word you've said.'

'Why not?' I frowned. 'I have no reason to tell lies.'

Martin shook his head. 'I think you're living in a fantasy world and making all this stuff up.'

This annoyed me. 'Listen, Martin, you only know what you read in the papers and half of that isn't as bad as what really goes on.'

'I still think you're a liar,' he insisted.

'Well, don't ask me these questions and you won't be disappointed.'

His jealousy was written all over his face. He had grown into a person who was always feeling sorry for himself. This was something I blamed our father for, because Martin had received the worst treatment from him during our childhood. Nevertheless, he had grown strong over the past few years and his toughness had gained him a bit of a reputation amongst the locals.

I felt that Martin hadn't realised that I had grown into a fit and strong young man and that I had changed significantly from the quiet youngest brother who had left home almost five years before to join the Marines. He was wrong in his assumptions, but I didn't want to labour the point and start an argument. We drank heavily for the rest of the night and it became something of a competition as to how much beer we could drink. Later in the evening, Martin was starting to become aggressive, and it made me feel uneasy.

'How tough are you, Steve?'

'Why?' I sighed and slowly shook my head.

'Because I want to know,' he snarled, and bared his teeth like an animal. His face was flushed bright red and his eyes stared at me like daggers. I could sense that something was going to happen and chose to try to avoid any form of confrontation.

'Well?' Martin continued.

'I'm going home, I'll see you tomorrow,' I replied and got up to leave.

He didn't look at me and continued to drink from his beer glass. I felt nervous and uneasy as I walked out of the exit door and could sense there was going to be trouble.

Within seconds, Martin appeared outside the club and rushed into the poorly lit street.

'Where do you think you're going, you little bastard?' he screamed angrily.

'I'm going home,' I frowned.

'Come here,' he continued to shout.

I turned and faced him and momentarily contemplated an attack.

'Come on, let's have a go,' he screamed, shaking his fists and baring his teeth once more.

He beckoned me to come towards him with his hands, but I didn't raise my fists. He wasn't my enemy, he was my big brother. I didn't want to fight with him so I thought better of it and backed down.

'No, Martin, I'm going home.'

This just seemed to make him even angrier and he lunged at me and head-butted me on the forehead. I looked at him with great disappointment and felt sad, very sad. Tears started to stream down my face.

'Come on, fight me,' he yelled. 'Call yourself a Marine, you're a soft piece of shit.'

I turned and ran across the quiet road to get out of his way, but he kept shouting at me that he wanted to fight me.

'No, Martin, I don't want to hit you, you're my brother, I love you,' I cried.

His anger continued. 'Fight me, fight me, fight me, come on.'

I turned and ran hard and fast and rapidly disappeared into the distance. He was no match for my high level of physical fitness and I soon left him far behind. I didn't stop until I was nearly home and could see my parents' house in the distance. I stopped to think for a while and gathered my thoughts on the events of the previous fifteen minutes. Although Martin lived near the working man's club, my instincts told me that he wouldn't go home, but would pursue me back to my parents' house. A small bush caught my eye. It was on the opposite side of the road on an embankment which ran down from a disused railway line. I knew from my infantry training on camouflage and concealment that I could sit in front of the bush, in its shadow, without being seen from the road. My emotions changed from sorrow to anger and I prepared myself so that I could sit still in my chosen area without being seen. I waited patiently for his arrival and felt sure he wouldn't disappoint me. I now thought of him as an opponent and felt keen to show him what kind of man his little brother had grown into.

Several minutes later, the silence of the still night was broken and my instincts were proved right as I watched him walk by on the pavement, only a few feet away from me. I could hear him cursing and swearing to himself as he moved, and yet he was so close that I could hear his heavy breathing. As he moved into the distance I cautiously followed close by, using the available shadows for cover.

When he reached our parents' house, he burst in through the unlocked front door. I was literally twelve feet behind him. He declined to switch on the hallway light and ran up the stairs in the darkness shouting as he went.

'Where is he? Where is the little bastard?'

'Where's who?' answered our father from his bedroom.

Martin didn't answer and I could hear him searching through the few rooms upstairs. As I entered the dark hallway, the floorboards creaked gently under the weight of my feet. I waited in the darkness; it was my best friend because I knew how to use it. I could hear him shouting upstairs and cursing my father before beginning his walk back down the stairs. I waited patiently at the bottom. He couldn't see me, but I was ready.

'Where is he?' he snarled.

'I'm here,' I whispered and stood in front of him.

His immediate action was to throw a punch between my legs, but he missed his intended target. I moved swiftly and began my attack. I hurled a powerful head-butt clean into his face and followed it up with several swift blows from my fists, before knocking him down to the ground with a well-placed foot sweep. I went crazy and laid into him with a hail of kicks.

I knew if it was him who was kicking me he wouldn't stop, and now he was down I intended to keep him there. He screamed time and time again, but I showed no mercy as he had pushed me too far too often and now he was going to learn the hard way. His aggression withered and he screamed in desperation for me to stop my attack.

'I've had enough, I've had enough, please don't hit me no more,' he cried.

Then my mother shouted down the stairs. 'Steven, stop it, stop it, please.'

I stopped and looked up at her. She was crying. I looked down to see Martin holding his head and face and thought, am I wrong? I placed my foot neatly in the back of his neck to prevent him from moving. I paused and sighed and let him get up and onto his feet. He looked at me with a sorry-looking battered face and blood streamed down from his nose and lips. For a moment, I could see myself in him. His face reminded me of mine on the morning I had looked into the mirror at 45 Commando several years before, beaten and shaken. He ran out of the open doorway and into the street. He moved a few yards away and turned to look at me. Tears streamed down his bloodstained face.

'I'm happy now,' he sobbed. 'I know you can do it.'

'You silly cunt,' I replied in a calm voice and shook my head slowly from side to side.

I watched him walk into the distance. I couldn't really say how I felt at that time. He was my big brother, but I didn't feel glad or sad to see him end up this way. However, I had put up with his aggressive attitude for a long time now and had had no choice but to give him what he was looking for.

My head ached when I awoke the following morning. I thought about the previous night and felt sad. I wasn't proud of what I'd done. I asked myself why I'd had to fight with my big brother. He obviously hadn't understood the life I'd been leading for the past five years or the type of person I'd become.

My alarm clock ticked loudly near my left ear on my bedside cabinet. It was twelve o'clock, midday, and I decided to get washed and changed and go out for a few beers to take my mind off things. I sat alone in the local pub and spoke only briefly to the locals to acknowledge their greetings.

After a great deal of thought and several glasses of beer, I came to the conclusion that the best thing I could do would be to cut my home leave short and return to HMS Warrior. My arm felt a great deal better, so I would be able to return to active duty early if I wanted to. My mind was made up, so I drank a few more beers and headed home to collect my things. When I walked in through my parents' front door, my head spun a little and I felt tipsy, light-headed and tired. Inside, I saw my mother as soon as I entered the living-room. She looked me straight in the eye and looked angry.

'Who the hell do you think you are?' she shrieked.

'What?' I exclaimed, opening the palms of my hands.

'Have you seen the mess of our Martin's face?'

'It wasn't my fault.'

'Oh yes it was,' she continued. 'You think you can go around beating people up just because you're a Marine. Well I'll tell you what you are, you're nothing, nothing.'

Her remarks upset me. She didn't understand or was not aware of the endless taunts and invitations to fight in the back garden that I had always received from Martin. I felt angry towards her.

'You think I did that just because I'm a Marine?' I shouted, and looked around the room. In a rage of temper, I pulled two Royal Marine wooden plaques from the wall and smashed them against another. Then I grabbed a glass-framed picture of myself dressed in ceremonial Blues uniform on the day I passed out of Marine basic training and smashed that against the same wall.

'You don't understand, you don't fucking understand,' I shouted loudly and tears streamed from my eyes. I felt broken-hearted. My family had once told me that they were proud of me and now they were against me. I didn't hang around and hurriedly packed my bags and slipped out through the open front door. As I left, I could hear my mother crying and calling out my name in the street. Maybe she didn't mean what she said, I thought. But there was no going back. I climbed into a nearby taxi, which sped off towards the town centre train station.

I felt all alone on the train and sat in a virtually empty carriage. Tears continued to pour down my face as I continuously went over the sad events of the past two days in my mind. However, the beer I had consumed helped me relax and I soon fell asleep.

A few hours later, the juddering motion of the train carriage awoke me as the train arrived at King's Cross Station in London. I had a horrible stale taste of alcohol in my mouth and felt dry and fairly dehydrated. To remedy this, I called into a nearby café and bought a hot cup of coffee before catching a tube back to Northwood.

'Back early aren't you, Steve?' asked one of the Marines when I walked in through the main gate of HMS Warrior.

'Yeah,' I sighed. 'I got bored with drinking with civilians who know nothing about nothing.'

I pushed the door to the Marines' accommodation block, which creaked open. There was a silence and my feet echoed in the corridor as I headed towards my room with my head down looking at the floor.

'Hello, Steve, you're back early,' a voice called out.

I looked up. It was Patrick, a short balding Irishman whom I worked with.

'Yeah,' I sighed.

'What's up? You look hungover and pissed off,' he continued.

'Yeah . . . I am.'

'Things not too good at home?'

'No . . . they're not.'

Patrick looked at me and then at his watch. 'It's nearly seven o'clock. Unpack your bags, Steve, and meet me in the NAAFI bar in ten minutes. Maybe a few ice-cool beers will cheer you up a little.'

'Yeah, cheers, Paddy, I'll see you in about ten minutes.'

The hot water from the stainless steel showerhead splashed off my head and naked body. It helped me clear my head and eased the tightness in my muscles acquired from sleeping on the train. My reflection looked back at me from the mirror in the shower room. Dark shadows hung below the sockets of my eyes and my face looked drawn and tired of its worries and encounters. I'll have a few beers with Paddy and put it all behind me, I thought, and hurriedly got dressed in some clean clothes and headed down to the

NAAFI bar. Inside, it was quiet, but this was because it was still quite early in the evening and most people didn't venture in until later.

'Here, Steve,' said Patrick as he passed me a pint of beer. 'Get your sorry-looking gums around this.'

A warm friendly grin covered his face. I liked him a lot as a friend and I also enjoyed working with him. He was a fit, wise and well-experienced Marine with over sixteen years' service under his belt. I always admired his coolness and tactful approach when addressing angry and obnoxious naval officers, who frequently complained about the behaviour of Marines within the security detachment. He always seemed to listen to what they had to say, give them an answer that seemed to confuse them, and smile and nod his head. Generally, they weren't sure if they had got their point across, but thought they had in some way because he always finished with a nod and an agreeing smile.

The same man had once attended an Army social function, where he verbally insulted an Army woman who had reacted by throwing a full pint of beer over him. He didn't flinch and gave her his usual warm smile before brushing himself down with the palm of his hand. He then casually left the bar and returned a short time later with a portable toilet full of human excrement. He walked up to the woman and poured its contents all over her head and body.

'Cheers, Paddy,' I replied and accepted the drink he had bought me.

Throughout the night, we drank heavily and consumed a great deal of a mixture of cider and Pernod topped up with blackcurrant. Later, I was very drunk and stood alone leaning against the bar. Paddy had left and most people chose to stay out of my way. I knew this because I saw them moving away from me when they entered the bar. When I sensed this, I decided it was time to leave and then staggered back to my room, where I lay awake on my bed.

The events from home flashed around in my mind like beams from a torchlight. My true feelings poured out of my eyes in the shape of tears. Although I had had very little choice in what I had done, I felt very much ashamed, and I despaired that the pride I had once brought to my family was now in tatters.

'Why . . . why?' I asked myself out loud as I clasped the palms of my hands over my eyes and sobbed heavily. Pictures of Martin beckoning me to fight him and the state of his face after I had beaten him kept repeatedly flashing into my mind. My feelings were very strong and I stood up and opened my boot locker. Inside, I found what I was looking for, my razor-sharp survival knife. I placed it on the table in front of me and stared at it. I felt like I wanted to kill myself.

I had no fear of dying. Back on the streets of Northern Ireland when I was involved in exchanges of gunfire with the enemy, I always felt the fear, but I was never afraid to die. This was no different. All I had to do was pick up the knife and either slit my throat with it or thrust it into my heart. The will to live was rapidly fading away in my confused and emotional state. I placed the ragged sharp edge of the start of the long shiny blade against my Adam's apple, with the intention of dragging it across. If this doesn't do it I'll just keep cutting, I thought.

Then I paused momentarily to think again. I pictured my mother in my head, standing at my funeral with the wind blowing and a lone Royal Marines bugler sounding the 'Last Post' before the soil was placed on my coffin, which would be draped in a Union Jack flag.

I loved the Marines and I loved my mother. Maybe the hurt would be too much for her, I thought. I wasn't afraid to die, but I felt an emptiness in my mother's heart which could never be filled. Oh fuck this, I thought. I'll telephone her and tell her how I feel about it all. The knife rattled on my small wooden table as I flung it down and went out into the corridor to use the telephone to call her.

A clicking noise sounded as the telephone receiver was lifted at the other end of the line. 'Hello . . .? Hello . . .? Hello . . .?' answered my mother.

Her voice triggered my emotions and I once again burst into tears and sobbed heavily, so much so that I couldn't find the words to speak.

'Hello, hello, is that you, Steve? Are you all right, son?' she asked.

'Mum, Mum, why, Mum? Why?' I sobbed.

'Calm down, son, it wasn't your fault. I saw Martin try to hit you between the legs and you retaliated,' she said softly.

'Mum, I feel like I want to kill myself,' I sniffed as I fought to control the tears.

'Don't be silly, son, it's not that bad.'

'But I feel ashamed, Mother, ashamed.'

Her voice changed from softness to the strict voice she used to use when telling me off as a child. 'Listen, son. I've told you, it wasn't your fault, and I'm not blaming you. Martin has been to see me and sends his apologies.'

'But Mother, every time I hit him, I could see my face in his face. It was like beating myself up.'

'Martin has told me, he pushed you too far. He wanted to test you.'

'But why, Mother . . . why?'

'I don't know, son, but he said he's sorry and that, for him, the war is over.'

'Is that what he said?' I asked curiously.

'Yes, he did. So go to bed and sleep it off. Everything will be OK in the morning.'

'OK, Mum,' I nodded. 'I'll call you tomorrow, goodnight.'

By the time I had returned to my room, my emotions had eased off and I felt a lot better. The sharp survival knife glinted against the moonlight, which shone in through the small window at the end of my room. I turned on the cold tap in my sink and cupped my hands to collect water and splashed it over my face. My reflection looked back at me again in the mirror. For a moment, I stood motionless, looking at myself. The thought of killing myself now seemed totally pointless and stupid. I shook my head and dried my face on a towel. As I climbed into bed I burst into a prolonged bout of laughter. I lay back and looked up at the ceiling. You silly bastard, I thought. It's a strange life we live.

CHAPTER TWENTY-EIGHT

THE WELSHMAN

For a few months, I remained teetotal and drank nothing with alcohol in it. Instead, I concentrated on my security duties and physical fitness training. I had always been extremely fit as a Marine, but got even fitter over this period of time. When I wasn't on duty, I was in the gymnasium working out. Early every morning, I pounded the many running routes that the Marines used around the area of the NATO base and worked hard pumping out the many exercises I had learned over the years. I excelled in fitness tests and generally came either first or second from groups of around twenty Marines. Also during this period, I kept out of trouble and even apologised to some people whom I had caused trouble with on previous occasions.

New expansion work started on the NATO base, which involved a number of civilian workers needing to gain access to the establishment. One of these workers was a scruffy-looking Welshman with brown curly hair, whom we nicknamed Taff. Taff or Taffy was a regular nickname for a Welshman or woman who mixed with people outside Wales.

He was a very loud person whom most of the Marines didn't take to. However, me and him became good mates, so they put up with his manner for my sake.

Me and Taff had such a laugh that we were out socialising all the time. He drank like a fish and held his own on heavy boozing binges. One night, we teamed up with a sailor and a couple of Wrens and headed for a disco at a naval base in Portsmouth, called HMS Dryad. One of the Marines in the security detachment had sold me an old Morris Minor car for £10. It was green with a wooden outer frame. It may have looked like an old banger but it ran like a dream. I hadn't passed my driving test yet but nobody even asked when I offered them a lift to the venue. The journey took about one and a half hours and we joked along the way. The occupants of the car were fairly humorous except for one of the Wrens who never seemed to smile or make any effort to join the conversation. She didn't bat an eyelid when Taff called her a miserable bastard and just stared out of the window.

The sailor was a petty officer in rank and a really good lad to get along with. He had a house in Portsmouth and offered to put us all up for the night after the disco had finished. We arrived at the naval base at around 7 p.m., when it was starting to get dark. A young Navy rank stood guarding the main gate and walked over to the car when we pulled up at the barrier.

'Any identification?' he asked.

'Yes,' I replied swiftly and waved a card in front of him, which I had pulled from my pocket.

'Thank you,' he nodded and raised the barrier, allowing us to proceed.

'That's a strange ID card,' commented the sailor. 'It looked like a beer mat.'

'It is a beer mat,' I laughed and drove into the car park.

Inside, the disco hall was pretty similar to the one at HMS Warrior and packed with people. The atmosphere was a lot calmer than what we were used to and everybody just seemed to drink and dance. Taff disappeared with a Wren for a while and so did the sailor a short time later. I chose to drink at the bar and converse amiably with the servicepeople around me.

It was an enjoyable evening and it went without incident. We were hungry and the sailor told us that there was a hot-dog stand open just around the corner. Great news, I thought. I could really murder a hot dog or two right now.

The hot-dog stand was made up from a small white caravan, which was chocked up on blocks of wood to steady it. The front had been converted into a long sliding window, which the owner slid back during opening times. Steam billowed out of the open window and a waft of hot dogs, hamburgers and fried onions filled our nostrils. There was a small queue of people and we stood in line awaiting our turn to be served. After a few minutes, I was next to be served. The owner was dressed in a white apron with a small white chef's hat on his head. He was around forty years old with a thin face and a shortly trimmed moustache. He just stood motionless staring at me as I placed my order.

'I'm not serving you,' he said.

'What do you mean, you're not serving me?' I replied.

'You were here last night and didn't pay me. You're a poor excuse for a sailor.'

I could feel the hairs standing up on my neck. 'I think you've got me muddled up with somebody else, mate. I've never been here before and I'm not a fucking sailor.'

'Yeah, I'm pretty sure it was you and you're not getting served,' he snapped, and asked the person behind me what they wanted to eat.

'Fucking twat,' I snarled. 'It definitely wasn't me. I'll give you something to remember me by,' I continued and bent down and grabbed a hold of one of the chocks of wood which supported the caravan. I slammed my shoulder hard against the structure and it lifted slightly, just enough for me to remove the piece of wood. Everybody, including me, rushed back out of the way as the caravan came crashing down onto its side.

'Aaaarrggghhh!' screamed the owner as the contents of his kitchenware, cooking materials and food scattered around inside the van. A side window opened and the owner crawled out with a till in his hands.

'I'm going to have you for this,' he scorned, waving one of his fists at me.

'Come on then, twat, let's see you do it,' I grinned.

At that, he turned and ran off. The queue had dispersed and just the sailor, the Wren and myself stood next to the wrecked hot-dog stand. I was still hungry and climbed into the caravan to try and salvage a couple of burgers or hot dogs. It was dark inside, but I could smell the food and soon managed to collect a couple of burgers and buttered buns. I also found some brown sauce and squirted some onto my burgers. When I climbed out, my friends had gone and a couple of naval policemen stood a few feet away with their hands on their hips.

Without hesitation, they grabbed hold of me and twisted both arms behind my back. My burgers fell to the ground, but I still managed to keep chewing part of one, which I was determined to eat. They frogmarched me to the guardroom and stood me at attention outside the duty petty officer's room. One of them knocked on the door and pushed it open. I could see the duty petty officer stood staring at me.

'Come in,' he shouted with a sense of urgency.

I walked in casually and stood in front of him. He was

dressed in uniform and had a familiar face that I felt I had seen before, but I wasn't sure where. He told me to sit down on a chair opposite his desk and then told the two policemen to leave.

'Fucking hell, I don't believe it,' he exclaimed.

'Don't believe what?' I asked.

'You don't recognise me, do you?' he asked.

'I do, but I don't know where from.'

He stood shaking his head slowly from side to side. 'I left the Navy a few years ago and on my last night of duty I arrested you at HMS Raleigh. I've since rejoined the Navy and this is my first night as duty petty officer and now I'm arresting you again.' He rubbed the palm of his hand over his face.

'I thought you looked familiar,' I replied with a smile.

'My brother is in the Marines now and I told him the story about you at HMS Raleigh a couple of years ago and he said he knows you and that you're a handful, but a good dedicated Marine.'

'That's flattering,' I answered sarcastically.

'Yes it is, and guess what I'm going to do?'

'Don't tell me . . . lock me up and throw away the key.'

'No,' he shook his head. 'My brother speaks very highly of you. I'm going to let you go without charge.'

'What?' I frowned, very shocked.

'Yeah. I don't like the hot-dog seller anyway, he's always ripping people off. He deserves what he got.'

I stood up. I wasn't sure if he was bluffing and taking the opportunity to get his own back for my behaviour now and also several years ago at HMS Raleigh.

'Can I go then?' I asked.

'Yes, go on, beat it,' he smiled.

I thanked him and left the office and then the establishment and went back to the sailor's house. He looked very surprised to see me when I arrived and invited me in. Inside, a warm fire was burning and the two Wrens and Taff were sat on cosy chairs drinking cups of coffee. I told them my story and they all shook their heads in disbelief. Taff grinned and opened a bag full of cans of beer before putting some music on. The miserable Wren never smiled at all and casually went upstairs to her allocated bed. Taff commented on what a miserable bastard she was and said he was going upstairs to shag her up the arse. We just laughed and sat and drank our beer. About twenty minutes later Taff re-entered the room and was completely naked.

'Fucking smell it,' he shouted. 'Fucking smell it,' and pointed at his erect penis. 'I've shagged her and she let me shag her up the arse, fucking smell it.'

We just laughed and carried on drinking before retiring for some sleep in the early hours of the following morning. Later that day, we drove back to HMS Warrior and throughout the journey I noticed the once miserable Wren smiling all the time as she stared out of the partially opened window.

On arrival, I parked outside the guardroom and went inside for a bit of banter with the Marines who were on duty. When I entered, I was told that my mate Craig had telephoned the guardroom and wanted to speak to me. I took hold of the hanging telephone receiver to speak to him.

'Hello, hairy arse, how's it going?' I said.

He didn't answer and there was a short silence, before I saw Craig enter the guardroom. He was grinning and all the other Marines were rolling around in fits of laughter. Hhhmmmm, I thought. I've been had. I had a suspicion of who was on the other end of the telephone. 'Hello, is that Craig?' I asked.

'Yes, it is,' answered a mature, deep, posh type of voice, which I recognised immediately. It was the commander-in-chief (CNC). He was the most powerful man in the Royal Navy and the Royal Marines. Apart from meeting the Queen of England and the Prince of Wales a few years previously, he was the most important person I had ever spoken to: and someone had called him for a practical joke.

'Do you know who this is?' he questioned as I watched all the Marines present holding their ribs to contain their laughter.

'Yes, I do,' I replied. 'Do you know who this is?'

'No, I don't,' said the commander-in-chief.

'Good, so fuck off,' I laughed, and replaced the telephone receiver as the other Marines collapsed into hysterical laughter.

A few minutes later, one of them patted me on the back and passed me a hot cup of tea. I pulled up a seat and sat at the front of the guardroom with my mate Craig and joked about the telephone call. Craig was a dog handler and had his Alsatian dog stood beside him. It was wearing a muzzle but was making fretting noises. I looked at Craig and then at the dog and realised why. The guardroom was responsible for holding the bosun's whistle, which was retrieved by one of the Royal Navy ranks to blow each day when they raised the naval flag at first light and lowered it at last light. The bosun's whistle was made of silver metal and was shaped like a small model cannon with a long barrel. Craig was waiting for the duty sailor to arrive in a few minutes' time to collect the whistle. I noticed that he was pushing the end of the whistle up the dog's arsehole, which was why the dog was whimpering.

I grinned at Craig and at all the other Marines who were waiting with excitement for the duty sailor to arrive to collect it. At last light and right on time, the duty sailor arrived and tapped on the one-way glass of the sliding window at the front of the guardroom. He was a black guy called Simms. He was dressed in his standard naval dress uniform. We all knew him quite well and found him very amiable and humorous.

'Here we go, lads,' laughed Craig as he pulled the sliding window open.

'Hello, Simms, mate,' Craig smiled. 'Give it a good blow for the Marines.'

'I'll see what I can do,' Simms smiled and grabbed the whistle from Craig's hand.

Then he marched smartly onto what the Royal Navy call the quarterdeck, where their flags fly.

We watched with interest.

The duty officer nodded his head to signal Simms to start blowing the bosun's whistle, whilst another sailor lowered the flags. Simms blew hard and then started to cough and splutter.

'Bloody blow the damn thing,' snarled the duty officer.

Simms tried again and then spontaneously threw up all over the floor and partially over the duty officer. The duty officer started to scowl and curse Simms and then beat him about the head with his clenched fist. The other sailor finished pulling down the flags and turned to the duty officer for his formal order to march off the quarterdeck to finish the process. The officer nodded to acknowledge him and they all marched off together. At the end of the quarterdeck, the duty officer brought all three of them to a halt and kicked Simms right up the crack of his arse before storming off back to the officers' mess.

Simms limped back to the guardroom to return the whistle and threw up once more when he was just a couple of feet away from the closed sliding window. Inside, we all rolled around in painful fits of laughter. Craig slid the window open and Simms' pale-looking face peered in.

'Cheers, Simms, mate, we owe you one,' laughed Craig.

Simms smiled broadly and then spat a few times on the floor. 'The fucking whistle tasted like shit and that cunt of a duty officer kicked me right up the arse,' frowned Simms.

'We'll see you down the bar when we've finished our duty and the beer is on us,' laughed Craig.

At 7 p.m. that night, I headed down to the bar. I wasn't on duty for a couple of days, so it seemed like a good idea. En route I walked down a narrow path. It was dark and there was very little lighting in that area. As I walked into the darkness, I heard a Marine dog handler called Mick shout a command to his Rottweiler guard dog.

'Stan, seize.'

I turned and in total disbelief watched the guard dog running towards me. Fear ran through me like a bolt of lightning. Everybody in the whole establishment knew who Mick's dog was. It was the most fearsome of all the guard dogs and was a Rottweiler bred with an attitude. I looked for somewhere to run, but knew it was pointless in the few seconds I had. The dog charged towards me and leapt up into the air when it was a mere couple of feet away. My heart was in my mouth as I felt its heavy weight knock me to the ground.

I lay there and felt practically helpless, waiting for the savaging that would follow. The dog sat on my chest and looked at me with its tongue hanging out. Mick rolled around in laughter and then I took a closer look at the dog whose weight prevented me from moving. It wasn't the ferocious Stan, but Mick's own pet Rottweiler that I once saw when I went to his home town for a drink a couple of months before.

'You bastard,' I laughed, as he pulled his dog from my chest and then helped me back onto my feet. It would have been hard to describe how relieved I felt, but I only saw the funny side and continued on my way to the NAAFI bar.

The bar was fairly quiet during that evening and I teamed up with a Marine called Benny. Benny was in his mid-twenties and came from the north-west of England. He had short brown hair and a face covered in freckles. He was about six feet tall with a deceptively skinny build. His performance in the gymnasium showed great inner strength and determination, way beyond what you would expect of someone with his appearance.

He was coming to the end of a nine-year career in the Marines and was only a few weeks away from leaving and joining the prison service. Like the majority of the Marine security detachment, he could drink like a fish and train like a highly tuned athlete the following day.

He introduced me to a couple of well-spoken civilian women whom he had invited into the bar for the evening and then persuaded one of them to invite me back to a house she was staying at, on a nearby posh residential estate. After the bar was closed we all bundled into some sort of mega sports car, which was driven by one of the women. We were quite drunk by then and so chuffed to be driven in such an expensive motor that we bared our buttocks out of the window as we drove past the duty guard. Our actions prompted laughter, wolf whistles and a round of applause from the Marines who looked on, as we drove out past the main gate.

A few minutes later we pulled onto a loose-stone-covered driveway, outside a house the size of a mansion. Wow, I thought, this is posh. One of the girls opened the big wooden door at the front of the house and invited us in behind her. Inside, there was a huge hallway, which must have been the size of my parents' house. We went into a living-room and sat down on a set of hard leather chairs. The room was massive and about the size of the dining hall back at HMS Warrior. A great big log fire blazed away in the background and the rest of the furniture in the room looked like antiques.

Benny pointed out a huge wooden globe and lifted the lid to reveal a hidden set of bottles of spirits. We wasted no time and poured ourselves a couple of large glasses of vodka before sitting down and chatting with our hosts. We sat and talked for a while and the two women referred to me as a commoner. They said I spoke with a working-class accent and dressed like a tramp. I didn't like their attitude towards me and had never been made self-conscious about my appearance before. I did feel quite insulted, as being a Marine was quite often a tough life. We would often have to endure hardship, no water or food for days and no nice warm beds to sleep in. We were only appreciated when wars were being fought or the newspapers wrote articles about us. These people lived in a world where they had everything and I guessed that they'd never really stopped to appreciate it.

After a while, I got fed up with all the snidey comments from the women and left the living-room to use the toilet. I walked down the hallway and pushed open the toilet door. I switched on the light and looked around. I felt flabbergasted at the luxury I saw. There was a huge bath that several people could fit into, two toilets, two sinks, two glass shower units and even glass chandeliers hanging from the ceiling. The floor had a lovely pink carpet with several small light blue rugs fitted around all the utilities.

I needed a crap, so I closed the big wooden door behind me and sat on one of the toilets. I looked around the room and felt quite sickened by the level of luxury that some people could afford. I was also quite pissed off by the way I had been treated and referred to as a commoner.

All these years I'd been training in the wastes of the Arctic, the fury of Northern Ireland and the cat and mouse conflict on the Greek/Turkish border in Cyprus. I'd accepted years of hardship with very little reward and now luxury was staring me in the face with these two ungrateful bitches enjoying it.

When I finished having a crap, I stood up and reached over for the toilet roll. I held a few sheets of it in my hand and felt a softness like I'd never felt before. Even the toilet roll was posh. I looked into the toilet itself and saw that my turds were jet black in colour. This was a familiar sight after a couple of days of drinking Guinness.

I'll show them, I thought. These bastards have all this luxury and I have a hole in my pocket and a hole in my arse. Fuck them; I'll give them something to laugh about. At this, I dropped the soft white tissue paper into the toilet and then proceeded to wipe my buttocks on the light blue and pink carpets. Layers of black crap rubbed off onto their surfaces and I also used the pink and blue curtains to finish the job off.

I smiled as I closed the door behind me, leaving a foul smell behind. Back in the hallway, I could hear Benny arguing with the women. They were calling his accent common and he wasn't very happy about it. He peered out of the living-room and smiled when he saw me.

'Come on, Steve, let's leave these stuck-up slags here and fuck off back to Warrior.'

'Yeah, let's go,' I replied.

Outside, we laughed together. Benny told me he had urinated into a couple of the spirits bottles whilst I was in the toilet and the women were in the kitchen.

'You dirty bastard,' I commented, and Benny just laughed.

CHAPTER TWENTY-NINE

HOME FOR CHRISTMAS

As usual when I arrived home on leave, I dropped my kit bags off and went straight out for a few beers. My mother and father were sat together in their house. They greeted me when I arrived and were in good spirits. When I entered the living-room I observed the familiar sight of one bottle of Olde English Cider for my mother and three or four bottles for my father.

After a brief chat, I left the house and headed for the local pub. To my surprise, my brother Martin was sat on a stool near the bar. He welcomed me with a big smile and a handshake and apologised for his behaviour the last time we had met. I was only too pleased to hear these words and gladly accepted his apology. Following this, he insisted that he bought the beers all night as his way of apologising. We sat down together and chatted amiably about life in general. It felt as if nothing had ever come between us and we had always got on well together.

After we had drank our last beer, we walked back to our parents' home. We wanted to share the good news with them that we had put the past behind us and swept our differences under the carpet. Martin had just turned his key in the front door lock, when we heard a bottle smash inside the house and then our mother scream. This was followed by another smash and a load of offensive abuse being shouted at our mother by our father. A heated argument was taking place. Over the years, this had become a regular occurrence.

'What's going on?' I questioned as I opened the living-room door.

My father was sat in his usual seat next to the fireplace with a twisted sour look on his face. My mother was sat on the other side of the room at the end of the sofa next to the window. Fragments of beer bottle glass covered her head and shoulders as well as the immediate area around her. There were also several small rips in the wallpaper where the bottle had been smashed against the wall. My father swore as he spoke and was obviously very drunk. His aggressive manner, coupled with the onslaught of foul language directed at my mother, annoyed me.

'What are we going to do?' asked Martin.

'Throw him out,' I replied sharply.

I grabbed a handful of his black curly hair and dragged him off his seat, back through the kitchen and outside into the back garden. Once outside, I kept the dragging motion going and hurled him face down onto a muddy patch of soil. He seemed to exaggerate the amount of force I'd used and he groaned loudly as he banged his head against a wooden fence. Without any feelings for him, I turned and walked back inside the house and locked the door behind me.

'He's coming back,' shouted Martin, who was peering out of the kitchen window.

CCRRRAAAAASSHH. The door caved in and crashed onto

the floor with my father on top of it. The heavy frame of the door missed my head by millimetres.

'Fucking hell,' I exclaimed quietly, with my eyebrows raised high.

I then switched off the lights, so that the room was in darkness and grabbed hold of one of his arms and twisted it up behind his back.

'Aaarrrgggghhhh,' he cried out in pain.

'Yes, pain bloody hurts, doesn't it?' I snarled and increased the pressure to hear him scream again.

'OK,' I growled. 'I'll leave you alone if you leave my mother alone. She's suffered enough pain through you, hasn't she?'

I twisted his arm further.

'Aaarrggghh. Yes, yes, she has.'

Martin switched the lights back on and I released the tight grip on my father's arm, before pulling him up hard to his feet and sending him upstairs to bed like a scolded child.

Martin and myself did what we could to repair the damaged door and re-attached it to the splintered door frame. We saw that our mother was sat crying in the living-room so we cleared the many pieces of glass away from around her body and I gave her a reassuring cuddle to let her know the danger was over.

Martin made three hot cups of coffee and we sat together to work at calming down her emotions and making her feel more comfortable and secure. It was a sad state of affairs, but my father's intolerant behaviour was a regular occurrence throughout the many years of our family's life.

Christmas Day came a week later. My mother and father had made up their differences and things were running smoothly again. Peter was home that day and he socialised with me prior to us heading home for Christmas dinner with our parents. We always sat down for dinner at approximately

2 p.m. and usually invited several of our friends around for a small party at 5 p.m., before heading off to the local boozer to carry it on until the early hours of Boxing Day.

Christmas dinner was a sight for sore eyes. My mother always made a big effort and the event always felt very special. Steam billowed up into the air from the perfectly cooked turkey, and mouth-watering vegetables filled our plates, complete with a lovely thick gravy. My father sat quietly at the table. He was in his usual drunken state, but for once he seemed in control. Unfortunately, Martin had decided not to join us as he had accepted a previous invitation from his mother-in-law. However, we did have a female guest called Rebecca. She was Peter's girlfriend. She was a petite woman, with short brown hair and a very freckly face. She seemed nice, but I knew very little about her. There was still one spare empty place left at the table, but Mother always set this for Santa Claus just in case he dropped in.

When we were all seated and dinner was served, Mother asked me to stand up and propose a toast. I gladly accepted the honour and stood up and raised my wine glass.

'Here's to a happy and joyful Christmas.'

'A happy and joyful Christmas,' everybody replied.

Our glasses chinked as we individually toasted each other and then we tucked into our scrumptious meal. Initially, there was very little conversation as we were too keen to eat our food, but afterwards we all sat and talked for a while. The mood was good and, for the first time in years, I felt at ease and relaxed. It was good to be home.

A couple of hours later, we cleared the dinner table and cleaned up, before our friends arrived a short time later. Each of them brought a bottle of alcohol of one kind or another and was dressed in fancy dress. We turned up the volume of the music and got everybody into the party mood. Smiling and happy faces filled the living-room and dining room and everyone sang Christmas songs together. My father was drunk and sat motionless with his head facing flat down on the dining room table, where he snored heavily.

The only incident that occurred was when I saw Peter push his girlfriend onto the floor during a brief argument. When he saw that I was watching him, he put his hands in the air before reaching out with his hands to help her back onto her feet. Nevertheless, the party carried on and turned out to be a great success.

At eight o'clock, we thanked my mother for her kind hospitality and made our way along to one of the local pubs. They too were hosting a party, for which we had all bought tickets. Inside, everything was in full swing. There were already a lot of people having fun and this got even better as we seemed to bring our happy party mood along with us. The atmosphere was electric: party poppers were being cracked every few minutes, filling the air with colourful streamers, and loud seasonal music pounded out of the new flashing jukebox.

Much later, things calmed down and a lot of people had gone home. I looked around the room to see who was still present and noticed Rebecca sat crying a few tables away. I looked for Peter but couldn't see him anywhere, so I went over to ask her why she was crying and where Peter was.

'Peter slapped me,' she sobbed.

'Hit you . . . why?' I exclaimed in a surprised fashion.

'I don't know,' she replied.

This made me angry as it reminded me of my father's behaviour. Was Peter becoming a wife-beater too, I wondered. I shook my head. 'I'm going to bloody hammer him,' I snarled, and stormed out of the pub.

My party and Christmas spirit withered away and I felt

very annoyed. He's a wife-beater just like my father, I thought. I'm going to knock it out of him. When I arrived back home, the house was in darkness and everybody had gone to bed. I switched on the living-room light and looked around. Both the downstairs rooms looked like a bomb had hit them. There were empty pint glasses and half-full beer bottles scattered all over the floor, along with loads of party streamers and pieces of food. Also, a strong smell of stale beer rose up into my nostrils from the carpeted floors. I crept quietly upstairs in the darkness and the floorboards creaked gently under my body weight. Peter's bedroom door was open and I could hear him quietly snoring.

'Peter . . . Peter,' I whispered, but he didn't stir.

'Peter . . . Peter,' I growled as I grabbed hold of him by his hair and shook him violently.

'Aaarrrrgggghhh, arrrrgghhh,' he cried out. 'What are you doing this for?'

'Why did you beat your girlfriend? Why did you beat your girlfriend?' I questioned in a heated voice.

'I don't know, Steve. I don't know,' he whimpered tearfully.

At that, my anger took over and I tightened the grip on his hair. He cried out in pain, but I wasn't listening. I dragged him out of bed by his hair and pulled his half-naked body down the stairs.

'No, Steve, no, please, no,' he cried out as I began to repeatedly punch and kick him around on the floor. Blood poured from his mouth and nose and formed a pool on the floor.

'Fucking woman-beater,' I shouted and kicked him one last time.

Then I stopped. I could feel my heart pounding and my pulse racing as I panted for breath. Peter rolled around on the floor crying and holding his wounded face.

'Get up . . . get up and go back to bed. You're a pathetic piece of shit,' I shouted.

He got up slowly and looked at me. He looked sorry, but also confused. Blood dripped down his badly bruised face. I told him to go upstairs and bathe his wounds and followed him into the bathroom. He sniffed and groaned when he splashed cold water onto his face and wiped it with a sponge. For a moment, I drifted back to my early days at 45 Commando and the night when I was dragged out of bed and beaten and I thought about the feeling of being hurt and the sorrow. Then I thought of the many times I had seen my father beat my mother and throw her around the room like a rag doll. No, he deserves it, I thought.

Following this, I went back downstairs and slept on the sofa. Early next morning, I awoke around 6.30 a.m. and got dressed into my PT kit and went for my usual run along the beach.

My head ached as I ran, but I pushed on and ran against the cold wind that blew in off the sea. After a few miles, I turned around and ran back towards home with the wind behind me. I was sweating heavily because I always trained hard, but also because I had drunk so much beer the night before. At 10.45 a.m., I got washed and changed and was still the only member of the household who was out of bed. I felt fresh and wide awake and was ready to enjoy some more of my home leave in the pub where we had been partying the night before.

It was quiet inside and only a few of the hardened drinkers sat on stools near the bar with their beer glasses full. I ordered a beer and pulled up a stool next to a lad I knew called Phil.

'Where's your Pete?' he smiled.

'Why?' I replied with a sense of curiosity.

'Oh, I thought he'd have been sat here with us by now.'

'No, he's still in bed,' I frowned.

'He had a rough time with that bloody girlfriend of his last night, didn't he?'

'Yes,' I agreed. 'The pillock slapped her for nothing.'

'Nothing?' gasped Phil. 'I saw her punch him in the face at least four times before he hit her back.'

'Are you sure?' I asked.

'Positive, Steve, she's a nasty one that one.'

I drank the rest of my pint of beer and buried my head in the palm of my hands. Tears slowly dripped down my face and I felt a deep, deep sorrow. I was wrong and now knew why Pete had looked so confused when I beat him. What could I say to him, though? The word 'sorry' seemed totally inadequate. I left the pub and walked home. Peter was leaving the house when I arrived. He didn't look at me, but I could see that his face was badly cut and swollen, along with a big fat black eye, which looked more like a septic lump of meat. We passed in the doorway and he calmly shut the door behind him on his way out. I sat alone in the quiet house. I held my face in my hands and sobbed heavily.

Unlike Martin, Peter had never tried to hurt me. He was proud of me when I became a Marine and was a great friend as well as a brother. What had I done? Everything had turned to rat shit and it was all my own fault. There was only one answer and that was going back to where I belonged, with the Marines. I sadly packed my bags and left, with great regret about my actions the night before.

Back at HMS Warrior, everybody was full of Christmas spirit and in the party mood. That is, everybody who wasn't on guard duty. I wasn't the only one who had returned from leave early and we all quickly got organised and arranged a night in the NAAFI bar disco, followed by a party in the Marines' accommodation block. Everybody was invited on the condition that they brought copious amounts of beer.

The Marines totally emptied one of the four-man rooms and put together a makeshift bar, made up of a couple of tables and a big long wooden board. Huge white camouflage nets, which were normally used in the Arctic during the Cold War, were draped down from the ceiling with colourful Christmas decorations attached. Somebody had provided a big ghetto-blaster, and there was a Christmas tree from some mysterious source. The room looked great.

There was a massive supply of beer bottles and cans stacked against one of the walls and plenty of beer glasses, which were provided by the NAAFI staff, who were also invited. We scheduled our party to start at 11.15 p.m. after both the NAAFI bar and a nearby pub called the Reindeer had closed. We then called the dog section and sped off down to the pub. Inside, it was bouncing with excitement, with '60s-style music being played on the jukebox and hordes of people dancing the night away, having a good time.

I drank with Diz and a huge Marine called Big Mac. He was over six feet tall with jet-black hair and built like a brick shit-house. A partially bald-headed Marine called Gerry also joined us. He was a fairly quiet man and rarely came out to socialise because he was married and lived with his wife, just a few miles from the NATO base. He joked with me about the police statement from my night at the US Marine base, and then he asked me to hold onto his pint of beer whilst he visited the toilet.

The vast numbers of people made the pub atmosphere hot and sticky. I saw sweat dripping from a lot of people's brows and down their faces. Diz was sweating too and playfully used my shirtsleeve to mop his soaking wet forehead. My old girlfriend Lucy appeared and called me a piece of shit. I told her to fuck off and then she told me to fuck off. I warned her that if she didn't leave me alone I would pour my beer over her. Then she told me I was full of shit, so I spat in her face and threw both mine and Gerry's beer over her head. She immediately looked like a drowned rat and ran out of the pub, scowling.

I saw a Wren who was a friend of mine approaching. She waved as she pushed her way through the crowd towards me, along with a group of females. I acknowledged her greeting and took the invitation to join her in conversation. She and her friends were in good spirits and joked about my falling asleep a few weeks before whilst having sex with her after a night on the town. She did admit I satisfied her needs when I awoke the following morning, but said it was a whole new experience for her.

A commotion coming from the toilet area attracted my attention. I couldn't see past all the people around me, but I could hear Diz's voice shouting aggressively. I was concerned that there was trouble for my friends and stood on top of a nearby table to get a better look beyond the crowd. Diz was going wild and a fight was in progress. I saw a long-haired man shaking his fists at him. Then a forceful blow thrown by Diz bust the man's nose and knocked him to the floor. Several other men with long hair joined in the fight and it looked obvious that they weren't service personnel.

A tall skinny man with long black hair ran out of the crowd towards Big Mac. He had something held in his hand, but I couldn't make out what it was. Then he raised it into the air to reveal a heavy beer glass with a handle on it. He smashed it hard onto Big Mac's head, who was currently busy punching somebody he had grabbed hold of. The glass smashed into pieces and amazingly Mac didn't flinch. He turned to the assailant and told him he was going to kill him after he had finished with the man he was beating with his big fists. Mac hit this man one more time and turned towards the attacker who had hit him with the beer glass. The attacker understandably seemed to turn white with fear.

'You had better start running,' warned Mac, as he raised his fists.

The young man took his advice and sprinted out of the exit door. Mac laughed loudly before giving chase. Meanwhile, Diz was still engaged in fighting against three others, so I decided to even the odds a little and steamed in with a flying head-butt which went straight into one of their faces. Blood splashed everywhere across his face and I followed up with another head-butt into his nose, which I felt crunch under the force of the blow.

Diz continued to fight with the other two and quickly knocked them both to the ground. There was blood everywhere and all the long-haired men bolted for the exit door together. They were beaten. Big Mac returned victorious a short time later and helped me calm Diz's temper down before we put the incident behind us and continued to enjoy the evening.

When the pub closed, we returned to Gurkha block to start our party, where everybody was dancing, drinking and having loads of fun. The atmosphere was great and everybody was laughing. I was feeling quite merry and tired so I decided to leave to get some sleep. The corridor outside was fairly quiet and the noise from the party became faint as I walked further away. A door in front of me creaked open and a Marine called Gruff stood staring at me with a serious look on his face. I'd known Gruff for over a year, but didn't get on with him. He was a loner and usually acted more like an old woman, moaning all the time, than a Marine. I moved to walk past him and he stood in my way.

'What's up?' I asked cautiously.

'You're always fighting with people, aren't you?' he snarled.

'So what?' I snapped.

'Why don't you have a fight with me?' he suggested and pointed to himself.

'Fuck off, tosspot, or I'll kick your fucking head in,' I snapped.

'Come on then, do it,' he beckoned.

I didn't need telling twice and threw an array of punches into his head and face. He returned one half-decent punch which spun me around, but I easily regained my balance and continued to fight him. Several Marines appeared from the party area and jumped in between us. They tactfully separated us and two of them escorted me outside the building and calmed my aggression down. They said Gruff was a tosser and that he wasn't worth it. I agreed with their comments but insisted that they should let me finish what Gruff had started.

After a few minutes of discussion and a mutual agreement that I was right, I headed back into the building to find Gruff. When I reached his room door it was locked, so I forced it open and off its hinges with a couple of shoulder charges. Gruff stood against the back wall with his hands in the air.

'I don't want a fight, I've made a mistake, a mistake,' he pleaded.

I looked at him for a few moments. 'Fucking tosser,' I sighed and turned and left.

Later, back in my own room, I locked the door and got undressed. I pondered the events of the past few days and shook my head as I climbed into bed. What a fucking week this has been, I thought, and closed my eyes and went to sleep.

CHAPTER THIRTY

ROYAL MARINES POLICE (RMP)

After two years' service with the NATO security detachment and a total of five years' service in the Marines, I had been granted a request for a career change to join the Royal Marines police (RMP). A lot of the other Marines found this quite amusing as I did have a reputation for being a reprobate, and a military policeman's career was the last thing that anybody thought I would choose. However, the quota system I had been on required a three-year return of service before I could leave the Marines, and joining the military police was, to my mind, a good way of serving my time without going back to the clerical branch.

In May 1988, I reported to Stonehouse Barracks in Plymouth along with about ten other Marines who had signed up for the RMP training course. The Royal Marines police were only thirty strong in personnel across the world and were normally assisted by both Army and Navy military policemen, who were a lot greater in number.

The course was sixteen weeks long and consisted of six weeks of studying military law with the Army's Royal

Military Police in Chichester, four weeks of vehicle driving and motorbike training at a Royal Marines establishment in Poole, three weeks' administration skills training at HMS Raleigh near Plymouth and three weeks' radio communications training at the Royal Marines Commando Training Centre in Lympstone.

The course was very interesting and involved a lot of studying, especially in the area of military law. During this phase of the course we were based at Chichester with the Royal Military Police (the redcaps). We all gelled quite well as a team except for one young Marine called Bernie. He was an eighteen-year-old who had very little experience of being a Marine as he'd only just passed out of basic training a couple of months before.

A black Marine called Kes, who was a good friend of mine, had previously befriended him. Kes and I served together in Northern Ireland and were very close friends. He had asked me to keep an eye on Bernie and said he was OK. However, Bernie's suitability to be accepted as one of our group was questionable. Nobody liked his sense of humour and he seemed immature for his age. Our first impressions gained him no points as we watched him rub his hands when the redcaps spoke about arresting soldiers and locking them up. The rest of us had several years' service under our belts and knew only too well that Marines let off steam from time to time. Arresting them for trivial offences resulting from this would be unfair.

This young man was a new breed. He hadn't really served much time as a Marine, or any time in a commando unit, and had wanted to be a policeman for one reason only, which was to add notches to his belt. Every Marine he could arrest would be a new notch for him.

I found the military law phase very interesting and began

to realise just how lucky I had been to get away with all the trouble I had caused over the years. However, sometimes we found the rules and law difficult to digest. From a Marine's point of view, we learnt that you could be arrested for a lot of antics that happened every day: antics that you readily accepted as part of the Marine lifestyle, such as getting drunk in your spare time and the odd bar-room brawl here and there.

We found the redcaps to be a different kettle of fish to us, as they joined the Army specifically to be policemen and seemed to be very proud of arresting Army ranks for any offence. They openly bragged about using excessive force to restrain the suspect or offender.

On a couple of occasions, our different lifestyles clashed. The course instructor accused me of having a guilty conscience because I never looked him straight in the eye when he was addressing the classroom. He was a bit shocked when I told him that he would probably get a good kicking if he looked at some of the other Marines the wrong way back in the commando units. On another occasion, he explained how he would arrest a squaddie (soldier) and throw him into the back of a military police van and then jump in behind him and kick him a few times. When he asked what the reason was for the resulting classroom silence, one of the Marines informed him that if he kicked a Marine in that fashion, the Marine would probably come looking for him sometime during the next day to return the compliment. He frowned and rubbed his chin.

Other differences were things such as physical training sessions. Royal Marines had a reputation for being exceptionally fit and we stood out from the crowd. Our dress and standard of cleanliness were always immaculate compared to the standard produced by Army ranks. This was always thrashed into us, right from the very start of our careers during our basic training. We were told that more ranks were killed during the Second World War from diseases caused by poor hygiene and a poor standard of cleanliness than were actually killed in battle. A sick or dying man on the battlefield is no good to the cause of winning a war.

During the training course, we got very little time to socialise and had to spend many late nights working on mock case-file scenarios and writing witness statements. It was hard work, but enjoyable. Bernie, however, did not get on with anybody and his lack of experience in the Marines showed. He continued to annoy most of us as he frequently commented about looking forward to making his first arrest. This caused a lot of uneasiness amongst our group as we'd all served on active duty in various places around the world and had made many friends within our corps. We were adamant that once we were qualified Royal Marines policemen, we would be lenient with drunks, reserved with fights, yet ruthless with thieves.

Bernie's attitude caused me a lot of headaches. Most of the other Marines wanted to beat him up for one reason or another, but I always put up resistance and protected him. I did get fed up from time to time and eventually telephoned my mate Kes to tell him how I felt. Kes told me that he had only served with him for a couple of weeks and would like to withdraw his request for me to look after him. I thanked him for his understanding and told everybody that Bernie would look after himself from now on.

At the end of the military law phase we went for a night out in Chichester. There were about seven of us in a group. We came across a wine bar and went inside. The interior was quite small, but the bar was quite busy. I noticed that a lot of people were drinking jugs of sangria. As I queued for a drink, I saw that the bar staff put lots of ice and fruit into the jugs, which meant that you actually had less volume of sangria. I was quick to switch on to this and asked for a jug of sangria with no ice and no fruit. A couple of the other Marines looked on and one of them made a comment. 'No fruit and no ice, because you get more in.'

'That's right, you get more in,' I smiled.

Then everybody started to buy jugs of sangria, repeating the slogan, 'No fruit and no ice because you get more in.' We all found this very funny, except the bar staff who really had no choice but to give us the value for money we asked for. A couple of jugs later, we were joined by another Marine, called Roddy. He was about the same age as me but fairly quiet. Roddy was a pleasant fellow, who didn't really drink alcohol. He asked what we were drinking and I told him it was a fruit juice called sangria. He smiled, licked his lips and ordered a jug.

As the night wore on, he seemed to get absolutely polatic on the sangria and we ended up having to carry him back to the barracks and put him to bed. Meanwhile, back in the barrack room, Bernie continued to piss everybody off with his poor attitude and tempers were beginning to flare. One of the other Marines threatened him and he stood next to me.

'Don't expect me to pull you out of the shit, you wanker,' I snarled.

His face dropped. 'Fuck you,' he snapped.

This upset me. I had stopped the others from beating him up on many occasions. On this occasion, however, I head-butted him hard on his forehead. I wanted to hurt him because I didn't like him either. However, I knew the head-butt directed at the forehead would not mark him and that he would get the message to get lost. He did get the message and stormed off back to his own room.

A couple of off-duty Army redcaps joined us for a cup of tea and we told them about our problem. We all hated Bernie and didn't want him finishing the course so that he could arrest our friends. We also knew that we would be kicked off the course for assault if we really did give him the beating we wanted to. With this in mind, I asked the two redcaps if they would go to his room and beat him up if we dropped them a few quid. They found this hilarious and agreed to do it for £15. When they entered his room, they began to shout at him, psyching themselves up for what was to follow. We watched through the open door as they started to taunt him. Then he started to cry like a little boy. The two redcaps quickly calmed down and bottled out of the beating they were supposed to give him. They shook their heads and walked out of the room. On the way out, one of them spoke to us.

'Sorry, lads, he's crying like a little immature kid. He's petrified. How on earth did he get through the Marines' basic training?'

'We don't know,' we answered together and shook our heads.

The following morning, I heard Roddy groan as he sat up in bed. Then he started shouting and cursing at himself as he went into the bathroom to get washed. A horrible foul smell came from his bed space area, so we went over to have a look. After a quick investigation, we all burst into laughter. The reason he wasn't happy was because he had been so drunk on the sangria that he had lost control of his bodily functions, and pieces of vomit, excrement and a wet patch of urine covered his mattress.

'Uuuurrrrggggghhhh,' we all laughed.

At the end of the course, we were awarded our specialist qualification as part of our graduation as Royal Marines policemen and were each assigned to police duties in various parts of the world.

The year was 1988 and the civilian prison officers had gone on strike. Consequently, I was chosen to report for prison duties at a prison on a converted RAF base in Deepcut, Surrey. (I don't know whether or not this base ever came to have any relation to the Deepcut Army Barracks, which are infamous nowadays, of course, due to the controversial military deaths there.) The prison held category-three civilian prisoners, who weren't regarded as being very dangerous. Because of the strike, the regular Army also sent some of its soldiers. These were assigned to guard duties on the perimeter of the prison, while the various forms of military police were assigned to the interior of the prison, policing the prisoners. The prison establishment looked more like a scene from Colditz than a civilian prison.

There were eight single-storey prison blocks, which were labelled alphabetically from A to H. Their appearance reminded me of the Maze prison, which was used to confine Irish prisoners back in Northern Ireland. The difference was that, because this building was part of an ex-RAF base, its interiors were laid out more like a military barracks than the usual prison cells that you see. Each prisoner had a small locker, a bed with a single sheet and blanket, a plastic cup, a plastic knife, spoon and fork, and they all wore the same clothes.

The main thing that struck me was that the black prisoners were segregated at night and confined to the H block. They could mix during exercise breaks, but this was very rare as it often caused trouble. This was symptomatic of a whole feeling of tension from the prisoners. They were like caged heat, waiting to burn up. Tempers often flared and we had to pull prisoners apart and separate them. The good thing was that they didn't hate us. In their eyes, we weren't screws (civilian prison officers) and only did this job because we had to. I did find a few of them quite humorous and was astounded at the number of them who claimed they were innocent of the crimes of which they had been convicted.

One of the prisoners, who came from Glasgow, claimed he had abseiled down a block of flats in Edinburgh during the early hours of one cold winter morning. He said his rope got tangled up and it forced him to climb into a flat through an open window. When he got inside, a woman passed him a sack full of money and jewellery and then started screaming, so he bolted out through the flat door and straight into a policeman who nicked him for burglary and breaking and entering. Rough justice, I thought!

After a few days, I began to settle into my new job and to get used to the duties associated with running a prison. One evening, I saw one of the cons pushing something into a small hole above one of the door panels. He then placed a piece of plaster over it to conceal it. After he had gone, I removed the piece of plaster to satisfy my curiosity. Inside the hole, I discovered a small pipe, which resembled a peace pipe, smoked by the American Indians. I guessed it must be something that they smoked drugs with and placed it back in the hole and replaced the piece of plaster.

About an hour or so later, a different prisoner came to the same place and removed the pipe from the hole. I followed him into one of the day rooms. Inside, I saw several prisoners sat together around a table, each taking a turn puffing smoke from the pipe. They noticed me as I entered and tucked the pipe away. Then they started to waft the smoke away using their hands. They looked disappointed that they had been caught and waited to hear what I had to say to them.

'That's a strange smell, gentlemen, has someone got smelly feet?' I asked. All their eyebrows raised and they all smiled at each other.

'Yeah,' one of them replied. 'Some of these filthy bastards have got smelly feet. It stinks, doesn't it?'

'Hhhhmmm,' I nodded. 'I don't care if your feet smell. Just as long as there's no trouble.'

'Yeah, no trouble, boss. No trouble,' they mumbled.

Following this, they started to treat me with a fair bit of respect. They spoke to me with ease and told me about their lifestyles and the mistakes which led to them being imprisoned. A lot of them were sentenced for drug-related issues with sentences ranging from six months to five years. Some were in for a second or even a third custodial sentence for smuggling and dealing in drugs. They said the money they were paid was too good to pass up and swore they would go straight back to the drug scene as soon as they were released again.

One night, I was stood in the exercise yard near an eight-foot interior fence, which bordered the dining hall. It was starting to get dark and I noticed one of the inmates was hanging around suspiciously. I asked him what he was doing and he said he was out for a bit of fresh air. Suddenly, a door creaked open from the kitchen next to the dining hall on the other side of an internal perimeter fence. Another inmate, who was on kitchen duties, appeared, carrying a box in his arms. He walked over to the fence and went to throw the box over.

'Whoops,' he exclaimed when he saw me on the other side of the fence. He cancelled his plan and turned to go back into the kitchen.

'Hey, mate,' I shouted. 'Throw it over.'

He smiled and threw the box over the fence. I caught it and had a quick look at its contents. I saw that it contained a few tins of curry, boiled potatoes and peas, and I passed it to the other con who was still having some fresh air.

Later, one of the cons I had made friends with came into my office and invited me into the day room for a curry and a chat. I was bored and hungry so I gladly accepted the invitation. They made me welcome and thanked me for turning a blind eye and allowing them to steal the food. During the meal our conversation came around to a problem that had occurred between two of the prison blocks. One of the blocks contained a lot of the black and Asian prisoners and the other contained white prisoners. Apparently, a couple of inmates from each block had been given a serious beating. The prisoners were adamant that the black and Asian prisoners were uneasy about the situation and had planned to riot at 2 a.m. the following morning. I listened with interest, but felt unsure as to whether to believe them or not. It wouldn't have been the first time they had tried to pull the wool over my eyes.

After the curry, I left and shared the information I had gained with a few of the other military policemen from the Air Force, Army and Navy. They all sat in our office with their arms folded and shook their heads. One of them laughed and said we should ignore anything that the cons said to us. I sat for a while and drank my tea. I would look stupid if I got it wrong, I thought. Nevertheless, I felt uneasy about the situation and walked around one of the corridors wondering what to do. If I did nothing and nothing happened, that would be fine. If I did nothing and something happened, that wouldn't, yet if I did something and nothing happened, I would be left looking like a prat.

I walked outside into the now dark exercise yard and looked in through the small dimly lit windows into the prisoners' dormitories. I watched them walking around and pacing up and down. They looked nervous and one of them kept looking at his watch.

Bollocks, I thought. One of the assistant governors is due

on his rounds at 1 a.m.; I'll report the incident to him. I spoke with the other military policemen and they said they didn't want to say anything about what I had been told.

'I'll do the talking and if I'm wrong I'll take the blame,' I said.

At 12.55 a.m., the door to our office opened and an assistant governor entered, along with a Royal Military Police sergeant. The assistant governor was a tall, skinny man, around fifty-plus years old with a balding head. He sat on a vacant chair on the opposite side of the table I was sitting at and asked us all if we had anything to report. As he spoke, I picked up a strong smell of alcohol and realised from his breath and dilated eyeballs that he was under the influence. Everybody except me shook their heads.

'Right, I'll be off then,' he said in a broad Brummie accent.

'Er, one minute please,' I interrupted, anxiously raising my hand to signal him to wait and listen to what I had to say.

'Yes,' he frowned with his thick bushy eyebrows raised.

'I have something to report. A couple of the cons have told me that there's been some trouble between a couple of the cell blocks and that the block that contains the black and Asian prisoners is going to riot at two o'clock in the morning.'

He sighed deeply before sitting back down at the table opposite me. He clasped his hands together and leant over towards me. He looked very serious.

'Do you fucking realise, now that you've fucking told me this, I'll have to get the fucking governor out of bed and he won't be fucking happy,' he snarled.

'This man is intoxicated,' I snapped to the sergeant who put his head down and looked at the floor. I looked back at the assistant governor.

'I'll tell you what, drunken arse,' I snarled. 'You fucking

stop here and wait for the fucking riot to start and I'll get the fucking governor out of fucking bed and I don't fucking care if he's not fucking impressed. OK?' I finished.

I don't know if it was because I sounded convincing or because I had mentioned the fact that he was intoxicated, but he agreed. Twenty minutes later, we were joined by the governor, who asked me to produce the prisoners who had given me the information and he then talked to them in private. Without hesitation, the block which contained the black and Asian prisoners was cordoned off with barbed concertina wire and some of the soldiers who were guarding the perimeter fence were brought inside to boost our numbers. All the military personnel, including myself, were dressed in riot gear and held riot shields and batons. At exactly 2 a.m., windows were smashed and a large group of black and Asian prisoners stormed out of their block shouting and screaming threatening words. As we came into view, they gasped at the sight of the waiting reception guard and stopped dead in their tracks. They looked at each other and seemed unsure of what to do. The governor intervened with a loudspeaker and ordered the prisoners back into their cells. Slowly, they backed off and returned inside their block without any further incident.

Thankfully, my information was correct, and my actions had earned the governor's gratitude. The assistant governor was moved to another prison a few days later.

This was the pinnacle of my six-week tour of duty at the prison. When it was over, I was reassigned to military police duties and deployed onto my fourth tour of the Arctic (which was a summer and autumn tour, unlike the previous winter ones). During this period, my social life was practically non-existent, so I intended to make up for it as soon as I returned to Plymouth.

CHAPTER THIRTY-ONE

THE INCIDENT

It was Tuesday, 25 October 1988. Shadows loomed in the corridors of the Marine accommodation block at Stonehouse Barracks in Plymouth. The Royal Marines military police occupied a large room on the second floor of a three-storey building, within which I was allocated a bed space on my return from the Arctic. Two other military policemen also occupied the room, both of whom I had previously worked with. One was called Mossey Carter. He was a fairly senior Marine with at least ten years' service under his belt. He was a short stocky man with bright blond wavy hair that was shaved around the back and sides. He was generally a very pleasant guy to get along with and was very popular with the ladies. The other was Bernie, who was the immature Marine with whom I had had the misfortune of working on my military police training course.

When I entered the room, I was greeted by Mossey, who was sat casually watching the television. He shook my hand and welcomed me back. 'Welcome back, Steve. How was the Arctic?'

'Cold.'

We both smiled and then arranged to meet up later at a pub called The Tube in Plymouth's infamous Union Street, at around 10 p.m. He said he would be accompanied by Bernie, which I wasn't too happy about as I'd heard he was still very immature. However, I realised he had become a friend of Mossey's so I nodded in agreement as I left the room. I headed for another pub in Union Street called the Prince Regent. Sam Olsen, a former Marine colleague of mine, had left the Marines a couple of years before to begin a new career as a mercenary in Angola. We were very close friends and had been in touch via the telephone. The last time I had seen him was over a year prior to this, when he had returned from his mercenary job abroad. During that meeting, he pulled a roll of fifty pound notes out of his coat pocket and put it into my hand. He told me that the roll contained a thousand pounds and said that he wanted me to have it. I smiled and declined the offer. I told him that our friendship was worth more than any roll of money he could offer me. Anyway, during our last telephone conversation, we had agreed to meet up once again at 7 p.m. that evening. Sam told me that if he didn't turn up at this time, his current mission would have been a failure and he would probably be dead.

I reached the Prince Regent public house at approximately 7 p.m. Inside, it was virtually empty and none of the faces I saw were familiar. Nonetheless, I ordered a beer and sat on a stool next to the bar. I waited until 7.30 p.m. but there was still no sign of Sam. Maybe he's been delayed, I thought. The place was still empty so I decided to go to the pool hall across the road to shoot some pool. The pool hall was full of civilians who warmly accepted my request to join them to play a few games. The pool hall didn't sell alcoholic drinks, so at 9.30 p.m. I bid the civilians farewell and headed back to the Prince

Regent pub to see if Sam had turned up. By this time, the pub was fairly crowded, but there was still no sign of my friend, so I purchased another beer and sat for a while.

At 10 p.m., I decided that Sam wasn't going to turn up and made my way across the road into The Tube wine bar to meet Mossey and Bernie as planned. Inside the busy bar, the atmosphere was warm and friendly. Mossey and Bernie had already arrived and were sat on stools around a table next to the bar. I smiled at them and bought myself a beer and sat down. Both men were in good spirits and we talked about our military experiences over the last few months. Bernie was boasting about several fights he had had in an effort to try to impress me. Mossey filled in the missing details from Bernie's accounts for me, explaining that Bernie had really made an arse of himself and had started several fights and come second in all of them. I shook my head and expressed my disapproval at his immaturity. He told me that he was sorry for the trouble he had caused and that he needed me to teach him how to box so that he could defend himself in a better fashion. I shook my head again and told him that he should only get involved in fights with people when someone caused trouble with him, and not because he felt that he'd got something to prove to people.

Shortly afterwards, we visited a couple of other pubs and then made our way to a nightclub called Boobs. This was a very busy place and more commonly known as a cattle market, as the women that frequented it were nicknamed cows and were very easy to get off with. We queued outside the club and I told Bernie how disappointed I was with his attitude whilst I'd been away. He shrugged his shoulders to this and agreed he still had a lot to learn.

Inside, the club was busy. There was a small wooden dance floor surrounded by walls covered with mirrors, and a long bar at the far end of it. A doorway was situated on the left-hand side of the dance floor, which led to a couple of bars upstairs. We made our way to the bar and bought a round of drinks. Within minutes of our arrival, Mossey was busy chatting up a stunning-looking woman and Bernie and I were left to talk together. During our conversation, I told Bernie that he really needed to learn to judge situations better, especially when it came to getting involved in street fights. He repeated that he wanted me to teach him how to fight like a boxer so that he could defend himself better and said that he would listen to the advice that I gave him. After we finished our pint of beer, I told Bernie I was going to the bar to buy another round and would be back in a couple of minutes.

When I returned, Bernie was no longer stood where I had left him, so I looked around the room. I saw him stood on the edge of the wooden dance floor next to a gaming machine. He was involved in a heated argument with a man about the same height, build and age as me. The man looked like a sailor. I was pretty good at judging this as my many years of experience taught me the things that made them stand out, such as the way they dressed and the type of haircut they had. I saw Bernie throw a punch at the sailor, which missed by a mile, and then the sailor grabbed him by the throat. I rapidly put down the two beer glasses I was holding and steamed in, pushing the sailor away from Bernie and onto the floor. I shouted at the sailor to back off and he got up and walked away to play on the gaming machine.

I decided that it would be best for us to keep out of trouble, because, realistically, we were military policemen now. With this, I suggested that we should both leave and head back to barracks. Bernie agreed, so we informed Mossey of our intentions and left the club together. On the way back, we walked along the backstreets, which led past the perimeter wall of the Marines' Stonehouse Barracks. The wall varied in height from four to six feet on the side we were on but dropped to about thirty or forty feet on the other side. I felt quite drunk and staggered a little as we walked. We discussed the events of the evening and I told Bernie that I wasn't very happy with his attitude as he'd caused the trouble but couldn't back it up.

He was very upset about this and went into a strange silence. Suddenly, he laughed and clipped the back of my head with the palm of his hand. I laughed too and did the same thing to him. Then I felt a foot trip me from the side and I fell down heavily onto the hard stone pavement. My momentum caused me to slide along the floor on my face and bare arms. I felt a bit stunned but quickly looked up to see if Bernie was backing me up against whoever had tripped me over. Then, to my total astonishment, I saw Bernie stood above me with his fists clenched. He was looking at me and laughing.

'Har har har, fucking so-called hard man,' he laughed.

'What? What are you playing at?' I frowned.

'You're telling me I can't fight. Come on then, big man, let's fight.'

I reacted instantly and palmed his boot away as he hurled a kick towards me. This temporarily threw him off balance, giving me enough time to get back on my feet. He steadied himself and started to run around me in circles, jumping in and out like a boxer and throwing punches, which I managed to block. I couldn't believe what I was seeing, but almost exploded with anger.

'Come on then, fuckdust, let's fight,' I screamed aggressively.

He ran in towards me and threw a sharp right punch, which I parried downwards with my right hand. Then I lunged forward with a forceful head-butt, which connected with his cheekbone around the area of his eye. He fell backwards under the blow and hard against the wall behind. Without pausing to stop and think I ran forward at him, grabbing hold of his throat with my left hand and his leg with my right. We were at the lowest point of the wall and the force of the grab caused him to pivot on the top edge of the wall. I momentarily held him there. He couldn't speak or scream because of the grip I had on his throat. I released the grip on his leg and used that hand to grab a hold of his jacket.

'Do you want to go over? Do you want to fucking die?' I screamed at him.

He shook his head. I paused for a moment and then released the grip on his throat to allow him to come back over to this side of the wall. At this moment, he turned and twisted out of his coat, leaving it hanging in my grip. He jogged a few feet away and turned to look back at me. His face was badly swollen and blood trickled from his lips. I threw his coat into his arms.

'Come on, Bernie, let's go back to barracks and get cleaned up,' I pleaded.

This felt like the best thing to do as things had got out of control and it was time to get cleaned up.

'No, no,' he shouted. 'I'm going to get you done for assaulting a Royal Marines policeman.'

'Don't be fucking stupid, you hit me first,' I replied.

He ran off into the distance and occasionally looked back at me. Oh, bollocks to him, I thought. I'll see him tomorrow morning. I headed back to the barracks and into our room. There was no sign of Mossey, so I assumed he had got off with the attractive woman he was talking to and must have gone back to her place for the night. I sat on my bed and shook my head. I was very disappointed with Bernie, and also very disappointed that he called himself a Royal Marine.

Fuck him, I thought, he doesn't deserve to be in the same room as me or Mossey. I'll throw his kit locker and bed outside the room. I then proceeded to do just that. I didn't notice at the time that the locker was screwed to the wall and that a couple of big chunks of plaster came away from the wall as I pulled hard to move it. When I had completed the task, I locked the door just in case he came back and tried to attack me in my sleep. I undressed, climbed into bed and fell asleep as soon as my head hit the pillow.

KNOCK, KNOCK, KNOCK, BANG, BANG, BANG, went my room door. 'Steve, it's Benny, let me in.'

I opened my eyes and saw that it was daylight. I still felt half drunk and saw that it was only 7 a.m.

BANG, BANG, BANG, went the door. 'Steve, it's Benny, let me in, I need to speak to you.'

Benny was a sergeant in the Royal Marines police troop. He had been a Marine for about twenty years. He had black spiky hair and gappy teeth and came from Leeds. He was very popular in the police troop, because he was one hell of a Marine and always very professional at his job.

I wonder if I'm meant to be on duty and have overslept, I thought. Still seems a bit early to me.

Knock, knock, knock, went the door. 'Steve, open the door. For fuck's sake, open the door,' shouted Benny.

'Er yeah, OK, Benny, I'm opening it,' I replied and opened the door.

Benny stepped inside. He looked pissed off and was slowly shaking his head from side to side.

'What's up, mate?' I frowned, holding my sore head with my hands.

'Anybody else but him. Anybody else but that fucking Bernie wanker.' He looked and sounded concerned, but things were unclear.

'What do you mean?'

'Fucking Bernie, he's fucking reported you for assaulting him last night and I'm here to arrest you. Any other Marine would have accepted that they got a kicking for shooting their mouth off. Yeah, I can guess what happened, I've heard about his attitude. But he's reported you and I'm fucking pissed off about it. I wanted you to work with me at 45 Commando Unit in Scotland, but now, because of that little shit, that won't happen. Get dressed and come with me down to the RMP office.'

Fucking hell, I thought, as I got dressed into uniform. As we exited the accommodation block, the RSM marched towards us. The soles of his highly polished boots made a thundering noise that echoed around the courtyard outside.

'My office, NOW!' he screamed.

I marched smartly into his office and saw that my sergeant-major from the RMP troop was already inside. He shook his head when I entered the room.

'I knew you were going to be trouble from the day I accepted you onto the military police training course,' he snarled. 'You're a violent bastard, Preece, and this time you've gone too far. We're going to throw the book at you.'

'Get your heels together when you speak to the sergeant-major, NOW!' screamed the RSM. He then stood about six inches in front of me and looked me straight in the eyes.

'Look at the state of your fucking eyeballs, they're like piss holes in the snow. Are you still drunk, PREECE?' he bellowed.

'No, sir.'

'Well, you could have fucking fooled me, lad,' he continued. 'You're a bully, Preece, a fucking bully, and we're going to get you banged away in Colchester prison for a long time. Do you understand?'

'Yes sir, but!'

'Don't fucking but me, lad, you're guilty as hell, and I know you are.'

The RMP sergeant-major cut in. 'Get yourself a solicitor, Preece. Get someone who understands you.'

I didn't reply. My eyes filled with tears as I saw my career slipping away before me. My life was the Marines; this was what I stood for. Now I was going to lose everything, because of Bernie. I breathed in deeply and then out slowly before being marched out of the RSM's office and down to the interview room at the RMP's offices.

The RMP's offices were situated a few hundred yards away from Stonehouse Barracks and were totally independent from everybody else. I was taken to the RMP sergeant-major's office and told to wait. A few minutes later, the sergeant-major stormed in through the doorway and started telling me how much he was going to make an example of me. He then suspended me indefinitely from being a Royal Marines policeman and told me I would be pending a court martial. I asked him if Bernie was also suspended and he said that there was no reason to suspend him, as he had done nothing wrong.

I was then taken into the interview room next door, where I was met by an officer from the Special Investigations Branch (SIB) who was waiting to interview me. The SIB are the military's equivalent to the CID of the civilian police. The interview room was small and shabby with red-painted walls and a bare wooden floor. There were two chairs inside and a large clock ticking away on the wall.

The interview commenced on 26 October 1988 at approximately 1 p.m. The SIB officer introduced himself and produced a paper pack, which contained several sheets of typed paper with questions on them and several other sheets of blank paper. He started to read from the preamble on the sheets before commencing his line of questioning.

The following is a faithful account of the initial questioning:

> SIB: I am making enquiries into an assault that occurred this morning in which Lance-Corporal Bernie Drudge claims that you attacked him whilst walking along Millbay Dock Road, near Stonehouse Barracks.
>
> I am going to ask you some further questions, but before I do, I must caution you that you do not have to say anything unless you wish to do so, but what you say may be given in evidence.
>
> You now have the right to the following:
>
> (a) Legal advice.
>
> (b) Request the presence of an observer at the interview.
>
> (c) Consult the Service Police Codes of Practice where applicable.
>
> You may exercise any of these rights now, but if you do not, you may do so later during the course of the interview.

I declined a legal adviser, as I felt fairly sure I could talk my way out of this. I'd done it plenty of times before. I signed the bottom of his form and indicated that I did not want a legal adviser present. Then the question and answering took place, which went along these lines:

> Q: Lance-Corporal Bernie Drudge alleges that whilst you and he were walking along Millbay Dock Road, Plymouth, about 0150 this morning, you attacked him for no apparent reason.
>
> A: Not really.
>
> Q: Would you tell me what happened?
>
> A: We were walking along the top of Millbay Dock

Road together and he clipped me around the back of the head, only in jest to start with. I clipped him just the same in jest and then he swept my feet away from me. I injured my left arm, I got up and he swung a punch at me so I head-butted him to defend myself.

Q: Where did you head-butt him?

A: In the face.

Q: I have interviewed Lance-Corporal Drudge this morning and he had a severely swollen and bruised left eye. Was the injury caused by you head-butting him?

A: Yes.

Q: He also has a grazed and swollen forehead. How was that injury caused?

A: I think he fell against the wall when I head-butted him.

Q: Lance-Corporal Drudge claims that you attacked him for no apparent reason and that initially you tried to throw him over a wall running alongside Millbay Dock Road. Did this happen?

A: No. I don't know where he's got that story from. The thing is, during the night I had to pull a sailor off him in a nightclub called Boobs.

Q: What was that argument about?

A: I don't know. I ended up arguing with the sailor as well to get him off Bernie and then we left shortly afterwards.

Q: Lance-Corporal Drudge stated that he saw you attempt to head-butt a person believed to be a serviceman whilst inside the Boobs discothèque, is this the incident you are referring to?

A: Yes.

Q: What was the argument about?

A: I don't know.

Q: How did you know he was a sailor?

A: He just looked like one.

Q: Lance-Corporal Drudge claims that the first time he saw this person was when he was falling onto his back next to him, and he believed you had punched him. Did this happen?

A: No.

Q: How well do you get on with Lance-Corporal Drudge?

A: Quite well.

Q: Have you ever had problems or words with him in the past?

A: No.

Q: Lance-Corporal Drudge claims that you and another lance-corporal continuously verbally and sometimes physically abused him whilst on the military police training course. Is this the case?

A: No, not me. He didn't get on with many people and I guess I spent a lot of the time looking after him and protecting him from everybody else on the course.

Q: What time did you leave the barracks last night?

A: Just before seven o'clock.

Q: Where did you go?

A: The pool hall in Union Street.

Q: Where and what time did you meet up with Lance-Corporal Drudge and Lance-Corporal Carter?

A: In The Tube wine bar at approximately 10 p.m.

Q: How much did you drink last night?

A: About seven pints.

Q: Were you drunk?

A: No.

Q: So seven pints is well within your drinking capabilities?

A: Yes.

Q: Lance-Corporal Drudge denies goading you or giving you any reason to retaliate against him and claimed that you were in an aggressive mood whilst in the discothèque. Why should he say this if it is not the case?

A: I don't know. Since I got back he's been telling me how many people he's had a fight with. So it looks like he's just trying to prove himself.

Q: I inspected Lance-Corporal Drudge's bed space this morning and noticed that his bed and locker were outside the room and in disarray. Also that there was damage to the wall it was fastened to. Can you explain this?

A: Yes. I put his bed and locker outside the room to block the doorway in case he came back to cause more trouble. The plaster must have fallen off the wall during the process and was an accident.

Q: I intend to terminate this interview pending further investigations. Before I do, do you wish to make a written statement?

A: No.

I was given the opportunity to read over the 'record of interview' and signed a declaration to confirm I had done this. Then the interview was terminated. I was allowed to go of my own free will and told to report to the administration block, where I would be assigned administration duties. I was also told that I was not allowed to approach or speak to Bernie or go anywhere near the RMP offices.

When I returned to the accommodation block, I saw that all Bernie's and Mossey's bedding and kit had been removed. Both of their bed spaces remained empty.

I felt dismayed and quite upset at the way things had

turned out. I couldn't understand why they had believed Bernie's version of events and not mine. Why wasn't he suspended as well, I wondered. I stared at the two holes in the wall and rubbed my chin. Hhhhmm, that'll be the charge of criminal damage, I thought. At that, someone knocked on the door. I opened it and saw a civilian industrial painter dressed in white overalls stood in front of me.

'Excuse me, mate, but I'm working on the new accommodation block next door. Could you tell me if there's a way through to it from this block?' he asked.

I smiled. 'Er, yes, mate, I can. But first, if I give you £5 will you seal those holes in the wall and paint over them for me?'

'Sure, mate, no problem, I'll do it now.'

I felt elated. I was about to remove the evidence of a possible charge of criminal damage from the scene.

Later that day, I received a telephone call from the SIB officer who had interviewed me. He laughed and congratulated me on covering up the possibility of being charged with criminal damage. However, he did tell me that they were still going to nail me to the floor with the other charges.

I wasn't interviewed again until 8 December 1988. This time, I had sought legal advice and acquired the services of a solicitor. The investigating SIB officer was a previous training partner of mine as we used to work out together in the gym. This interview went as follows:

Q: On the evening of Tuesday, 25 October 1988, what time did you go out?

A: About 6.45 p.m.

Q: Where did you go?

A: The Prince Regent public house to meet a friend. Prior to this, he had told me that if he wasn't there by 7 p.m. he wouldn't be coming.

Q: Did your friend arrive?

A: Unfortunately not.

Q: Where did you go after that?

A: To the pool hall across the road for a couple of hours.

Q: Did you consume any alcohol at the pool hall?

A: No. They don't sell it there.

Q: What time did you leave the pool hall?

A: About 9.30 p.m. to go back to the Prince Regent public house to see if my friend had arrived.

Q: Had he?

A: No.

Q: It has been said that you met up with Lance-Corporals Drudge and Carter at The Tube wine bar at approximately 10 p.m. that evening. Is that correct?

A: Yes.

Q: What time did you arrive at Boobs nightclub?

A: Around midnight.

Q: How much beer did you drink during the course of the evening?

A: Around seven pints.

Q: During your time in Boobs nightclub, was there an incident involving you and another man?

A: There was an incident, but it was initially caused by Lance-Corporal Drudge.

Q: Can you tell me about this?

A: Yes. Bernie was arguing with some guy who looked like a sailor. I intervened to stop the argument and the sailor went to push me away, so I pushed him back against the gaming machine. I then turned to Lance-Corporal Drudge and told him we should leave before anything else happened.

Q: Did you in fact knock this man to the floor?

A: No.

Q: Can you explain how a witness states he stood between you and the other man and that it had nothing to do with Lance-Corporal Drudge?

A: No.

Q: So you are adamant that you intervened to stop trouble between Lance-Corporal Drudge and this other man?

A: Yes.

Q: When you left Boobs, who were you with?

A: Lance-Corporal Drudge.

Q: Where was Lance-Corporal Carter at this time?

A: He was occupied with some female.

Q: When you left Boobs, what was the atmosphere like between you and Lance-Corporal Drudge?

A: Fine.

Q: Can you explain what occurred as you and Lance-Corporal Drudge were walking along Millbay Dock Road?

A: Yes. We were walking along, holding a conversation about some fight he'd been involved in during the previous week. Then he clipped me across the back of my head with the palm of his hand.

Q: Why did he do this?

A: In jest I think, he was laughing.

Q: What was your reaction to this?

A: I clipped him across the back of his head and we both started laughing.

Q: What occurred next?

A: We carried on walking for a few metres and Bernie swept my left leg across the back of my right leg.

Q: What effect did this have?

A: Momentum carried me forward on to the floor, scraping the skin off my left arm.

Q: How did you take this?

A: I realised he wasn't joking any more, so I stood up and he shouted at me and threw a punch into my face.

Q: What was he shouting at you?

A: 'Come on then, fight me.'

Q: What happened next?

A: He started running round and round me, throwing punches. On his second punch, I head-butted him in the face.

Q: Did he fall to the ground when you head-butted him?

A: No, he fell against the wall.

Q: Did you take any other action against Lance-Corporal Drudge, apart from head-butting him?

A: No. After I head-butted him he fell against the wall. He looked at me and shouted with his fists clenched and then he ran off down one of the side streets.

Q: What did you do then?

A: I walked back to the barracks.

Q: It has been alleged that also during this incident, you picked up Lance-Corporal Drudge or tried to throw him over the wall running along Millbay Dock Road. What do you say to this allegation?

A: No, I never, the wall is above my head.

Q: Do you think you are capable of picking up Lance-Corporal Drudge?

A: I don't know.

Q: Do you carry out any extra form of physical activity to increase your performance as a Royal Marine?

At this point, I became agitated as my interviewer often trained with me himself in the gymnasium and knew very well that I maintained a very high level of physical fitness.

The following notes were added to the record of interview:

Time: 4.43 p.m. Interview terminated at this stage on request of Lance-Corporal Preece's solicitor.

Time: 4.48 p.m. Returned to the interview room. Comments from Lance-Corporal Preece's solicitor.

The reason that Lance-Corporal Preece was unsure about the question was that he believes the question may have been prompted by the interviewer's own personal knowledge of him and wished to clarify that it was a proper line of questioning on that account.

Time: 4.50 p.m. Interview recommenced.

Q: Do you carry out any extra form of physical activities to increase your performance as a Royal Marine?

A: Yes.

Q: What does this include?

A: Running, weight training, circuit training, and pretty much what most Royal Marines do.

Q: Lance-Corporal Drudge is adamant that all the aggressive actions stemmed from you with no provocation from him.

A: No, that's not true.

Q: Why do you think he would say these things?

A: I don't know, maybe he was drunk.

Q: Were you drunk?

A: No.

Q: Would you consider he was drunk?

A: Yes.

Q: What made you think he was drunk?

A: He was slurring and staggering as we walked back.

Q: Have incidents like this occurred before between you?

A: No.

Q: Why, suddenly, should this happen on this occasion?

A: I don't know, maybe he had too much to drink.

Q: How well do you know Lance-Corporal Carter?

A: Fairly well.

Q: Lance-Corporal Carter actually says that in Boobs nightclub he had to break up an incident with you and another man. Can you explain this?

A: I don't know if he actually came over whilst the incident was going on between the three of us. If he did, then he may have been the reason why the sailor backed off from us.

Q: 5.10 p.m. I consider there is sufficient evidence to justify disciplinary action being taken against you for the assault on Lance-Corporal Drudge on the morning of Wednesday, 26 October 1988, which is an offence against the Service Disciplinary Acts. A report will be submitted without delay. You do not have to say anything unless you wish to do so but what you say may be given in evidence.

A: Yes. OK.

Q: Do you wish to make a statement?

A: No thanks.

I was then given the opportunity to read over the record of interview with my solicitor.

Later, photographs were taken both of Bernie's injuries and mine, and also of both sides of the wall along Millbay Dock Road. I was then suspended indefinitely from Royal Marine police duties and put to work in an administrative job in the headquarters of Commando Forces, pending a date to be set for my court martial. I waited patiently to see what I would be charged with, and was initially told that my charge would be attempted murder. This charge was subsequently lessened to grievous bodily harm (GBH), and then to actual bodily harm (ABH), but at the time, it really seemed like they were going to accuse me of trying to kill Bernie Drudge. This was a bitter pill to swallow, and even more bitter when I had to tell this to my parents over the telephone.

My mate Diz was transferred from HMS Warrior to a troop called Air Defence Troop at the same location as myself, so I teamed up with him again socially and also made a new pool of friends. Bernie's popularity with the other Marines within the barracks hit an all-time low and he was told to quickly move out of the barracks and into remote accommodation, as it was no longer safe for him to stay there. The military police went to Boobs nightclub to obtain a copy of the security videotapes from the night of the incident. They wanted to obtain video evidence of the incident with the sailor. However, the videotapes had mysteriously disappeared, and truthfully I had no idea who had removed them.

CHAPTER THIRTY-TWO

A PARTNER FOR A WEDDING

Music poured out of the jukebox in the Prince Regent public house in Union Street, Plymouth. It was twelve o'clock on a Saturday afternoon. Briggs leaned over the bar to order the first round of drinks.

My eyes caught the attention of an attractive young woman standing next to the bar. She looked about twenty-one years old and had long red streaky hair. A tight white dress with small blue spots clung to her shapely figure, down to the top of her knees. She was standing with another girl, who was roughly the same shape and age as her. I smiled at her and then laughed as I watched her turn her nose up to shun my advances.

'Here, Steve, grab this,' said Briggs as he held out my drink.

'Hold on to it for a second, Briggs, I'm going to have a word with that girl in the spotty dress.'

I approached her. 'Excuse me, snotty,' I beckoned to her.

'I beg your pardon,' she exclaimed in a very posh voice.

'If you stick your nose up at me once more, I'm going to grab hold of it and pluck all the snot out of it.'

'Uuurrrggghh, that sounds absolutely disgusting. I don't

know what you mean,' she shrieked. She's naive as well as stuck-up, I thought.

'I bet you don't know what it's like to have a good night out, do you?' I asked her.

'Oh, I don't know what you mean.'

'What's your name?'

'It's Kerry.'

I grinned to myself and decided to try my luck and ask her out for a date. After all, a slap in the face would not be an unusual occurrence for me. 'I'm called Steve. Meet me in here tonight at seven-thirty and I'll show you what a good night out is.'

'Oh well, why not,' she shrugged. 'Seven-thirty it is.'

I exchanged smiles with her and rejoined Briggs.

'What's happening, Steve?' questioned Briggs.

'I'm meeting her in here tonight at seven-thirty.'

'God only knows what state you'll be in by then.'

'I'll be OK,' I replied and smiled at her again as we left the pub.

We spent most of the afternoon drinking and playing pool in a pub called the General Moore. The pub was named after a Marine major-general who led the land assault during the Falklands War in the South Atlantic Ocean in 1982, and the walls were covered in Marine pictures, medals and insignia. It was a very popular pub with the Marines.

'It's nearly seven o'clock, Steve, are you still going to meet that posh tart in the Prince Regent?' Briggs called out to me across the busy bar.

'Oh shit, yes, I nearly forgot.'

By this time, I had had quite a lot to drink and felt very merry. The bright yellow T-shirt I was wearing was covered in beer and chilli sauce stains from a kebab which I had eaten earlier in the afternoon.

'I'll see you later, in Cascades,' I shouted to Briggs, and left through a side exit door. Kerry smiled at me when I entered the Prince Regent pub. She was now dressed in a short black skirt and a tight red jumper. Her two bulging assets stuck out prominently and pointed in my direction.

'Hello, Steve,' she beamed. 'I bet you thought I wouldn't have the nerve to turn up, didn't you?'

'Well, I did have my reservations,' I smiled.

'What happened to your T-shirt? It's filthy.'

'Never mind my clothes, what would you like to drink?'

'Oh, I'll have a dry white wine please.'

I bought us both a drink and engaged her in conversation. Her posh accent was easy to understand, but unfortunately she found it a constant effort to decipher my strong northern accent. She told me that this was the first time she had been into the pubs in Union Street and that I was the first Marine she had ever spoken to. She also commented that my evening-wear was a lot different from other men she had been out with. I laughed. She must be excited by the chilli stains, I thought.

The next pub we went into was called The Two Trees, and was situated just a few yards away. A lot of the Marines I socialised with often drank here. Kerry smiled at me as we walked inside. This was a whole new experience for her. Here she was, out on the town with one of those nasty lot of Marines whom her friends had warned her to stay away from.

My friend Diz and another Marine called Sonny shouted a greeting to me across the crowded bar. Kerry stood patiently next to me. She was waiting . . . waiting for me to buy the next round of drinks.

I looked at her. 'Kerry.'

'What?'

'Do you believe in equal rights between men and women?'

'Oh yes . . . I really do.'

'Have you got any money?'

She looked puzzled. 'Yes, I've got ten pounds actually.'

'Good. Spend it. I'll have a bottle of lager.'

'Oh, yes, OK,' she replied and queued at the bar.

Diz and Sonny came over to join me. This will be an experience for Kerry, I thought, as both men were wild-natured and had very little respect for the opposite sex.

'Who's the tart?' asked Sonny in his broad Scottish accent.

'Yeah, who's the tart?' repeated Diz.

I laughed. 'She's some snotty-nosed bitch whom I met this afternoon. You wouldn't believe how naive she is.'

'Oh really,' answered Sonny sarcastically. 'And I suppose she doesn't fuck on the first date?'

We all laughed together. This was common practice between the three of us. We had an agreement which we'd made some months before, that if any one of us brought a girl down town into the pubs of Union Street, then the other two could give her as much abuse as possible. If the woman was able to withstand the sarcastic insults and related bad behaviour then she'd passed the test and there would be no further hassle. On the other hand, if she failed to handle the abuse then it was tough at the top.

Kerry returned with our drinks. She smiled at Diz and Sonny to greet them. 'Aren't you going to introduce me to your friends, Steve?' she smiled.

'Yes, of course. Diz, Sonny, this is Kerry. Kerry, this is Diz and this is Sonny.'

They both exchanged warm smiles with her and shook her hand.

'You look like a nice girl,' said Sonny. 'Do you fart or shit in the bath?'

Kerry's face dropped. 'I beg your pardon?'

'Do you wear small white ankle socks and have piss stains in your knickers?' continued Sonny.

Diz quickly joined in. 'Do you look at the toilet paper after you've wiped your arse on it?'

'I . . . I . . . I really couldn't say,' stammered Kerry.

We all burst into laughter. Diz's hand disappeared up the back of Kerry's short tight skirt. She slapped him across the face. 'Do you mind?' she shrieked.

Half an hour or so later, both Diz and Sonny got tired of dishing out the insults to Kerry and knocked it off. She didn't like their rude behaviour or warped sense of humour, but chose to remain by my side. Shortly afterwards, they left to go elsewhere to drink and Kerry commented that she was appalled by the fact that I could stand there just laughing while she put up with their insulting comments and behaviour. Then she went quiet and stood staring into my eyes.

'Steve.'

'What, Kerry?'

'You're a bit of a lad, aren't you?'

'Yes, I suppose I am.'

'And . . . and your friends.'

'What about them?'

'They're animals, aren't they?'

'Yes, I suppose they are.'

'Well,' she continued, 'you must understand, I've never met people like them before.'

I laughed and pointed at the bar. 'Get the beer in, Kerry.'

She leaned closer and whispered into my ear. 'I haven't got any money left.'

'Good, you can go home now,' I smirked at her.

She clenched her fists by her side and shook her head before rapidly leaving through the exit door,

A week later, I saw her again in the Prince Regent pub and declined to speak to her. I could see her glancing at me across the bar via an angled mirror on the wall. She walked up to me and tapped me on the shoulder. I turned around and said hello as if I hadn't noticed her earlier.

'I still like you, you know, Steve,' she smiled. 'I really do.'

'Would you like to come to my friend's wedding next Saturday?' I asked. 'I'm the only one who hasn't got a partner to go with.'

'Oh, yes please, I'd love to.'

The following Saturday, I met Kerry at eleven o'clock in the morning. One of my friends, called Pods, was getting married to some posh hoity-toity girl at one o'clock and I wanted to get to the church early. Kerry commented on how smart I looked in my black tuxedo suit, cummerbund and dickey bow, but I didn't have the heart to tell her I'd bought it all from a second-hand clothes shop for fifty pence the week before.

The woman Pods was marrying came from a very wealthy family and had loads of money. They'd previously put out a wedding gift list for people to buy presents for them, but everything on it was out of my reach, as a Marine's wage didn't quite meet the requirements. I had mentioned this to them and they told me to just get them what I wanted. I appreciated the gesture and had had a good look around for presents to buy them. In the end, after a lot of thought, I settled for a box of plastic soldiers for the groom at a price of seventy-five pence and a nice mini plastic tea set for the bride, at a bank-breaking cost of one pound and twenty-five pence. This wasn't as bad as it sounded, as another Marine had bought them a Mars bar.

We arrived at the church in a taxi, as did the majority of the groom's guests, who were virtually all Royal Marines.

However, the bride's upper-class side of the family arrived in limousines and Rolls-Royces, all of which were chauffeur driven.

The church ceremony went very smoothly and we all commented on how beautiful the bride looked. Pods looked very smart too and was dressed in his best dress Blues uniform. Afterwards, there was a photograph session and then we were ferried by bus to a remote country mansion house. Inside the house, we were greeted by a toastmaster who announced our names. I told him that Kerry and I were Mr and Mrs Preece and he shouted this out loud to announce our entrance. We were all given glasses of champagne and an opportunity to talk with the bride and groom. I approached the bride, who gave me a kiss and thanked me for the nice presents. She smiled and said that it was just what they'd always wanted.

After an hour or so, we were told to make our way through to the garden, where the reception would be held in a huge white marquee, which seemed about half the size of a football pitch. The interior was beautifully decorated with temporary wooden flooring and lots of sets of chairs, tables and candelabra. There was a wooden dance floor in the middle surrounded by arches covered in floral decorations. Huge multi-coloured silk sheets lined the ceiling and draped down in places with neatly tied bows. Kerry seemed at home with the setting and even knew a couple of the posh guests who were related to the bride. However, I felt a little uneasy, as I hadn't been accustomed to such lovely high-class surroundings as this before.

We were shown to our table and we sat down. I looked at the many rows of cutlery laid at each place on the table and hoped that I could copy from somebody else when it came to using the correct pieces. I looked around and noticed several other Marines whom I knew, and exchanged smiles with a few to say hello. Some were dressed in their best Blues uniform, complete with military medals, and looked very smart for the occasion. Kerry asked me why I wasn't dressed in my Blues and I told her it was because they were at the dry cleaners. This was true, but what I didn't tell her was, even if I did have immediate access to my Blues uniform I wouldn't have worn it, in case I got into a fight and got blood on it.

A lot of the Marines' eyes lit up when a couple of waiters wheeled two trolleys into the marquee next to us. One contained a couple of barrels of beer and another was filled with numerous bottles of spirits. Then the food was brought in and each of us was served by a waiter. The food was outstanding and of the highest quality. Kerry realised I didn't know which pieces of cutlery to use for each dish and soon put me on the right lines.

After the meal, we all tucked in to the alcoholic beverages and soon got into the swing of things. A lot of the Marines, including myself, were drinking triple measures of spirits with every pint of beer we drank and we were soon very merry.

One Marine, called Dave, fell asleep at his table and snored heavily. Others were having food fights and playing games that resulted in drinking more beer if you lost. The equal numbers of toffs who were scattered around our area were highly amused and watched the gremlin-like behaviour of the Marines with interest.

The bride's father stood up and shouted for order. He was ready to make his speech. He was a chubby man, aged around fifty-five with short brown hair. He spoke with a posh crisp voice in the Queen's English.

'Order, order,' he shouted. 'Quiet, everybody, please.'

Slowly, everybody calmed down the chat and looked

towards the bride's father. Only a faint snore coming from Dave could be heard, but this didn't seem to matter.

'Ladies and gentlemen, this is one of the happiest days of my daughter Becky's life, and we're all gathered here today to celebrate it. Her mother and I are very proud of her. She's gone from being a hard-working student at university to a hard-working manager in a large human resources corporation. She's chosen to marry a Royal Marine, whom I welcome with open arms into my family. So, ladies and gentlemen, please raise your glasses and let's drink a toast to the happy couple and in particular to my daughter Becky.'

Everybody raised their glasses of bubbly into the air.

'To my daughter, Becky.'

'Becky,' everybody repeated together.

At this moment, Dave stopped snoring and woke up from his long deep sleep. He raised his glass into the air and shouted.

'To Becky, and all who sail in her.'

Then he collapsed onto the table in front of him, which crashed down onto the floor. All the Marines burst into laughter and then somebody turned on the disco music to drown out the commotion.

Kerry expressed her disgust with Dave's behaviour and asked me to dance. I nodded my head in agreement and walked over to her. She smiled at me and gave me a kiss on the cheek. I bent down and threw her onto my shoulder in a fireman's carry. She screamed at me to put her down, but I ignored her pleas. People stepped back out of my way as I ran towards the dance floor. I ducked down to get us through one of the arches that surrounded the dance floor. Then I heard a loud ripping noise and Kerry screamed again. I turned around and saw half of Kerry's skirt dangling from the half-toppled arch. I put Kerry down and started to dance facing her. She shrieked with anger and I saw that the top of her tights and her underwear were exposed. Her cheeks were bright red and she sprinted out of the marquee at great speed. I jogged out after her and saw her pass by in a taxi as it sped off into the distance. I shrugged my shoulders in disappointment and went back into the marquee for some more fun. I never, ever saw Kerry again.

CHAPTER THIRTY-THREE

A CHAIN OF CATASTROPHE

One cold winter morning, I was working out in the gymnasium. Sweat dripped down my face as I neared the final exercises of my training circuit. The door to the gym opened and the new regimental sergeant-major walked smartly in. He was a tall smart fellow in his late forties with jet-black hair. He was well respected by everybody for his many years' service with the SBS.

It was obvious he was coming to see me, as I was the only person in the gym. He had a serious look on his face when he called me over to speak to him. He told me that my mother had been knocked down by a car and was in intensive care in a hospital close to home. She had suffered serious head injuries and was in a critical condition. I felt dismayed by the news but kept myself composed. The RSM told me to go home for a week and see my family and not to do anything silly, such as going absent without leave (AWOL) pending my up-coming court martial.

I acknowledged his advice and caught the train home. Once there, I went straight to the hospital, where I was met by my father and both my brothers. I then saw my mother lying unconscious in bed with heart-monitoring machines and blood drips attached to her battered body. I looked at my father who was sat opposite her on the other side of the bed.

'She doesn't deserve this,' I snarled at him. 'Not after all you've put her through over the years.'

He frowned and put his head down. I looked back at my mother and then at my two brothers who looked totally bewildered and sad.

'Come on brothers, let's go and drink some beer,' I suggested, and we left the hospital.

A week later, my mother was still ill but had regained consciousness. She was awake but incoherent from the heavy impact of the car that had knocked her down. My father remained by her bedside and I found out that he had quit drinking alcohol on the doctor's advice. He looked like shit, as the many years of boozing had taken their toll on him. He had a problem with his skin hanging loosely from his body and was worried about his health. I listened to his concerns about his ailments but offered little sympathy as I departed to return back to Plymouth.

Two days later, I was sat in the galley (dining hall) at Stonehouse Barracks. I felt disappointed when I was told that there were no chips on the menu. This was because the kitchen only had new potatoes, and it was common practice not to make chips out of them. I saw the duty chef sergeant walk into the room and shouted to him. He walked over, but he looked unusually nervous.

'What's the crack, no chips, a Marine without chips is like a fish without water,' I exclaimed to him.

He looked at me and shook his head. A sad look covered his face and he opened his mouth but no words came out. We had always got on quite well so I was confused by his actions and then he turned and walked away. Oh well, keep your bloody chips, I thought. A few minutes later, he returned with the duty officer who also had a serious look on his face.

He came over to my table and asked if he could have a word with me in private. I agreed and got up to go with him. I looked at the chef sergeant to express the disappointment I felt because he had involved the duty officer in my complaint about the lack of chips. However, he didn't even look at me and stood in the background. The duty officer led me into a small side room and told me to sit down. He looked at me and paused for a moment. I don't believe this, I thought, it's gone a bit too far over a plate of chips.

'Er, I'm afraid I have some bad news for you,' said the officer quietly.

'Yes, I know, no chips,' I replied.

'No, no nothing like that. I'm afraid one of your parents has died.'

'Oh shit, my poor mother.'

'No, I'm afraid it's your father.'

'My father?' I frowned.

'Yes, your father has died.'

'How?'

'Heart attack, I'm afraid. Are you OK?'

'Yeah, I'm OK, but that bastard owed me ten quid.'

The officer looked at me. He didn't laugh or smile at my smart remark, but I didn't care at that moment. I had too many bad memories about the way our father had brought us up. All the hardship, all the violence and the lack of fatherly love that I had always wanted as a child. Later, the RSM came to see me again. He told me that he was sorry about my run of bad luck and that my current court martial date would be put back a couple of months. He told me to go home, give my family some support while they put my father in the ground, and not to do anything silly, such as going AWOL. It felt like déjà vu. I acknowledged his advice and packed my case to head home.

As I drove home, I thought about my father. Although I felt hatred for him, deep down I still had love for him and privately I shed a few tears. My world was starting to collapse around me.

When I got home, I saw that all the front-window curtains were drawn, to signify that there'd been a death in the house. I went inside and drew them all open. My two brothers sat quietly together in the front room. They said hello and both looked down at the floor.

'Come on,' I said, pointing at the door. 'Let's go and get pissed.'

I spent the next few days by my mother's side at Martin's house, where she was convalescing. She was still suffering from her traumatic head injury and was almost totally oblivious to our father's death. Although both Martin and Peter went to see my father lying in state at the mortuary, I refused to go, and I also stood firm on my decision not to let our mother see him. I didn't want my last memory of him to be one of looking at his dead corpse in a coffin, nor did I want my mother to suffer this.

On the day of the funeral, I dressed in my Lovats, the light-coloured number two uniform. I chose this form of dress so that I could wear my Green Beret. My father always boasted about how proud he was of my service in the Marines and in particular of how proud he had felt on the day he had watched my passing out parade and the presentation of the Green Beret. Also, I had made a decision on behalf of my family to have our father cremated. I did this because I could picture my mother coming out of her head injury and back to her senses and screaming and clawing at his grave to try to get him back. I also made this decision because my father had always said that he wanted to be thrown into the docks, where he had worked for the past twenty years, when he died.

Peter cracked a joke as we stood outside our parents' home awaiting the arrival of the hearse and the accompanying cars and relatives: 'I'm just going to the shop. If the hearse arrives in the next few minutes, put him on a low gas until I get back.'

Martin and I smiled and shook our heads. The funeral service went very well and the church was packed with people. The hardest part was supporting my mother as she stood at the front of the church. She was slightly aware of what was going on, but still not totally coherent. Later, after the cremation, I told everybody who was present that we didn't want anybody to come back to our house for a wake. We wanted to be left to grieve in peace.

The next day, my two brothers and I took our father's ashes onto the docks. A security guard approached us in a van and asked what we were doing. We told him that we were fulfilling our father's dying wish and he acknowledged that he'd known him and drove off.

I opened the lid and started to pour some of the ashes into the water. Then I passed the container to Martin, who also poured some out and passed it to Peter. A cold wind blew and then Martin started swearing because the ashes were blowing all over him and he looked white like a ghost. Peter and I both laughed and threw the empty container into the cold dock water and watched it sink down into the dark depths and out of sight.

That night, we went into town and drank lots of beer till the early hours of the morning. Only I headed back to our parents' house, as both Martin and Peter had their own homes now and our mother was still staying with Martin. I was very drunk when

I staggered in through the front door. Once inside the front room, I sat and paused for thought. I could feel the emptiness and for the first time I felt the hurt of my father's death. I shouted out loud: 'FAAATTTTTTHHHHHHHEEEERRRR.'

My parents' dog barked loudly from the back kitchen, where it was locked in. Tears streamed down my face and I could feel a deep dull pain coming from my diaphragm. It wasn't physical pain, it was emotional pain. Even though he hadn't been the father I had always dreamed of, he was my father and now he was gone forever.

I saw his coat lying on the back of a chair and I put it on. It made me feel warm. In fact I felt so warm that I decided to go outside to see how well it would shield me from the cold. I closed the door behind me and stood staring up at the sky. A few moments later, I tried the door and found it was locked. I knew nobody was there to answer the door so I went around the back of the house and sat in the empty coalhouse. I was cold, freezing cold, but I couldn't remember how I had managed to get locked out of my home. It started to rain heavily so I tried knocking on the door again. I stood there confused. I knocked on the door, even though I knew nobody was inside to let me in. The dog continued to bark loudly. I went back to the coalhouse and lay down on the cold concrete floor. I was both wet and cold and was starting to shake, probably because all the alcohol I had consumed had lowered my resistance to the cold weather.

Bollocks, I thought. I'm going to kick the back door in. I stood up and started to kick the back door with as much force as possible. The dog barked wildly. The door and its frame buckled heavily under the blows but no matter how much I kicked it, it just wouldn't give. The rain poured heavily. I stopped and went back into the coalhouse and lay down on my back. I was shaking like mad with the cold and my hands felt numb. To warm them I placed them in my pockets and then I felt something sharp and hard. I pushed deeper into my pockets and my hands started to warm up. As some feeling came back into them I realised what the sharp object was. It was my front door key. I got up and shook my head. I went back to the front door and opened it. Inside, I felt a great warmth. I took off my coat and went into the back kitchen. The dog jumped up at me and licked my hands and face.

'Good boy,' I said. 'Good boy.'

I felt proud of him. He was old now and had always been a good dog. I looked at his small carpeted space under the table. His food bowl was full so I dropped down onto my knees and started to eat it with him. He wagged his tail and rubbed his head against me. I thought, maybe it would be a good idea to swap beds with him, just for one night. I picked him up and took him upstairs and placed him on my bed and threw the quilt over him. He stared at me with a look of joy on his face so I left him there and turned out the light. His carpeted bed space wasn't comfortable, but if it was good enough for him then it was good enough for me.

Next morning, I awoke early. The dog had somehow managed to open the doors and was sat opposite me with his tail wagging. I looked at the door, which was badly damaged. My head ached so I put the kettle on and made a cup of tea. There was a knock at the door and I answered it. It was a friend of mine called Jim, who was a joiner.

'By hey, you look rough, Steve. Was it a heavy night last night?'

'Yes, it was. I got locked out and tried kicking the back door in to get in. The door is wrecked. Is there any possibility of you getting a replacement door and also fixing the door frame?'

'Yeah, sure, Steve.'

KNOCK, KNOCK, went the front door again, so I looked out of the window. Two men stood outside. They were dressed in suits and were carrying books under their arms.

'Who is it, Steve?' asked Jim.

'Fucking Jehovah's Witnesses.'

'Don't answer the door, they'll go away.'

KNOCK, KNOCK, KNOCK, went the front door again. I picked up the dog with both hands and went to answer the front door. When I opened the door, the two smartly dressed gentlemen smiled and opened their books.

'Here, FUCK OFF,' I shouted, and threw the dog at them before slamming the door shut.

'Bloody hell, Steve,' exclaimed Jim. 'That was a bit strong. I thought you liked that dog?'

'Yeah, I do, but he's left dog hairs all over my bed.'

Later in the day, Jim replaced the damaged door and fixed the door frame. It was a good door that, I thought. A bloody good door.

The last couple of days of my leave I spent training hard in a local weightlifting gym. On the second to last day, I bent down to pick up a very heavy weight and felt something tear in the lower part of my back. Unbearable pains shot through the base of my spine and down into the back of my legs. I knew immediately that the damage was serious and went straight to the doctor's. He told me that I had slipped a disc and that it would get worse before it got better – if it ever did get better.

The car journey back to Plymouth was a long one, taking me about six hours. By the time I arrived in Plymouth, my legs were starting to seize up. The pain in my back became unbearable and I found it hard to work the clutch and brake pedals without hurting myself. I drove straight to a Royal Naval Hospital near Stonehouse Barracks.

As I approached the barrier next to the security guarded entrance I tried pressing the brake pedal to halt the car. However, my legs had seized up so much that no matter how hard I tried I just couldn't press my foot down on the pedal. Then CRAASSHH, my car smashed through the barrier. I cried out with pain and then pulled up the handbrake as hard as I could, bringing the car into a skid and then to a screeching halt. Two security guards were stood next to my car shouting at me to get out. I calmly wound down the window and told the two men that my back and legs had seized up and that I was stuck in the car and couldn't get out. They shook their heads and smiled at each other before calling medical staff to come to my assistance.

I spent the next week in a hospital bed in traction and was given an epidural to numb the pain. I was excused duties for the next couple of weeks and told to take as much bed rest as possible. I took this advice seriously, but quickly got bored with doing nothing all day and all night.

One of my friends, called David Seed, came around to see me. David was a big guy with black hair and a big square jaw. He had been a Marine for about four years and came from London. He sympathised with me about my run of bad luck with my mother's accident, my father's death and my back injury and suggested that we go into town for a few beers. I pondered on the idea for a short while, but I didn't need much persuading. Some of my mobility had returned and as long as I didn't lean forward I wouldn't be in pain. Consequently, I agreed and headed into Union Street to socialise with David.

We started drinking at around 1 p.m. and continued with a pub-crawl around a lot of the pubs in the area. We arrived in a pub called the Clipper Bar in Union Street at around 11 p.m. By this time we were very drunk. The Clipper was a small pub with lots of naval memorabilia scattered around the walls. It was fairly popular with the Marines and served an excellent pint of Guinness. After a couple of pints, David was so drunk he fell asleep with his head resting on the bar. I smiled and slowly shook my head; I'd drunk him under the table. I got up from my seat and staggered into the toilet. I was going to relieve myself before waking David and heading back to barracks. Whenever I went into a public toilet I always chose the urinal that was furthest away from the door. This was a good habit I had learnt over the years: it defended you against the possibility of someone attacking you from behind and smashing your face against the wall. If you were using the urinal furthest away from the door you could see anybody who came into the toilets behind you.

On this occasion, I went into the toilets and walked over to the urinal furthest away as normal. The door opened and three fit-looking men with short military haircuts walked in. One had ginger hair, one had dyed blond hair and the other had brown hair. They looked like Marines but they weren't familiar to me. For some reason or other, I actually sensed straight away that something was wrong. I felt vulnerable, as not only was I very drunk, I was also harbouring my very serious back injury.

I turned towards them. 'What's up, lads?' I asked cautiously.

The smallest of the three answered my question. 'You've been looking at his girlfriend so we're going to kick the shit out of you.'

'But I'm in no fit state, I've been on the drink all day.'

'We don't care,' he answered.

'But I won't be able to fight as I've got a bad back injury.'

'We don't care,' he snarled and threw a punch at me. I blocked the punch and surged forward to throw a flurry of punches at my attackers. Unfortunately, as I threw my first punch a great pain ran through my lower back, causing me to stop dead in my tracks. Then I felt a great onslaught of kicks and punches coming from the three strangers. This knocked me down to the floor and the three repeatedly kicked and punched me until I was knocked unconscious.

The next day, I awoke in hospital. I could feel the heavy swelling and bruising around my head, eyes and face, and also my mouth. A nurse told me that I had eleven small skull fractures, swelling to both my eyes and a broken nose. The teeth in the bottom of my mouth had also been badly chipped. Above all, my back was in agony, and lightning bolts of pain ran up and down my whole body. I was in a bad way.

I was given a painkilling injection by a nurse and fell into a deep sleep. Later, when I awoke, there were several of my Marine colleagues sat around my bed. They looked like the Mafia. They were unhappy about the beating I had taken and wanted to seek immediate revenge. They even knew who the three men were who had attacked me, and my assumptions were right, they were Marines. When I learnt this, I asked my colleagues not to get involved and told them that I would resolve the matter my way once I was fit again. They all agreed and respected my wishes.

Next, I was visited by the familiar Royal Marines police, who told me they wanted me to make a statement about the attack and that my assailants would be punished accordingly. I wasn't the slightest bit interested in talking to them and told them I couldn't remember anything. I had already made my mind up that I would work hard at getting fit again and seek vengeance in my own way against my attackers.

CHAPTER THIRTY-FOUR

THE CONSPIRACY

I stayed inside the barracks for the next few months and worked hard at getting myself back into shape. I made good progress with my back injury and was training hard once again in the gymnasium. A new date was set for my court martial. It was to be held on 10 October 1989. The final charges against me were published as follows:

First Charge: COMMITTING A CIVIL OFFENCE CONTRARY TO SECTION 70 OF THE ARMY ACT 1955. THAT IS TO SAY ASSAULT OCCASIONING ACTUAL BODILY HARM CONTRARY TO SECTION 47 OF THE OFFENCES AGAINST THE PERSON ACT 1861.

In that he at PLYMOUTH on 26 October 1988 assaulted Lance-Corporal [DRUDGE], Royal Marines, thereby occasioning him actual bodily harm.

Second Charge: FIGHTING CONTRARY TO SECTION 43 (a) OF THE ARMY ACT 1955.

In that he at PLYMOUTH on 26 October 1988 without

reasonable excuse fought with a person unknown.

Third Charge: DRUNKENNESS CONTRARY TO SECTION 43 (1) OF THE ARMY ACT 1955.

In that he at PLYMOUTH on 26 October 1988 was drunk.

Thankfully, the attempted murder charge had been reduced to grievous bodily harm first and then reduced again to actual bodily harm. However, the charges were still serious enough to sentence me to a long term in a military prison with the added possibility of being dishonourably discharged from the Royal Marine Commandos. I was also indirectly warned by an officer whom I got along with to keep out of any form of trouble in the run-up to the court case, as the officer in charge of the Royal Marines police wanted to make an example of me and was not happy that I didn't have any serious previous offences to put in front of the judge on the day of the court martial.

My fitness training continued and I was assessed as being fit enough for a forthcoming three-month tour of arctic warfare training in Norway. Once there, we were based at a place called Hunderfossen, which is situated a few miles from Norway's capital city, Oslo. When we weren't training out in the cold wilderness we would pass the time in our NAAFI bar. The bar was set up in a big wooden log cabin. The cabin was our dining hall during the day and then turned into a bar at night. Initially, I chose to stay out of the bar so that I could avoid getting into any more trouble, but as the weeks of training went by my will-power was beginning to waver. The first two times I went into the bar to socialise I was approached by two Marine policemen who seemed intent on trying to annoy me. I remembered the warning I had received from my officer friend and asked the duty sergeant if he would remove the two MPs from the bar. This wish was granted, as other Marines backed up my belief that the MPs were trying to set me up.

Following this, I once again chose not to frequent the log cabin bar for a couple of weeks. Then catastrophe struck. A friend of mine called George had been out celebrating his fifteenth year in the Marines. During the evening, he had drunk a pint glass full of a spirits cocktail. He had lost consciousness and was carried back to his room and left on his bed to sleep it off. Tragically, George had vomited in his sleep and had choked to death on it. He was pronounced dead the following morning and I felt quite sickened when I heard the news.

That night, I decided to go back into the bar to drown my sorrows. When I walked inside, I saw a group of servicemen sat together whom I didn't recognise. I noticed them because their conversation went quiet when they saw me enter the bar through the wooden swing doors. I ignored the silence and purchased a two-litre box of wine. Then I sat down with a Marine I knew called Arnie. He too was sorry to hear about George and joined me for a couple of drinks. Arnie commented on how quickly I had consumed my box of wine, but I just shrugged my shoulders and went back to the bar to purchase another. When I approached the bar, I walked past the crowd of strangers who once again went quiet. I ignored them and ordered my wine. All of a sudden, I felt someone slap me on the back of my head. I turned around, but no one was there. I looked at the crowd of strangers and noticed they were all smiling. I frowned and turned my head back towards the bar. Then I felt another slap on the back of my head. Once again, I quickly turned around and nobody was there. The strangers were all laughing, which made me feel angry.

'Is this some sort of joke or what?' I snarled at them.

They didn't answer and just kept on laughing. This annoyed me even more and I felt like I was going to explode.

'OK, if that's how you want to play it, get outside, I'll fight the fucking lot of you,' I shouted. They stopped laughing and just stared at me.

My temper exploded. 'Fucking get outside and fight me now, bastards,' I screamed aggressively and shook my fists in their direction.

My friend Arnie ran over and stood between me and the group of strangers to cool things down. They started to smirk so I surged towards them. Arnie moved in fast and intercepted my attack by holding me around the waist. Another Marine joined him and the two of them pushed me back towards the exit door.

'Come on, Steve,' shouted Arnie. 'Can't you see they're trying to set you up?'

Arnie and the other Marine continued to push me back into the exit swing doors. I lifted my right hand up and pushed with my palm to open the door. As I pushed it, a small pane of glass smashed under the force and made a small cut on the inside of one of my fingers. A few seconds later, I was outside in the snow. Arnie talked to me for a while to calm my temper down and walked with me back to my accommodation block. He told me that he hadn't seen who'd hit me on the back of the head, but believed it was a planned move to get me into trouble. He then told me to get some sleep and said it would be best if I didn't go back into the bar for the rest of the evening. I agreed and got into bed.

The following morning, I was arrested and interviewed by the Royal Marines police. The following is an abridged account of my record of interview:

RECORD OF INTERVIEW – Thursday, 2 February 1989 at 8.45 a.m.

Royal Marines policeman (RMP): I am making enquiries into an incident which occurred about 2200 hrs on Wednesday, 1 February 1989, in the NAAFI bar, Hunderfossen Camp, Norway, when a window in one of the entrance doors was broken.

I am going to ask you some questions, but before I do, I must caution you that you do not have to say anything unless you wish to do so, but what you say may be given in evidence.

You now have the right to the following:

(a) Legal advice.

(b) Request the presence of an observer at the interview.

(c) Consult the service police codes of practice where applicable.

You may exercise any of these rights now, but if you do not, you may do so later during the course of the interview.

I asked for a Marine sergeant called Barker to be present as an observer. I did this because I knew I had been set up. Sergeant Barker was my boss and arrived within minutes of my request.

Q: Were you in the NAAFI bar, Hunderfossen Camp, Norway, on the evening of Wednesday, 1 February1989?

A: Yes.

Q: At what time did you enter the NAAFI bar?

A: 1900 hours.

Q: Who were you with?

A: I was on my own.

Q: How much did you drink during the course of the evening?

A: A couple of bottles of wine.

Q: Anything else?

A: No.

Q: Did you consider yourself to be drunk?

A: No.

Q: Did you talk to any members of the Royal Marines police troop during the evening?

A: I didn't recognise anybody in the bar who belonged to the Royal Marines police troop. There were a few strangers whom I didn't recognise in the bar.

Q: Can you give me your version of how the window in the entrance door was broken?

A: Somebody slapped me on the back of my head when I was standing at the bar, waiting to get served. I turned around and saw a group of men sat at a table behind me, whom I didn't recognise, all laughing and looking towards me. I said, 'Who did that?' and then they started shouting at me. I shouted back at them and was quickly pulled away by Marine Arnold, who was trying to defuse the situation. He grabbed me around the waist and pushed me back towards the exit door. I put my hand up to open the door and my hand went through it.

Q: So in your view it was accidental?

A: Yes.

Q: Every witness I have spoken to states that you started shouting abuse at people who were sat next to the bar for no apparent reason. Is this the case?

A: I was slapped across the back of the head.

Q: Did you threaten these people?

A: Not really. We exchanged a few heated words, but nothing physical happened.

Q: So you think all these witnesses are lying?

A: Somebody is making a mountain out of a molehill. I know I've been set up here and so do you.

Q: Several witnesses state that they saw you lash out at the exit door window, causing it to smash. Is this correct?

A: No it isn't. It's a swing door. I pushed it with the palm of my hand.

Q: So it was accidental?

A: Definitely.

Q: Did you shout abuse at these people?

A: I retaliated. What would you have done if someone slapped you on the back of the head for no reason?

Q: I'm not the one being interviewed, Marine Preece. You are. So in your view, you did not start the incident?

A: No.

Q: Even though all the witnesses stated you did?

A: All I did was retaliate.

Q: Did you use foul language towards anyone in the bar?

A: There was a fair bit of foul language, but it wasn't all coming from me.

Q: Did you say to the door sentry as you left the building, 'They won't fight me,' or words to that effect?

A: No I did not.

Q: But you admit that you were swearing and threatening people?

A: I wouldn't say threatening, but I did let them know I wasn't very impressed.

Q: Did you shout, 'Come on you fucking bastards, I'll take you all outside,' or words to that effect?

A: I can't remember what I shouted.

Q: And you cannot recall shouting or using abusive language towards people at the bar?

A: I didn't say that.

Q: So if someone shouted at you, 'Come on you fucking bastard, I'll take you outside,' you wouldn't feel threatened?

A: I don't know.

Q: So in your view you were not being abusive?

A: Everyone was being abusive. The group towards me and me towards them.

Q: So in your view you were not being abusive and all these people are lying?

A: I didn't say that.

Q: And you say the resulting broken window was an accident?

A: Yes.

Q: I consider there is sufficient evidence to justify disciplinary action being taken against you for using threatening, abusive, foul language likely to cause a disturbance at about 2135 hours on Wednesday, 1 February 1989 in the NAAFI bar, Hunderfossen Camp, Norway. A report will be sent to your commanding officer without delay. You do not have to say anything unless you wish to do so, but what you say may be given in evidence. Do you wish to make a statement?

A: No thanks.

The interview was then terminated and I was given the opportunity to read over the record of interview along with my observer. Later that day, I was summoned to the RSM's office and informed that I would appear in front of the commanding officer to answer to the following charges:

SECTION 70 OF THE ARMY ACT 1955
– CRIMINAL DAMAGE,

SECTION 43 A (6) OF THE ARMY ACT 1966
– USING THREATENING WORDS.

The Royal Marines policemen who were apparently visiting the base on that particular evening submitted three statements. All three of them said that I threatened them for no apparent reason and also that I purposely smashed the exit door window with my fist. My only defence was that I had cut one of my fingers on the glass when my hand went through the pane. The military doctor submitted a statement saying that it would be impossible for me to sustain an injury on the inside of my hand if my fist had been clenched when it hit the window. He therefore said that my injury was consistent with my version of events.

My officer friend told me that he believed I had been set up, but by this time I found this more than obvious. I appeared in front of the commanding officer a few days later to answer to these allegations. I didn't hold out much hope of beating these charges, as generally it was a foregone conclusion that you were found guilty when you appeared in front of the commanding officer. However, I had no intention of relenting easily. I pleaded guilty to the charge of using threatening words but pleaded not guilty to the charge of criminal damage. I then refused to accept the commanding officer's punishment and asked to take my rightful option of trial by jury at court martial. This action made the RSM absolutely furious and he marched me into his office to discuss it. I told him that I knew I had been set up and that I knew this was a conspiracy. He practically pleaded with me to accept the commanding officer's punishment, which I found astonishing. But I knew they were worried about the embarrassment this would cause and also the related costs of another court martial. Eventually, I agreed to plead guilty to the charge but only after the RSM promised me that I wouldn't be fined any money for it.

A few minutes later, I was back in front of the commanding officer, who told me that he had found me guilty of the charge of criminal damage and that I would have to pay a combined fine of £100 for the two offences. This was a great disappointment as the doctor's evidence was not even brought into consideration, and also the words of the RSM had been worthless bullshit. The officer commanding the Royal Marines police had been successful in his quest to obtain a military offence report on me, ready to present to the court-martial panel a few weeks later. In summary, the past few months had been a chain of disasters.

CHAPTER THIRTY-FIVE
THE COURT MARTIAL

Shortly after returning to the UK, and to Stonehouse Barracks in Plymouth, I went to visit the solicitor who was dealing with my court-martial case. His name was Grant Davison and he had a small office on the outskirts of Plymouth city centre. He was about six foot tall, slim with short dark hair and in his late forties. He was well spoken and easy to get on with. His office was small and seemed to be almost buried in hundreds of volumes of law books.

I visited him several times and repeatedly went over the events of the early hours of Wednesday, 26 October 1988. There were only a couple of weeks left to the court date, which had been set for Tuesday, 10 October 1989, almost one year after the incident. Mr Davison expressed concern about the lack of credible witnesses. He said that the court's decision could rest on a law term called *mens rea* (the frame of mind of the accused at or around the time of the alleged crime or incident). If Bernie Drudge could prove I actually did assault the sailor in Boobs nightclub that night, then it could be assumed that my state of mind was such that I did assault him during our journey back to Stonehouse Barracks. However, if this couldn't be proved then it would be my word against his and it would be down to Mr Davison's sheer professionalism to discredit him in front of the court. I told him I would put some thought into it and try to come up with a witness from the incident in Boobs nightclub.

As I walked away from his office, I felt dismayed. I knew for sure that I didn't have any credible witnesses. I still had no idea who had taken the CCTV tapes. It could have been someone trying to protect me, but it could also have been someone trying to protect Drudge. This puzzled me, as well as the fact that, even though nothing had been proved, I was suspended indefinitely from the Royal Marines police, and yet he was allowed to carry on. It seemed to be a foregone conclusion that I was the guilty party and that he was sweet and innocent. It was as if somebody, somewhere, was protecting him.

I spent the next week discussing possibilities with my friend Diz about who I could possibly call as a witness. Several of my Marine friends even offered to act as false witnesses as long as I could give them as much detail as possible. Their support cheered me up, but I declined their offer, as I needed somebody independent of the Marines. My nights were becoming sleepless. When I did manage to nod off to sleep, I regularly dreamed about the court martial. Each time, the dreams seemed to get worse and I was glad when I awoke to realise it was just another bad dream. My back injury had totally healed now and I worked hard at my fitness in the gym. During one of my training sessions, I passed a Marine in the entrance doorway, who asked me where the showers were in a strong Welsh accent. I gave him directions and continued into the gym to start training. After a short warm-up, I started pushing out a few press-ups on the floor.

Then it came to me. The Welsh Marine's accent rang a few bells. Of course, I thought: Taff, my Welsh civilian mate from HMS Warrior. He would be perfect, as not only was he not a serviceman, nobody here knew he was a friend of mine. This meant that I could say I was introduced to him after the incident through a mutual acquaintance, and that he then told me he was there that night and had seen what had happened.

I immediately got up and went to give my Welsh friend a ring. I managed to get hold of him without any problem and explained my situation to him. Even before I broached the subject of asking him to be a witness, he actually suggested it to me. I was overjoyed, and agreed to write down as much information as possible and send it to him through the post. This stroke of luck gave me some hope. At least this time it was me who had the hidden joker up my sleeve.

A couple of days later, Taff called to tell me that he had received and read the information I had sent him. He asked me any queries he had, to clear up any possible anomalies, and agreed to meet with my solicitor a couple of days before my appearance in court. This went as planned, but my solicitor hinted that he thought Taff's presence at Boobs nightclub on the night of the incident was questionable. Although he seemed to have his suspicions that I'd recruited a fake witness, though, I must have managed to reassure him. He said he would like him to appear in court and that he would only call him if he really thought he needed to.

On the eve of my court case, the details of the court martial were published in the unit's daily routine orders. One copy was placed outside the barracks' main gate on a wooden noticeboard attached to the perimeter fence. It read something like the following:

COMMANDO FORCES – ROYAL MARINES
ROUTINE ORDERS
DISTRICT COURT MARTIAL

1. A District Court Martial will convene at Royal Marines Barracks, Plymouth, at 1000 hours on Tuesday, 10 October 1989, for the purpose of trying the undermentioned accused person:

Marine Steven Preece.

Commando Brigade Headquarters and Signal Squadron Royal Marines.

2. The Officers mentioned below are to assemble at the Court Martial Centre at 0930 hours:

President: Major C. Gate, Royal Artillery

Senior Member: A Captain to be detailed by the officer commanding Commando Logistic Regiment, Royal Marines.

Junior Member: A Lieutenant to be detailed by the officer commanding 59 Independent Commando Squadron, Royal Engineers.

When I read the routine orders, I got butterflies in my stomach and felt a great dread. Shortly afterwards, I was summoned to the regimental sergeant-major's office, who told me to collect my kit and report to the guardroom for detention in the cells.

I did this and sat alone in the solitude of the quiet prison cell. Early in the evening, I had three visitors. The first was my officer friend, who brought me fish and chips. He sat and had a cup of tea with me and wished me luck on behalf of the majority of officers from the officers' mess. Next it was the regimental sergeant-major. He also sat and had a cup of tea with me and gave me some chocolate. He told me I was a good Marine and that I should accept the punishment awarded. He said you can't beat the system and that he expected me to get at least eighteen months' detention in Colchester military prison. He concluded that he would gladly welcome me back to his unit on completion of my sentence. Before he left, he wished me luck on behalf of all the senior non-commissioned officers from the sergeants' mess. Lastly, my mate Diz came to visit me. He brought a couple of cans of beer and drank one with me. I talked to him about how much I missed my father, and I became quite emotional. He consoled me and tried his best to cheer me up. Before he left, he wished me luck on behalf of all the corporals and Marines in Air Defence Troop.

I sat alone staring at the red stone walls. The full year I had waited to appear before this court martial had been the worst year of my life. My mother had been knocked down and had suffered severe head injuries. My father had died. I had badly damaged the vertebrae in my lower back. I had been beaten up whilst struggling with my back injury and had suffered severe injuries from this. Finally, I had been set up with the charges brought against me in Norway. Bollocks, I thought, I really don't care what happens to me next.

During the night, I hardly slept at all and I felt very hot and restless. I couldn't stop thinking about the court case. I lay on my bed and repeatedly went over the events of the evening of the incident in my head and also over what I had said at the interviews that followed. My final thought was that I hoped Taff would turn up, just in case we needed him. I did doze off in the early hours of the following morning, but only for a couple of hours. I was awoken around 6 a.m. by the duty guard to tell me to get washed and clean my kit. I did this and was then handcuffed prior to being escorted by a guard of two Marines to the dining hall to get some breakfast.

In the dining hall, other Marines kept wishing me good

luck and telling me that they'd be thinking of me throughout the day. At least twenty or more came up to my table and shook my hand or patted me on the back.

At 8.45 a.m., I was stood inside my cell waiting for my escorts to march me down to the court-martial centre. I was dressed in my Lovats uniform with a white belt, which showed the Marines' locket union, a black pair of highly polished and studded parade boots and my Green Beret. My escorts arrived in the same code of dress uniform and marched me down to the court. I knew both of the Marines who were escorting me and felt comfortable with them as they quietly joked about the event.

The court-martial centre was located in a room above the Royal Marines police headquarters, which was a couple of hundred metres away from Stonehouse Barracks. On arrival, I waited in a room outside the courtroom for my solicitor to appear. A couple of Royal Marines policemen released my guards from their duties and told them to come back at 5 p.m. to escort me back to my cell. As I patiently awaited my solicitor, I watched a few officers I didn't know and a judge making their way into the courtroom, before closing the door behind them.

The entrance door opened and my solicitor walked in. He was dressed in the customary black robes and grey wig. He smiled at me and nodded his head to acknowledge my presence. Then he turned to the two RMPs.

'Excuse me, gentlemen, but could you tell me who owns that great big jeep that's parked in front of the entrance to the courtyard?'

'Yes, sir, we do,' responded one of them.

'Oh, that's good. Would you mind moving it, because I can't get my Rolls-Royce in?'

Both RMPs seemed flustered by the request and rapidly

disappeared out of the door to move their vehicle. Mr Davison laughed. 'I haven't really got a Rolls-Royce, I just wanted a couple of minutes in private to have a few words with you. How do you feel?'

'I'm ready, Mr Davison, come what may, I'm ready.'

'Good, so am I.'

At 10 a.m. the door to the courtroom was pulled wide open and an order was shouted out by the adjutant (senior disciplinary officer) to the two RMPs who were guarding me.

'March in the accused.'

One of the RMPs took charge. 'Marine Preece, ATTENTION. QUICK MARCH, LEFT RIGHT, LEFT RIGHT, HALT.'

I marched as ordered and then halted on his command. I was then instructed to remove my belt with locket union and my Green Beret. This was because the accused at a court martial is being tried without honour and therefore cannot wear the insignia of the regiment or unit he serves. I removed them and stood before the court.

The courtroom was large with a high ceiling and a shiny wooden floor. All sounds echoed around the room, including the voices of the people in court. The court was furnished with a long, heavy wooden bench, which had a large Union Jack flag draped over it. This was where the judging panel sat. In the middle of the panel was a judge advocate, who wore black robes and a grey wig. On his left, there was a Royal Marines captain, who was in his mid-fifties. On his right, there was a major from the Royal Artillery and next to him was a young lieutenant from a commando-trained Royal Engineers unit. In front of them, on the bench, I saw a silver military sword, which had been placed on a small stand. On my left-hand side, I saw the prosecuting officer who was also sat at a heavy-looking wooden bench. This was a stunning woman from the Army legal service. She had long dark hair which was tied back, and a figure some women would kill for. She looked like butter wouldn't melt in her mouth. Next to her sat the adjutant, who appeared to be acting as an assistant to her. On my right-hand side was my solicitor. He was sat at a small wooden bench with a spare seat that was placed there for me. In the middle of the courtroom was a single wooden seat. This was to be used as the witness stand.

The judge stood up and momentarily stared at me before reading from a sheet of paper.

'Marine Preece, you have been brought before this court today, charged with the following offences. As I read out the charges, state your plea of guilty or not guilty.

'For the charge of committing a civil offence contrary to section 70 of the Army Act 1955, that is to say assault occasioning actual bodily harm contrary to section 47 of the Offences Against the Person Act 1861.

'In that he at Plymouth on 26 October 1988 assaulted Lance-Corporal Drudge, Royal Marines, thereby occasioning him actual bodily harm.

'Do you plead guilty or not guilty?'

'Not guilty, your honour,' I answered nervously.

'For the charge of fighting contrary to section 43 (a) of the Army Act 1955.

'In that he at Plymouth on 26 October 1988 without reasonable excuse fought with a person unknown.

'Do you plead guilty or not guilty?'

'Not guilty, your honour.'

'For the charge of drunkenness contrary to section 43 (1) of the Army Act 1955.

'In that he at Plymouth on 26 October 1988 was drunk.

'Do you plead guilty or not guilty?'

'Not guilty, your honour.'

'This court is now in progress. Marine Preece, be seated.' He pointed to the vacant seat next to my solicitor. The judge called for the prosecution to state her name, rank and service number, which she did. He then asked her to state her case.

'Your Honour, Marine Preece is a very experienced Marine who has served in the Marine Corps for over six years. During his service he has gained a reputation for being a man of few words. In plain terms, he readily accepts violence and would also not hesitate for one second to offer or to use it.

'During the early hours of Wednesday, 26 October 1988, Marine Preece attended Boobs nightclub in Union Street, Plymouth, along with Lance-Corporal Drudge and Lance-Corporal Carter, both of the Royal Marines police troop. During the evening he had consumed a lot of alcohol and was drunk. At one point during his time in Boobs nightclub, he fought with a person unknown and, in front of Lance-Corporal Drudge, he knocked this man to the floor with his fists. Later, whilst walking back to Stonehouse Barracks, Marine Preece attacked Lance-Corporal Drudge without provocation. During this attack, he brutally assaulted Lance-Corporal Drudge, causing severe injuries to his head, eyes and facial areas. Also, not being content with the beating he had inflicted on his colleague, he then tried to throw him over a wall, which has a forty-foot drop on the other side. Only sheer luck saved Lance-Corporal Drudge from certain death, in that he managed to break free from Marine Preece's grip and run away from him.

'Your Honour, these are the facts of the case and they are undisputed.'

When she had finished delivering the case on behalf of the prosecution, she stood and waited for the judge to acknowledge her. He did this by nodding his head and then stood up and looked towards my solicitor.

'Please can you state your name and professional position, and present your case for the defence?'

'Yes, your honour,' Mr Davison replied politely, before stepping out from his seat to introduce himself and address the court.

'Your Honour, Marine Preece is a very experienced Marine who has served in the Marine Corps for over six years. During this time, he has served in the Arctic during the Cold War, Cyprus, the streets of Northern Ireland and also in the civilian prisons during the recent prison officers' strike, for which he was commended. He is a Royal Marine through and through and dedicated to his job, his fellow Marines and the service of this country. He is not reputed as a violent man, but as a man who stands his ground and defends himself when he is attacked or threatened, which is exactly what you would expect from a member of the elite Royal Marine Commandos with his length of service and experience.

'During the early hours of Wednesday, 26 October 1988, Marine Preece attended Boobs nightclub in Union Street, Plymouth, along with Lance-Corporal Drudge and Lance-Corporal Carter. During the evening, he had consumed several glasses of alcohol, as did Lance-Corporals Drudge and Carter, but he was not drunk.

'In Boobs nightclub, the far less experienced Lance-Corporal Drudge picked a fight with a person unknown: a fight which was quickly defused by Marine Preece, who soon after suggested that Lance-Corporal Drudge should leave with him to prevent any repetition of Lance-Corporal Drudge's unacceptable behaviour.

'After leaving the nightclub, they both walked back to Stonehouse Barracks. During this journey, Lance-Corporal Drudge complained that he lacked the skills and knowledge of Marine Preece, especially on the street. He then, without provocation, attacked Marine Preece and knocked him onto the floor. Marine Preece quickly got back to his feet and defended himself from the attack of Lance-Corporal Drudge. Consequently, Lance-Corporal Drudge fell first against the wall and then onto the floor, which is how he sustained most of his injuries. Knowing that he had bitten off more than he could chew, he then fled the scene.

'Your Honour, I put it to this court that Marine Preece is not guilty of being drunk, is not guilty of fighting with a person unknown and is not guilty of assaulting Lance-Corporal Drudge. Nor did he, at any time, attempt to push or throw Lance-Corporal Drudge over a wall. In fact, the location where the incident took place shows that it would be impossible to lift a person of Lance-Corporal Drudge's size and build over the wall unaided.

'I further put it to the court that it was Lance-Corporal Drudge who fought with a person unknown in Boobs nightclub. He'd had too much to drink and was trying to prove himself to the more experienced Marine Preece, who then decided to leave the nightclub because Lance-Corporal Drudge's behaviour was unacceptable. Later, on the journey back to Stonehouse Barracks, Lance-Corporal Drudge wasn't satisfied with being pulled away from the unknown man he tried to fight with and decided to fight with Marine Preece. However, during the fight he had started, he came off worse and sustained injuries. Marine Preece did not assault Lance-Corporal Drudge as alleged. Lance-Corporal Drudge assaulted Marine Preece and then ran off and cried wolf when he realised he had picked on the wrong man.

'Your Honour, I also put it to this court today that Marine Preece is not guilty of these allegations against him and that this fact is emphatically undisputed.'

The judge accepted the delivery of the defence and once

again recalled the prosecution, who asked for Lance-Corporal Drudge to enter the court and take the witness stand. I turned and looked at the open doorway and watched him march in. He stated his rank, name and service number and sat down in the witness stand and swore an oath with his right hand held on a bible. I watched him as he chanced a brief glance in my direction. I felt very angry towards this immature and inexperienced Marine who had been responsible for tearing my career into shreds. I stared deep into his eyes and could sense his fear before he looked away.

'Lance-Corporal Drudge, how well do you know Marine Preece?' asked the prosecution solicitor.

'Fairly well, ma'am,' he answered in a nervous voice.

'Would you say he is an average Marine?'

'No, ma'am, he is renowned for his physical fitness, boxing skills and aggressive nature.'

'Objection, your Honour, the prosecution is leading the witness,' my solicitor interrupted.

'Yes, I agree. Adjutant, please remove that from the record,' he ordered.

The prosecution rubbed her chin and momentarily paused for thought. The court remained silent, waiting for her next line of approach.

'Lance-Corporal Drudge, it has been alleged by Marine Preece that you got into an argument with another serviceman whilst socialising in Boobs nightclub. Is this the case?'

'No, ma'am, this is completely untrue. It was Marine Preece who actually fought with the unknown serviceman.'

'It has also been alleged by Marine Preece that you attacked him whilst walking back to Stonehouse Barracks. Is this the case?'

'No, ma'am, it was Marine Preece who attacked me. He

then tried to throw me over the wall.'

'No more questions, your Honour,' she smiled and walked back to her seat.

My solicitor stood up and cleared his throat before beginning his line of questioning.

'Lance-Corporal Drudge, how long have you been in the Marines?'

'Nearly two years, sir.'

'So when the incident occurred nearly a year ago, you had more or less just come out of basic training?'

'Yes, sir.'

'Would you consider yourself to be mature?'

'Er, yes, sir, I would.'

'Lance-Corporal Drudge, during your Royal Marines military police training, did you fit in with the rest of the Marines on the course.'

'No, sir, I didn't really get on with them.'

'Objection, your Honour,' snapped the prosecution solicitor.

'Overruled. Continue with your present line of questioning, Mr Davison,' the judge answered.

'Is it not true that you were said to be immature during this course and also had not really got on with any of the other Marines?'

'Er, I don't know what you mean.'

'I put it to you, Lance-Corporal Drudge, that you had very little experience as a Marine when you attended the military police training course and that you didn't get on with anybody because of your attitude. I also put it to you that you had a run-in during this course with Marine Preece and that later, during your night out together in Plymouth, after Marine Preece had returned from his tour of duty in the civilian prisons, you took the opportunity to seek revenge for the bad feeling that existed between you both. Consequently, you have made false allegations about Marine Preece fighting with a person unknown, and being drunk and assaulting you, when in fact your immaturity pushed you to assault the unknown serviceman in Boobs nightclub, when you'd had too much to drink. And later, during your walk back to Stonehouse Barracks, it was in fact you who had assaulted Marine Preece.'

'Er no, no, it wasn't like that,' he stammered.

'No more questions, your Honour,' smiled Mr Davison.

My solicitor then requested that the charge of drunkenness be withdrawn, as there was no evidence to support this. The judge agreed, as did the rest of the members of the court-martial panel.

'The charge of drunkenness is withdrawn,' announced the judge.

Shortly afterwards, we stopped for a lunch break and I was given some sandwiches and placed under guard of the Marines police. At approximately 1 p.m., my friend Taff arrived and was shown in to the same room as myself. He surprised me, as he was dressed like a perfect gentleman, complete with a three-piece suit, briefcase and umbrella.

'Don't ask,' he smiled. 'I've bought all this shit from a second-hand shop as I want to look the part.'

When my solicitor returned, he greeted Taff and then told us both that he would only call him to the witness stand if he had to. He continued that he now had to prove *mens rea* (the frame of mind of the accused around the time of the offence committed). If he could disprove that I assaulted the serviceman in Boobs nightclub, then the court would possibly favour my story about our walk back to Stonehouse Barracks. On the other hand, if the prosecution could prove I did assault the unknown serviceman, then the court would judge my frame of mind as being unsound and might favour Drudge's version of events.

The court reassembled and both Drudge and myself were separately called to the witness stand to give more details on our versions of events. Lance-Corporal Carter was also called to the stand but he offered very little information about what had happened in his presence in Boobs nightclub. This gave me a warm feeling inside, as I knew he saw a great deal more than he chose to tell the court.

Late in the afternoon, my solicitor requested that the charge of fighting with an unknown person be dropped, and after a short discussion with the panel the judge withdrew the charge. This left the final charge of assault occasioning actual bodily harm, which in itself was a strong enough charge to send me to Colchester military prison for nine months' detention.

Before the court was adjourned that day, Mr Davison put Taff on the stand. As good as he looked and as posh as he tried to sound, the prosecution tore him to pieces. So much so, that had the charges of drunkenness and fighting not already been dropped, then I would have been found guilty on both counts. At 5 p.m., the judge banged his hammer on the bench and closed the court for the day. My original guard of the two Marines from Air Defence Troop returned and escorted me back to Stonehouse Barracks, where I was placed back in the cells.

That night I was visited by the regimental sergeant-major, who congratulated me on winning the first day. He continued that, in his opinion, I would not beat the charge of actual bodily harm and would be sentenced to nine months' imprisonment. He concluded that I would be welcomed back into his commando unit on completion of my sentence.

That night I sat alone in my prison cell and stared at the

star-filled sky through the bars on the cell window. I was restless, and felt unhappy about the events of the last twelve months. The remaining charge worried me. I went over and over the definition of assault in my mind, which I had learned at the military law school in Chichester. (Assault: the intentional application of force to the person of another, either directly or indirectly without their consent, or the threat of such force by act or gesture, if the person threatening has or causes the person threatened to believe he has the present ability to effect his purpose.) I couldn't make my mind up whether my actions fell inside or outside this definition. I decided that I didn't care what happened to me any more and tried to get some sleep. It took me until the early hours of the morning to finally drift off. I started to dream about my late father. I saw him standing at the back of a public bus on top of a red empty beer crate. He had a full bottle of beer in his hand and held it out to propose a toast to me.

'Not guilty, son,' he smiled and drank from the bottle. Then I heard the cell door keys rattle and awoke to greet the guard commander, who told me to get washed and go with an escort of two Marines to get some breakfast before the second day of the trial.

After breakfast, I waited in my cell until my escorts arrived to take me back to the court-martial centre. Prior to their arrival, I was once again visited by the regimental sergeant-major, who reiterated his comments on my guilty verdict.

'I'm sorry, sir, but you're wrong. I'm going to be cleared,' I smiled.

He shook his head and returned the smile as my escorts marched me away. Once at our destination, the two escorts shook my hand and wished me luck before handing me over to the military police. My solicitor had already arrived and was waiting to greet me. He smiled and then expressed his worry about Taff's performance the day before. However, he did say that he thought we had gained a lot of ground and that beating the fighting with an unknown person charge had to give us the edge over the case for the prosecution.

I stood outside the closed courtroom door and prepared myself to face the court for the last charge of actual bodily harm. I felt good about the dream I had had the previous night. My father had never been there when I needed him in my life, but I felt as if he was with me now.

I was told to stand to attention and then the courtroom door opened.

'March in the accused,' the adjutant shouted.

I smartly marched into the courtroom and stood before the court. When I halted, I felt a warm sensation run through my body. I looked towards the judge and the panel. The judge smiled at me, which I found peculiar. I looked at the Royal Marines captain on his left-hand side and watched him wink at me. He looked at the medals I wore on my uniform and smiled at me. I felt confused and looked towards the officers to the right of the judge. The major from the Royal Artillery Regiment smiled at me and so did the young commando-trained lieutenant from the Royal Engineers who was sat next to him. I stated my rank, name and service number and sat down as instructed by the judge.

All of a sudden, I strangely felt I had gained the favour of the court. The judge called for the prosecution witness to enter the courtroom. But the way he did this surprised me. The judge rubbed his forehead. 'Bring in the prosecution witness, er, Jack the lad,' he instructed the prosecution solicitor.

With these words, I looked at the panel and realised I had well and truly gained the confidence of the court, because all of them were smiling at me again. Lance-Corporal Drudge marched in, swore an oath to tell the truth, the whole truth and nothing but the truth and took the witness stand. He sat down and looked worried.

The prosecution solicitor walked into the middle of the courtroom and expressed concern about the allegation of Drudge being pushed over the wall with the forty-foot drop. My solicitor stood up and approached the bench. He looked at me and then at the prosecution witness and then smiled at me. Then he spoke directly to the judge.

'Your Honour, I would respectfully like to request having a word with you in your private chambers.'

The judge smiled at him and said yes. I was then marched out of the court into the adjacent room outside, where I waited with two Royal Marines policemen. I paused for thought, but felt totally confused as to what was going on.

Approximately fifteen minutes later, the judge and Mr Davison returned to the courtroom and closed the door shut behind them. Then the door opened and I was ordered to march in.

'March in the accused,' shouted the adjutant from inside the courtroom.

I marched in once more and halted in front of the panel. I immediately felt elated as all the officers in the panel were wearing their caps and I knew this was a sign that the court was closed. All the officers were smiling at me again.

The judge stood up. 'Marine Preece, of the charge of assault occasioning actual bodily harm, the court finds you not guilty. This case is now concluded and the court is closed.'

'Marine Preece,' shouted the adjutant.

'Sir.'

'Replace your belt and locket union.'

'Yes, sir,' I replied and put my Marine Corps belt on. This meant that my honour was being restored.

'Replace your Green Beret,' continued the adjutant.

'Yes, sir.'

I smiled and replaced my Green Beret. I stood smartly to attention and felt ten feet tall. It was all over now and I had been victorious.

'Marine Preece, about turn, to your duties, quick march.'

I did an about turn and proudly marched out of the courtroom. I waited outside for my solicitor, who was busy shaking hands with the judge and the panel. Drudge quickly made himself scarce and was driven away from the court-martial centre in a waiting vehicle. Mr Davison casually walked out of the courtroom and lit up a cigar. We shook hands and I thanked him for his services. He smiled and congratulated me on winning the case.

The two escort Marines from Air Defence Troop returned and stood in the doorway. One of the RMPs approached them and asked why they had returned. They said they had heard the great news and wanted to be the first to congratulate me.

Ten minutes later, I walked into the dining hall back at Stonehouse Barracks to get a cup of tea. The hall was full of Marines, who immediately started cheering when they saw me and then started throwing me up into the air. The same day, Drudge was told to pack his kit and leave to catch a flight to a place called the SHAPE (Supreme Headquarters Allied Powers Europe) in Belgium. I never saw him again.

A week later, I put together a redress of complaint letter and presented it to the commanding officer. It read as follows (I have omitted some purely administrative details):

REDRESS OF COMPLAINT

1. I have the honour to make a Redress of Complaint following my acquittal at District Court Martial (DCM) on 11 October 1989.

2. The complaints that I wish to have redress for are as follows:

(a) I was suspended indefinitely from the Royal Marines police (RMP) branch at 0835 hours on 26 October 1988 by [the officer commanding Royal Marines police branch]. This was before any statements had been taken or my chance to give my account of the incident of the alleged assault against Lance-Corporal [Drudge]. [. . .] Subsequently, even though Lance-Corporal [Drudge] was involved in the incident he was allowed to remain with the Royal Marines police troop. Consequently, my promotion to corporal was frozen.

[. . .]

(d) I have been under a lot of stress whilst awaiting court martial, which also placed my family under a great deal of stress as they were worried about my future. In June this year, my mother was involved in a serious car accident and was taken into intensive care with serious head injuries. Three weeks later, my father died of a heart attack on 13 July 1989. Whilst I do not claim that the death of my father was due to his worry about my court martial, I would say that it may have been a contributing factor along with the accident to my mother.

[. . .]

3. I wish to request the following:

[. . .]

(b) That I be reinstated as a Royal Marines policeman.

(c) That my promotion to corporal be reviewed.

[. . .]
I have the honour to be,
Sir,
Your obedient servant,
Marine [S. Preece]

I was subsequently granted both of my requests. I was reinstated as an RMP, and the question of my attending a junior command course (leadership course) to assist my promotion from lance-corporal to corporal came under review. It turned out, however, that a damning report on my conduct had been submitted to the review board during the lead up to my trial. It was compiled by the officer commanding the Royal Marines police troop, but not signed. It contained a D grade, which, of course, was below the required standard. I also learned that my superiors had previously failed to complete another report for the six-month period prior to this, and only sent a fax to the review board stating low marks and the recommendation of another D grade. This meant that I wouldn't be allowed to attend the course, and effectively blocked my chances of becoming a corporal.

My pride was at stake here, and I felt that I had been cheated of my long-awaited promotion, so I officially challenged both of the reports. The commanding officer responded encouragingly, stating in his letter that the reported comments were 'not balanced and unacceptably damning', and that the situation was 'a shoddy example of maladministration'. He strongly recommended that special reports be raised to cover these reporting periods.

There was one important factor, however, which partly underlay the commanding officer's reasons for looking into my promotion, and which, conversely, underlay my reasons for not pursuing it any further. Prior to the court martial itself, I had put in a request to prematurely end my career in the Marine Corps. At the time, I'd been at a very low ebb. My father's death and the prospect of a long imprisonment had destroyed my enthusiasm for the Marines. Now that I'd been acquitted, though, the commanding officer was perhaps expecting me to change my mind. He wasn't at all keen for me to leave, and he actually tried very hard to talk me out of it. Over the course of these last few months, however, I had resolved to stand by my decision. I explained my reasons why to the commanding officer.

Firstly, I told him that times were changing, and that Drudge was part of a new breed of Marines who were different in nature to me. Many now came from better educational backgrounds but lacked the streetwise education of the old-style Marines. If they were told to do something, they would ask why. They socialised less, they drank less beer and they went home every weekend instead of going into town to get drunk and have some fun. They were also very quick to report any threats or actions of violence, which resulted in others being court-martialled in circumstances similar to mine. I said that I didn't feel I had a place amongst these new Marines, whose values and notions of loyalty were so different to my own.

I also told him that I thought the amount of money we were paid was crap. He frowned at this and asked, 'How much do you think you are worth, Preece?' My answer was, 'A lot more than this, sir, we all are.' A Marine's wage in 1990 was less than a meagre £25 per day (yes, I know – peanuts). We had to pay for our food and accommodation out of this. We were charged income tax, and were even told that we would have to pay poll tax (when it was introduced in 1990), just like everyone else. However, I don't know if this was actually enforced, as I left before it was fully sanctioned.

Lastly, I mentioned that I had acquired a number of injuries over the years. I was still very fit, but had intermittent problems with my knees and back. These injuries were common amongst the old-style Marines, but some of them just soldiered on.

The commanding officer accordingly granted my request, and I was given a release date of 8 May 1990. I was then given the option of not returning to the police troop after all, but remaining in my administrative job instead. After a great deal of thought, I chose not to return to the RMPs. The Marines police had tried their best to make an example of me, and I had beaten both them and their judicial system. I knew that, if I carried on, it would only be a matter of time before they tried to pin something on me again. This knowledge only strengthened my resolve to leave. I had now passed the point of no return and, in just over half-a-year's time, I would be moving on.

CHAPTER THIRTY-SIX

THE FINAL CHAPTER

Seven months passed and my release date was soon on the horizon. I was only one week away from leaving the Marines, so I organised a customary night on the town with my colleagues. Even though the purpose of the night was to say goodbye to my friends, it was also my opportunity to seek revenge on the three Marines who had beaten me up and put me in hospital when my back was injured.

I felt highly excited when the big night came around. Thirty-five other Marines had arranged to attend. However, there was some scepticism amongst my friends. One of them, who was called Wicksy, asked to have a private word with me in my room. I listened carefully to what he had to say. He told me that he really wanted to come with me on my farewell night out, but expressed concern that he knew there would be trouble. He told me that he had the greatest of respect for me as a Marine, but really didn't want to get into any trouble. I smiled at him and told him that there were no hard feelings. I appreciated his honesty and realistically I knew he was right. It had been nearly a year now since I'd been beaten up. I thought about it every day and my blood boiled when I frequently saw one of the three Marines who had attacked me, every time I went out on the town. He was a tall skinny man called Spencer. He had brown spiky hair, a thick walrus moustache and a jagged scar on his right cheek. I chose not to approach him, though, until my back injury had healed and my pending court martial had been resolved. At times, this was difficult, because he always stared at me and smiled when he saw me.

As fate would have it, all three of these Marines were in town on the night of my organised leaving celebration. I'd gained this information from a good source within the Marine organisation. One of the three had just returned from a deployment on a Falklands patrol vessel called HMS *Endurance*, another had just returned from a six-month active service deployment in Northern Ireland and Spencer had always remained in another commando unit in Plymouth.

We started at 5.30 p.m. in a pub called the Phoenix, which was just yards away from the infamous Union Street. The quiet pub was instantly filled when all my Marine colleagues arrived. We laughed and joked about a lot of the antics we had got up to over the years as well as holding some quite serious conversations about experiences gained during various military conflicts around the world. I felt really comfortable with everybody who was present; we were good friends and had shared a lot of hardship together during our careers.

At 7 p.m., my best friend Diz arrived. He smiled when he saw me and bought a round of drinks. He passed me a pint of beer and whispered in my ear, 'I've just seen one of them lads who beat you up go into one of the pubs nearby.'

My ears pricked up and I gave him my undivided attention. 'Which one?'

'The big bastard with ginger hair.'

'Which pub?'

'The Star, just around the corner.'

'Is he alone?'

'Yes.'

I put my pint of beer down on the wooden bar and asked the lone barmaid to look after it until I returned. A few of the other Marines asked where I was going, but I just told them I was going to see somebody and would be back in a short while. Diz smiled at me again.

'I don't suppose you want any back-up, do you?'

'No thanks, mate. I'll sort this out myself.'

I slipped out of a side door and headed down the street towards the Star public house. The door creaked when I opened it and the few people that were inside turned around to see who was entering. The big ginger Marine was stood at the bar and noticed me as I approached and stood next to him. I pretended that I didn't know him and ordered a pint of beer. When I got my beer, I remained leaning against the bar next to him and drank half of it. I could feel his eyes staring at me as he watched me drinking.

'Do I know you from somewhere?' he asked.

'Did you have a good deployment in Ireland?'

'It was a bit rough. Is that where I know you from? Your face looks familiar.'

I smiled and drank the rest of my beer. The glass made a thudding noise as I placed it heavily down on the wooden bar. I turned and immediately rained a number of thunderous punches into his face. The force of the blows knocked him backwards and onto the floor. Then I repeatedly kicked him around the area of his head and face.

'What does it feel like to be kicked when you're down, you fucking bastard? I'm the one you beat up in the Clipper Bar with Spencer.'

With these words, I slammed a few more hard kicks into the beaten man, before calmly walking out of the pub. The door creaked shut as I exited. Outside, I panted for breath as I made my way back to the Phoenix pub. I felt better now, but I also felt angry, really angry about what they had done to me. One down, two to go, I thought.

When I re-entered the Phoenix pub, my friends just smiled at me and passed me my beer. Nobody asked any questions and we all just continued talking as if I had never left.

A short while later, we moved on to the General Moore. For the next hour or so I put all my efforts into chatting with as many of my colleagues as possible, and moved around the many conversations taking place. At approximately 9.30 p.m., I saw the second of my assailants as he entered the pub with another man, whom I didn't recognise. This was the one who had just returned from spending six months on HMS *Endurance*, the Falkland Islands patrol vessel. I continued to converse with my friends and intermittently watched him as he chatted with his friend and drank his beer. Then came my opportunity. I saw him pass his beer to his friend and walk off in the direction of the toilets. I swiftly passed my beer glass to Diz and followed him.

When I stepped through the doorway, I could see my assailant using one of the urinals nearest the door. His back was facing me as he relieved himself. Without hesitation, I stretched out my right arm with the palm open and ran straight at him, slamming his face hard against the wall. The whole of my body weight was behind the blow as his face made impact on the white tiled wall.

'Aaarrrggghhh,' he cried as blood splashed from his nose and mouth onto the wall.

He struggled to put his penis back into his trousers as I grabbed hold of the back of the jacket he was wearing and dragged him backwards onto the floor. I immediately slammed a few kicks into his head, which made loud thudding noises. He groaned and kept struggling to put his manhood back into his trousers.

'This is fucking déjà vu,' I screamed at him. 'This is for the kicking you and your two mates gave me in the Clipper.'

'I'm sorry,' he sobbed. 'We didn't know who you were.'

I gritted my teeth and swung a few more kicks into his head and back. I puffed and panted heavily and stood over him. I was so angry that I felt like I could just explode.

'Well, now you know who I am,' I snarled and kicked him once more before turning and walking out of the toilets.

My friends smiled when I returned and again asked no questions. They were ready to leave and move on to the next pub further down Union Street. At approximately 11 p.m., we entered the Clipper Bar. It would be poetic justice to find Spencer in here, I thought as we entered.

I looked around the packed bar room to see if I could see him, but he wasn't there. All of a sudden, another face stood out in the crowd. Fate seemed to be putting all the bad eggs into one basket on the same night. It was the Marine who had dragged me out of bed and beaten me up when I had first joined 45 Commando Unit back in 1983. However, I chose not to approach him until either he left the pub or we were ready to leave the pub. I continued chatting with my friends without losing sight of him. Later, we were ready to leave so I decided to make my move and approached him. I stood in front of him and stared deep into his eyes. He seemed to instantly recognise me.

'You've come for me, haven't you?' he frowned.

I nodded my head and smiled, before launching a head-butt hard into his face. The blow knocked him backwards and down onto the floor next to the bar. Blood splattered across his face and his half-empty pint glass smashed on the floor a few metres away. A woman screamed loudly and the crowd of people around us rapidly dispersed.

'That's good enough for me,' I smiled, before turning and walking out of the bar. I felt great and couldn't believe that I'd also got the opportunity to settle an old score from six years ago.

At approximately midnight, we made our way to a nightclub called Roots, which was very popular with a lot of the Marines. I knew Spencer was already inside as I had been informed of this by a couple of my friends. By this time, I had consumed a lot of alcohol and was quite drunk. However, this did not dilute my anger and determination to complete my revenge.

I walked straight to the front of a queue of people who were waiting to enter the club and was given a welcoming nod by one of the two doormen, who was a friend of mine and always let me in without queuing or paying.

The club was small and dark inside and consisted of a wooden dance floor and a small bar. When I entered through the internal swing doors I scanned the people who were stood waiting to get served at the bar. I couldn't see Spencer, but could almost feel his presence nearby. I looked into the shadows across the crowded dance floor and then, all of a sudden, I saw his brown spiky hair and then his scarred face looking straight at me. I felt ready, alert and eager to take him on. He was the last piece of the jigsaw puzzle I had started at the beginning of the evening.

Instead of the usual snidey smile on his face, he looked serious, very serious. My blood seemed to boil and I surged towards him, unconcerned about the people I knocked out of the way, who stood between him and me. From the corner of my right eye, I saw a tall figure of a man moving rapidly towards me. I instantly knew he was with Spencer. Without removing my attention from my intended target, when this man was close enough I struck out with a swift uppercut punch, which hit him hard on the chin and knocked him backwards and against a wall.

Spencer picked up on my actions and ran towards me with his teeth gritted. He threw a right punch, which I blocked with my left hand and then he followed it up with a left punch, which I blocked with my right hand. Without even a moment of hesitation, I thrust my head forward into his face with all my body weight behind it. I actually felt his nose and mouth crack and blood splattered into the air around him as he fell to the floor. I moved in to finish him off, but saw that he was out cold. It was over, so I tactfully backed away. My anger seemed to mellow and I felt like a huge burden had been lifted from my shoulders.

A couple of the nightclub's doormen appeared and used smelling salts to bring him around. Then they lifted him up and showed him to the exit. One of them, my friend, returned a few minutes later and told me that Spencer had gone. He smiled, patted me on the back and passed me a fresh pint of beer. I sat alone at a table in one of the dark corners and went to sleep.

When I awoke, I was back in my room at Stonehouse Barracks. It was daylight and I could hear the birds whistling outside. I wasn't sure how I'd got back there, but was told later by Diz that my friends carried me back because they couldn't wake me up.

I spent the next couple of days waiting in anticipation for the Royal Marines police to come and arrest me. Thankfully, they never came, and my final day in the Royal Marines arrived without incident. On my last morning, I went for a final workout in the gymnasium. On the way back to my room

I saw Spencer and the other two Marines I had beaten up walking in a group towards me. I initially felt like turning and running away, but something inside me told me to stand my ground. When they got close, I casually sidestepped to my right so that I would walk directly past them. Although I didn't focus on returning their glances, I could see that all their faces were swollen and badly bruised.

'Steve, can we have a word with you?' requested Spencer in a calm voice.

'Look, I thought we settled this the other night. I don't want to fight you all together, but I will if that's what you want,' I snapped back.

'No, no, that's not what we want. We want to say, we accept what you did to us last night. We didn't know who you were, we're really sorry.'

I looked at the three of them and for a moment I felt good about the injuries I had inflicted on them.

'Yeah, you look fucking sorry,' I laughed and continued on my way.

During lunch, I was continually approached by other Marines whom I knew, who shook my hand and wished me good luck with my move into civvy street. Afterwards, my boss called me into his office and handed me an exemplary testimonial, which described my career in commando forces. He also gave me a written reference, which closed with, 'the Royal Marines cannot afford to lose men of Mr Preece's calibre.'

Just before I left my room in Stonehouse Barracks for the last time, I was visited by my best friend, Diz. He shook my hand and gave me a big hug. He told me that he would miss me and wanted me to keep in touch, which I said I would. He also said that I was leaving the Marine Corps with the greatest of respect from the other Marines. He continued that he thought I was a soldier's soldier, with the honour of a warrior and the heart of a lion, and also that he thought Marines would continue to talk about me for years after I had left. I smiled and slung my kit bag over my shoulder.

Just before I walked through the archway of the main gate for the last time, I stopped for a few moments and gazed across the busy parade square. I didn't know what would be in store for me once I passed through the gates into civvy street. On paper, I was no longer a Marine, but mentally nothing had changed. I smiled. I've done my bit, I thought, it's time to move on. I wonder what the big wide world holds for me . . .